I DIDN'T COME HERE TO MAKE FRIENDS

I DIDN'T COME HERE TO MAKE FRIENDS

CONFESSIONS OF A REALITY SHOW VILLAIN

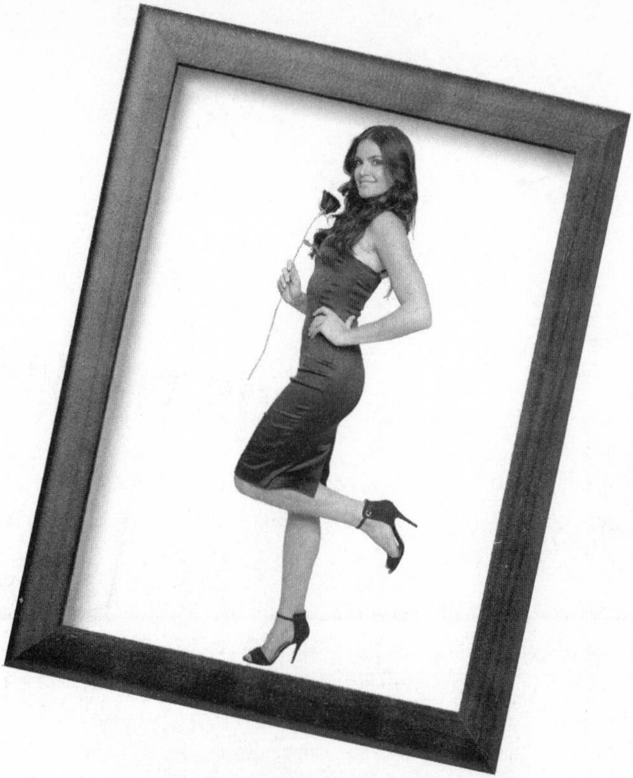

COURTNEY ROBERTSON

WITH DEB BAER

AN IMPRINT OF HARPERCOLLINS PUBLISHERS

Unless otherwise indicated, all photographs are courtesy of the author.

This is a work of nonfiction. The events and experiences detailed herein are all true and have been faithfully rendered as remembered by the author, to the best of her ability.

HarperCollins books may be purchased for educational, business, or sales promotional use. For information please e-mail the Special Markets Department at SPsales@harpercollins.com.

FIRST EDITION

Designed by Paula Russell Szafranski

Library of Congress Cataloging-in-Publication Data has been applied for.

ISBN 978-0-06-232665-2

14 15 16 17 18 OV/RRD 10 9 8 7 6 5 4 3 2 1

For my hero, my dad,
the one man who's
never let me down

CONTENTS

PROLOGUE: The Proposal 1

Birds, Bees & Birthday Suits 17

Catwalking & Starfucking 33

Malibu Barbies & Ben 65

Whine & Roses 91

Buffets & Breakdowns 109

Fly-Fishing & Fighting 119

Doody & Dipping 129

I Do's & Don'ts 149

Boning & Babs 161

Back to Reality 169

Paps & a Smear Campaign 183

Ranting, Raving & Cheating 197

Engaged & Dating 209

Building & Breaking 237

Rebound & Renew 245

EPILOGUE 260

ACKNOWLEDGMENTS 263

PROLOGUE

The Proposal

I'd been staring out the window at the majestic Matterhorn in Switzerland for at least ten minutes, a camera hovering mere inches from my face. I was filled with anxiety but tried as hard as I could to look both calm *and* pensive. I pushed aside thoughts of the camera filming me to focus on the man I was here for, the man I hoped was about to ask me to marry him. By the third take I felt on the brink of tears, but we needed these contemplative shots for the finale episode. I wanted to get it right quickly—and avoid having America witness "the high-stakes drama" of a very public meltdown. On his proposal day, former Bachelor Jason Mesnik felt an irresistible urge to run to his balcony and wail like an old Italian woman at a funeral. When I watched it on TV, I thought he looked ridiculous, but now, as I sat in his place, I understood why he was moved to man-tears.

It didn't help that I kept catching glimpses of my face in the window reflection. Ugh, I didn't look pensive. I looked like a loser! I cursed myself for not practicing in the mirror last night. I remembered from past modeling jobs that if I looked straight ahead at this exact angle, the camera would only catch the whites of my eyes and I'd look like a zombie. On national television. *Perfect.* So I shifted my glance away from the Matterhorn toward the camera a tiny bit. At least now I couldn't see my goofy reflection. And I wouldn't get snow blindness.

What else was running through my head besides avoiding bad angles? Ben Flajnik. My love. My soul mate. My future husband—*if* he proposed today. I'd know in just a few hours whether this would be the happiest, or the most humiliating, day of my life.

I'm not the kind of person who normally gets nervous, but on this morning I was wracked with nerves, my stomach twisted in knots. I thought about our first date in Switzerland, when we flew around the very mountain I was staring at in a helicopter. It was so romantic, but also pretty scary. While safety is a must, to win the Bachelor's heart you have to do more than look hot in a bikini. You have to be able to participate in an extreme sporting event—in a bikini. Let's be real. Nobody ever says, "No, I absolutely will not swim with sharks," because it pegs you as totally boring, high maintenance, and unable to handle adversity in a relationship. It's an automatic ticket home in *Bachelor*-land.

But I wanted to go home that minute. With Ben as my fiancé. I was truly in love with him. *Wasn't I?* A few nights ago, someone had given me a strange warning. "Courtney, Ben's a snob," she proclaimed. Why would she say that? I'd never seen that side of Ben. He did use the word "lovely" a lot, and not ironically. And when I met his mom, Barbara, a few days earlier at Ben's chalet, the first question she asked me was, "Why didn't you go to college?" which made me feel totally inadequate.

"Okay, we got it," the crew announced, and, finally, my Matterhorn selfies were over. *Thank God.* I'd been doing interviews all day, every day for almost three months and I felt like a caged animal. This suite at the Grand Hotel Zermatterhof in Switzerland was a total mind fuck, too. It wasn't relaxing or soothing at all. The room was creepy and old and depressing, like a haunted house. A bell tower across from my bedroom went off every thirty minutes. Since I didn't have a cell phone, computer, television, or music, it was the only sound I heard. The bell was not only deafening, it was driving me insane.

At this point, I was also getting totally paranoid. It was so hard not to start bawling just thinking about the possibility of Ben and Lindzi ending up together. The whole time I was on *The Bachelor*, twelve long weeks, I rarely broke down on-camera. I held everything in until I was in the only truly private place available to contestants—the shower. Finally alone, I would weep like Jason Mesnik. "Never let them see you sweat" was my motto. But thinking about Ben proposing to Lindzi had me on edge, prepared to lose it at any given moment.

As I got ready that morning, I tried not to think about Lindzi and her super cheesy jokes. She had a weird habit of talking in the third person, starting every sentence with "Cox believes . . ." or "Cox loves . . ." I think she enjoyed shocking people with her last name and even threw her dad, Mr. Cox, into many conversations for good measure. I didn't want to think about Lindzi. Instead I thought about Ben and his—cox. We'd had sex three times in the Fantasy Suite at a hillside chalet in the beautiful Swiss town of Interlaken, so I couldn't wait to be with him again.

My stomach dropped for what seemed like the five hundredth time. *What the heck would I do if he didn't propose to me?* I couldn't imagine it not happening. I deserved a fairy-tale ending. I had started to seriously think of Ben as my boyfriend after I'd introduced him to my family in Arizona on our Hometown Date, and I was convinced we were together. If he broke up with me, it would be the ultimate betrayal, especially since he secretly told me on our Fantasy Suite date that he was madly in love with me. I knew I was head over heels in love with him, but could he possibly have been lying to me? It had crossed my mind a few times that maybe Ben was only doing the show to promote his winery in Sonoma.

I tried to push the thought out of my brain, but that night I prepared myself for the worst-case scenario—having my heart smashed into a million pieces. In my mind, I forced myself to rehearse my answer if he dumped me or said he just wanted to keep dating casually. I couldn't just stand there, mouth hanging open. I decided that I would simply say, "Never contact me." Then I'd walk off in silence and completely ignore him.

The uncertainty of what was going to happen kept me up all night long. I tossed and turned, only getting a measly few hours of sleep. I didn't want to be out of it or groggy on the potential day of my very public engagement, but I just couldn't fall asleep.

Honestly, I probably could have taken horse tranquilizers and it wouldn't have affected me. Though my eyes were burning from a restless night, when the cameras swooped in at 6:00 A.M. to film me getting out of bed, I was wide awake and already pumping with adrenaline. Luckily, I was warned about the ambush, so I'd borrowed a floral, booby-revealing nightie, since I usually wear old T-shirts and sweats to bed. A few minutes before the crew came in, I sprang out of bed, brushed my teeth and hair, and splashed cold water on my face. (I'd wished I had an ice cube to rub all over my face. It's the oldest trick in the book on modeling shoots to not look puffy and like you just woke up.) Then I crawled back into bed, and waited for everyone to come in and "surprise" me.

After shooting me getting out of bed—and gazing with concern at the Matterhorn (again!)—they started to film me putting on makeup and my proposal dress. After a few interviews, I took the dress off and didn't put it on again until three hours later so it wouldn't get wrinkled. I hated that dress. I had picked it out three days earlier with the fabulous Cary Fetman, stylist for *The Bachelor.* Both Lindzi and I had to choose from the same eight dresses. I was so disappointed. I thought I'd be wowed—instead, as I walked around reviewing my choices, I thought, *Is this it? This can't be it.* I knew immediately that Lindzi would pick the really girly, poufy, navy blue tube dress with feathers. I ended up with a black dress with sequins, long black gloves, and a white cape. Yes, a white cape.

Under normal circumstances, I would not have been caught dead in that outfit. If I had known that there would only be a few dresses to choose from, I would have brought my own. I had pictured myself in a white gown, with long sleeves and a low back. I never would have dreamed of getting engaged in this! C'mon, black leather gloves? Cary thought I should take them in case it was freezing out. I practiced taking the left one off in one quick motion, if Ben kneeled down. (Funny enough, the one thing Lindzi and I got to keep from the whole *Bachelor* experience was our finale dress. I'm saving mine for a future Halloween party. She sold hers and gave the money to an animal shelter charity.)

So, I thought the dress was an epic fail, but should all go according to plan my ring would be gorgeous. My handler told "jeweler to the stars" Neil Lane exactly what I liked—cushion cut with a pave setting. Also, like a gift from God, Chris Harrison's makeup artist walked into my room and worked her magic on the day of. I was so thankful for this. The only other time I had my makeup professionally done was on the first night of filming at the mansion in Malibu. Other than that, the girls did their own hair and face every day. I certainly know how to do my own makeup for modeling assignments, but I wasn't sure how that would translate to high-definition, wide-screen television. I was hoping I didn't look like a hooker or a drag queen the whole time. I was actually concerned for some of my housemates, like Blakeley Shea, who spent three hours getting ready every day, and Lindzi, who had thick, black eyeliner tattoos, which unfortunately made her look like she slept with her makeup on 24/7.

Okay, that was kind of mean. I'm not going to lie. I was a bitch to some of the girls in the house. Hindsight is 20/20, right? After the proposal, I ultimately owned up to my behavior on "Women Tell All," when the cast came together to rip me a new one and make me cry on-camera (well played, ladies). But I'd just like to say that at this point during filming, I honestly did not know I was going to be portrayed as the worst villain in *Bachelor* history, a.k.a. "America's most hated." I genuinely thought I was being funny. It's sort of like those contestants on *American Idol,* who really have no clue that they can't sing. I guess I found out the hard way that stand-up comedy is not my forte.

Back to the Matterhorn. While I was in the makeup chair, I overheard one of the producers say that the makeup artist had *just* left Lindzi's room. I realized one of two things: either they gave me the later time slot for makeup because they knew I hadn't been able to sleep or—even better—Lindzi was starting filming first, which would mean Ben was going to propose to me after he sent her trekking back down the mountain.

Wow, this is really almost over. Today was officially the end of "the journey" and the last day I would see all the people I had spent every day and night with for the past twelve weeks. It was bittersweet. The crew and producers had become like family to me. I was sad and, at this point, so nervous I could barely speak. But I had one last confessional to do. They brought me into an empty hotel room, decorated with the requisite display of burning candles. My favorite producer walked in. He was the only one I'd been able to open up to. He asked me, "What are you thinking about?"

"My family," I said. I had a huge lump in my throat. I couldn't swallow or breathe. My heart actually hurt. Every emotion came rushing to me, like a flashback of my life. I thought about what my dad would say if he were here. And of my ex-boyfriend Chris.

Although I'd lost track of the date, I realized it was very close to Chris's birthday, and I couldn't help but feel guilty that I may end up engaged on the very day. But Chris had his chance. After locking eyes at a stoplight in Scottsdale in 2000, we had ended up dating on and off for seven years. I wanted to get married but he wasn't ready. We saw each other before I went on *The Bachelor* and he told me he loved me but wanted to support my decision to move on.

Another ex wasn't so diplomatic. *Desperate Housewives* and *Dallas* star Jesse Metcalfe also called me before taping began and tried to talk me out of it. "Fuuuck, this guy is going to pick you," he moaned. But his words were hollow. We also dated on and off for six years and had crazy chemistry. I tried three solid times to make my relationship with Jesse work, but he always disappointed me. He'd call me one night and then I'd see him the next day on TMZ on a date with another woman.

All of my relationships leading up to Ben were ultimately disappointing. I'd dated *Entourage* star Adrian Grenier (sweet but noncommittal), Reese Witherspoon's now-husband Jim Toth (down-to-earth but too old for me at the time), and "regular" guys like my ex Dylan, who liked to lie passed out on my couch and have me bring home a

Subway sandwich for him after I worked my butt off all day. It seems like I've gotten around, but the truth is I can count on three hands the guys I've slept with. And I've never cheated on anyone.

So Ben seemed to be what I'd been looking for my whole life. He said he was ready to get married and knew what he wanted. He was funny, smart, and owned his own business. He seemed like a real man to me (though oddly he did like Justin Bieber's music more than a twenty-nine-year-old man should) and we had good sex—so far. That was very important to me. If the sex had been bad, I couldn't accept a proposal. As crazy as it seemed, *The Bachelor* had truly brought me to the man of my dreams.

AT 1:00 P.M., after hours of waiting and pacing, I finally got escorted to a helicopter decked out in my horrendous cape and gloves (Cary, the stylist, had taken an emergency eleventh-hour train trip to Milan, Italy, to get me matching black boots). I was terrified, but also over the moon in love. I prayed Ben was, too. As the helicopter lifted, I couldn't stop myself from crying. I looked to the producer sitting right next to me with tears in my eyes, and he nodded his head. The cameraman sitting across from me in the jump seat had tears rolling down his cheeks as he filmed. The pilot looked back at me, and asked, "Are you okay?" He'd been watching me cry, and I think he was actually concerned. I felt a little scared. As we flew over a cliff, I saw Ben standing there, and a sense of calm came over me. He was the reason I was still here. He was worth it all.

When we landed, I stepped out of the helicopter, remembering to be careful of the blades. I mean how much would it have sucked to make it this far and then have my head sliced off? I refused to die in this dress. I saw *Bachelor* host Chris Harrison smiling, and the look on his face gave it away. *I'm getting engaged! Or I'm getting dumped. Help.*

I couldn't see Ben from the spot where we landed. It was really quiet and it seemed to be just Chris and me. I'd worried that it would be freezing outside, but it was warm and now I was stuck wearing that darn cape. I didn't realize it at the time, but looking back, I was channeling Cruella De Vil without the Dalmatian spots.

Chris greeted me with a hug, and asked, "Can I take your cape?" *I thought you'd never ask, Chris.* I didn't want to get engaged or broken up with wearing it. I would feel silly. I gave him the cape and he extended his arm for me to take it. Chris had been nothing but nice to me this entire time, and I felt very comfortable with him. He was like a machine. I could tell he wasn't nervous at all. We started to walk toward the top of the hill. I tried to make small talk with him, to get some of my nerves out.

While we waited, I thought about what I was going to say to Ben when I saw him. I had it memorized and was playing it over and over in my head. We started moving again and finally made it to the top of the hill. I wondered how Ben felt at this moment. I hoped he was in a good place, and that if he had sent Lindzi home that it wasn't too emotionally draining on him. I'd tried to shut off the idea that he'd been dating other women the whole time, but I also wanted him to be happy. And if Lindzi was his choice, then so be it. Okay, that was a lie. I'd have flipped out.

But then, just like in a classic rom-com, I saw Ben again, standing patiently in a gorgeous valley in front of, what else, the Matterhorn. He looked so handsome and was wearing my favorite suit, a dark blue Hugo Boss with a skinny velvet tie. He'd worn it during a Rose Ceremony back in San Francisco and I'd told him how sexy he looked. I felt like it was a secret sign that he was wearing it again for me. I just wanted to run up to him and hug him. I was always so happy to see him. He flashed me a big smile and waved. I waved back. Chris pointed out the path, gave me a hug, and said, "Good luck."

As I walked to Ben, I shouted hello in a voice that came out just a little bit too chipper. My heart was racing, and part of me wondered if I'd even be able to get out what I had to say without fainting. *I can do this,* I thought. *I have to tell him how I feel.* We greeted each other with a hug, and I took a deep breath. *Here I go*: "I'm a little nervous," I told him.

He took my hands. I took another deep breath. "Ben, I just want to thank you for this amazing experience." I started crying on-camera but this time I didn't care. "Thank you for making me believe in true love again. You're the best thing that has ever happened to me, and I would be the luckiest girl to have you. I will love you forever." As tears rolled down my face, he gave me a quick kiss. I thought this was another good sign.

He took a moment while I composed myself. "You kind of took my breath away there," he said, smiling. "What a journey, what a journey. It has been an incredible road getting to this point with you through all of the ups and downs. We have encountered real signs of what life could be, from our first date in Sonoma, where I felt we were on this same path, this wavelength of sorts where we understood each other.

"To Belize, where I had a moment—past, present, and future—on top of the ruin. It always seems like whenever I'm with you I have this incredible moment. I can see myself with this woman for the rest of my life. And I want you to know I think you are an incredible woman."

My eyes were totally focused on his face. "*But,*" he said suddenly,

"I had promised myself that I wouldn't get down on one knee again unless I was certain it was forever." Last season, he'd been humiliated by Bachelorette Ashley Hebert, who not only slept with him in the Fantasy Suite but let him propose before she rejected him by lifting him back up by his elbow.

My heart dropped, and in that moment I realized he was about to dump me. I was so frazzled I forgot that every single Bachelor does the "*but*" sentence with the winner for dramatic effect. They've done it every time! And yet, I felt all the blood rush out of my face, which started twitching uncontrollably. I could tell I was frowning.

"*But* I want to tell you," Ben started up again, "that you are my forever and I have waited a really, really long time to tell you that I'm in love with you more than you will ever know and that this whole experience and journey has been worth it every step of the way."

This was the first time Ben told me he was in love with me on-camera. When he started to kneel down, holding my hands the whole time, my heart felt like it was going to burst. "So with all that said, Courtney"—he opened the ring box—"will you marry me?"

I tried to wipe tears away from my eyes, but that long black glove was in the way. Oh no! I forgot to take it off. "Yes, of course, I will! I love you so much." I whipped the glove off, and he placed the ring on my finger. As he got up I said, "I will love you forever."

He repeated it back to me: "I will love you forever." We hugged and kissed and said, "I love you so much," like three times.

"I was hoping you would say yes," Ben told me.

"Any doubt?" I asked him.

"You never know," Ben said.

"This is the best day of my life."

"Mine, too," he answered quickly. "But there's one more thing I have to do." He reached beside him and picked up the final red rose. "Courtney, will you accept this rose?" he asked with a familiar smirk on his face.

"Yes, I do," I told him. We kissed passionately.

I heard loud cheering and clapping. We were finally done filming! It was a miracle! I looked around, but couldn't see anyone. Ben pointed to a far-off area. "Everyone is over there." All of the producers, *Bachelor* creator Mike Fleiss, Chris Harrison, jeweler Neil Lane, and the cameramen were all watching us. It was then that I realized, *The show is over*! We can finally be together the way we want to be, normally, without cameras around us!

Then Ben and I had our first private conversation as the future Mr. and Mrs. Flajnik. At first it was wonderful. "Did you ask my dad?"

"Yes, I called him yesterday. We had a great chat." I gave him a big hug and kiss. This made me so happy.

I whispered, "How did it go with—her? Are you okay?" I never liked to say the other girls' names to him. I tried to pretend it was just the two of us all along. I would joke and say "what's her butt" or "that other girl," instead of Lindzi. But I genuinely felt bad for her at this moment. I hoped she wasn't really devastated and hurt. Maybe they did really have a connection. I wondered why he would have an overnight date with her *and* Nicki Sterling? The same type of overnight date where he told me that he was in love with me? I questioned the sincerity of the words he told me, but brushed it aside.

One of my number one concerns this whole time had been that he was just here to promote his winery, and that he was just really good at saying all the right things. The doubt started to creep back in again.

I was also hoping we were really engaged. What if off-camera he said we should take things slow, and just be boyfriend and girlfriend? I'd have to ask him all of these things later. At that point, I was just trying to enjoy the moment.

We filmed the last scene of us running off together, down a hill toward the Matterhorn, while helicopters hovered over us. We embraced, kissed, and then Ben picked me up and spun me around. We saw everyone run out and start cheering and clapping again. That's a wrap! We were done! I was overjoyed. Ben and I were now able to be together. I could call my family.

As we filmed our first and last interview together, I was beaming. "I'm the happiest girl in the world," I declared. Ben agreed: "I'm the happiest guy in the world!" It felt like a perfect fairy-tale ending, that is, until I made my first joke as the future Mrs. Flajnik. A helicopter flew overhead with a wooden box hanging from it, probably carrying equipment inside. I pointed to the box and blurted out, "Is Lindzi in there?" The whole crew died laughing, but Ben covered my mouth. He didn't seem to get my sense of humor just yet.

We all loaded into a nearby train, and started our trip back into the picturesque city of Zermatt, where Ben and I would get to stay in our own private ski chalet for the next two nights. Neil Lane was standing next to us on the train. I walked over and gave him a big hug and thanked him for designing the beautiful engagement ring, which I later learned cost a whopping $80,000. Neil asked to take a picture with us, and I said, "Of course!" I was hoping to get a copy of the snapshot to remember this day myself. Ben did not seem happy about the photo op and ignored Neil. "He's a weird dude," Ben whispered to me. For the first time ever, I saw a different side to him. He was being standoffish and antisocial, and it made me feel uncomfortable. I didn't understand why he was being so rude.

I tried to focus on our romantic destination, which was so exclusive Brad Pitt and Angelina Jolie had recently stayed there. We'd have our own chef, sauna, Jacuzzi, masseuse, and most important, we could call our parents and share the news. I was so excited. I couldn't wait to be alone with Ben. The next two days would be the most uninterrupted time we'd ever spent together. On our overnight date, in between our sex sessions, we stayed up all night talking because we wanted as much time together as possible. In the Fantasy Suite we'd lain in bed facing each other, listening to Bon Iver, with a fire crackling. Around 5:00 A.M., my eyes started closing. I fought so hard not to fall asleep, and apologized that I couldn't stay awake any longer. About an hour later, I opened my eyes and Ben was still awake watching me sleep. It was one of the most intimate, special nights of my life.

When we arrived at the ski chalet, I saw it was three stories high, with floor-to-ceiling glass windows. We walked into the master suite and the first thing I saw was an incredible view of, yes, the Matterhorn. Our room already had a hundred lit candles (of course), and a romantic fire going. I felt a huge sense of freedom, and the weight started to lift off my shoulders. I saw my bags, and was happy to have all of my things with me, including random snacks I'd collected along the way—apples, teas, granola bars. It's weird but my personal belongings brought me comfort.

I looked around the suite. This is where Ben had been staying this whole time. I saw his clothes hanging up, and all of his things very organized in his closet. It made me feel closer to him to be staying in his room. We lay on the bed facing each other and stared into each other's eyes. I ran my hands through his hair. I told him, "I love you." His eyes filled with tears. I couldn't tell if these were happy tears or sad tears, but it pained me to see him cry. I realized in that moment that I had so much to learn about him, and it made *me* a little sad. I thought to myself, *It's okay. I will learn all of his faces, looks, moods, and what makes him happy. I will make him happy every day for the rest of his life. I have so much love to give and I will give it all to him.* I rolled on top of him, wiped his tears away, and kissed him. I wondered if he was thinking about his father, who'd died five years ago. I started to well up, too.

We should have been celebrating our engagement, not bummed out. So I said, "Let's get out of these clothes." We closed and locked the door and took our first shower together. It was really "lovely," as Ben would say. We made love in the shower, then in the bed.

After our steamy shower, I would have loved to have a romantic dinner à deux in our fabulous chalet in just our bathrobes. Instead, at Ben's request, we got dressed to have dinner with a couple who had worked on the show. After twelve weeks of no privacy, I was desperate to ditch all these people. But Ben had already made this executive decision without even talking to me about it first. He also ordered a $2,500 bottle of wine and later got in trouble for it from the producers.

For the next three days we ended up having every breakfast, lunch, and dinner with the couple. Every. Single. Meal. The second night we all watched *Finding Nemo* together. I was horrified to learn that Ben knew every line, which he recited during the movie. The boyfriend and I kept looking at each other across the room and rolling our eyes, but Ben and the girlfriend seemed to be having a grand ol' time. Sensitive Ben admitted to crying while watching movies on the road together. I did not like the fact that he was watching movies with her at all.

So, while I was trying to get to know my fiancé in the first few days after our engagement, he flirted with this woman and shared inside jokes. Later, when I gingerly told Ben that I was uncomfortable with their friendship, he shrugged it off and said that she was like a sister to him. Then he said that he thought it was healthy to be able to flirt in a relationship. And that she had a great body and "the best" boobs.

I worried I may have gotten engaged to the biggest boob of all. Had I just made the biggest mistake of my life?

On the final morning at the chalet, I woke up at 5:00 A.M. to take the train back to Zurich, so I could finally fly home. It was only a few days into our engagement and I was back to traveling without my fiancé. Of course, my flight home had been booked separately from Ben. I wasn't allowed to be seen in public with him for the next four months, until after the finale aired. So while I flew home, Ben went skiing across the border in Italy with that other couple.

Right before I got on the train I had to take off my engagement ring and hand it over. To make sure the show's finale remained top secret, I couldn't be spotted wearing it. "I'll just wear it because it'll be safer that way," the production assistant said.

As the train pulled out of the station, I glanced over at the production assistant's hand, and I seriously couldn't believe *my* ring was on her finger. Then I stared out the window pensively at the Matterhorn. But this time, I didn't have to try to look concerned. It was effortless.

1

BIRDS, BEES & BIRTHDAY SUITS

My mom warned me that men would cause me nothing but trouble and heartache. From the minute I was able to comprehend words she began lecturing my older sister Rachel and me about the evils of the opposite sex. The monologues began every night at six o'clock on the dot as we sat around the dinner table in our house in Scottsdale, Arizona.

"Men are pigs," she first declared to me in third grade, while sipping a glass of wine on spaghetti Sunday. "It's all about sex or getting some." A few years later, on taco night, I remember her philosophizing over a margarita: "Girls, always remember men are scum." My father, in my humble opinion, was not a pig or scum. He was always home for dinner on time at Casa de Ninas, as he called it. He'd usually stay quiet during these diatribes, though occasionally he might throw in "it's pretty much true" or "there is some truth to that."

My mom had pretty good reasons not to trust men. Her own father disappeared before she was born, so she never met him. Her high school sweetheart not only was abusive, but he also got her pregnant at nineteen (introducing my older half sister, Amy). They got married, but divorced three years later. And while my dad is the sweetest guy, a total softy, it's no secret that he was quite the ladies' man in his younger days. In addition to being extremely handsome, outgoing, and charismatic, he lived in L.A. in the swingin' seventies and had the good fortune of being roommates with Kurt Russell when he was starring in Disney movies like *The Computer Wore Tennis Shoes*. They called their dilapidated house the Goat's Nest. Yes, Kate Hudson's stepdad was my dad's best friend. "We were happily single," my dad fondly recalls. "We hosted many great parties at the Goat's Nest. Kurt was a very fun person to hang out with." Because my dad was kind of a chick magnet, for my entire childhood my mom was constantly worried he would have an affair. My sister and I would often overhear them fighting about it. If he came home one minute late, Mom would grill him about where he'd been and who he'd been with. My mom always said my dad's motto was "deny, deny, deny."

As passionately as my mom hated men, they passionately loved her. A 5'2" beauty with big boobs, she was courted by the richest, most successful guys in town—including a famous musician and a 6'7" basketball star on the Phoenix Suns—even though she came from nothing. After her disastrous first marriage, she grew a thick skin and became notoriously intimidating. She was not easily impressed by potential suitors. My dad, who moved to Arizona and enrolled in ASU's business school, ultimately won my mom over by making her laugh and pretending like he didn't care too much. On their first date, he picked her up in his burgundy Buick Regal, smoked with the windows up, and took her out for drinks instead of the expensive surf 'n turf dinners she'd been getting from other men. He may not have rolled out the red carpet, but his sense of humor and hardworking ways won her over. She felt like he had a promising future and would take care of her. So after dating for three years and avoiding his marriage proposal, my mom finally caved and said, "I do." Today, thirty-four years later, they're still together.

For my mom the bottom line with men was simple: with the exception of my father, men were disgusting and to be avoided at all costs. As Rachel and I got older she became paranoid. She was convinced that "perverts" were going to snatch us right off the street, or that a male family friend would kidnap us from school. If a family friend tried to pick us up, they'd have to know the secret Robertson family code word, which was "douchebag." As for strangers on the street, we practiced a drill over and over again so I was prepared to escape their filthy clutches. After I identified the pervert, I'd drop my backpack and run like hell. I actually had to implement the plan when a scary guy got out of a truck and followed me home from the bus stop one afternoon. Practice made perfect. I immediately ditched my bag and left the pervert in my dust.

Perverts weren't only limited to men in creepy vehicles. I also wasn't allowed to go to the local Big Surf water park because my mom didn't want dirty old men to ogle me in a bathing suit. Not being able to go to a water park in Arizona? In the scorching heat of summer? Not fun.

For all of my mom's lectures against the male species, I was organically a guy's girl. I couldn't help it. I was a tomboy and played soccer and war with all of the neighborhood boys in our front yards. I was a hopeless romantic and dreamed of having one true love like

I saw in my favorite movies *My Girl, Beauty and the Beast,* and *Aladdin*. But in my house, I couldn't just announce on meatloaf night that I had a crush on my adorable neighbor, Dallas. My mom was too scary, plus then I'd have to sit through a mind-numbing sermon about being an independent strong woman, which at nine years old, was also not fun.

Because I was terrified of my mother's wrath and didn't want to disappoint her, I got really good at crushing on boys behind her back. I was so good I actually had a secret boyfriend named Ryan for three months in sixth grade. He was the cutest guy in our class and I set my sights on him fearlessly. One afternoon a bunch of kids were hanging out on a hill. All the girls were just sitting there being lame, so I started rolling down the hill, even though it'd make me sweaty and grass stained. But Ryan noticed me. He came over and said, "I want to roll down the hill, too!" My mom may have been a ballbuster, but she'd also drilled it into me to be a leader, not a follower.

My very first kiss was with Ryan during a strategic game of spin the bottle at my friend Bri's house. Never one to play games, I just cut to the chase and pointed the bottle right at him. After a shot of Binaca we ran off to the bathroom for some tonsil hockey. As one might expect, the kissing was totally amateur, an alien tongue slobbery mess. I decided to give him a chance to hone his skills, so Ryan and I got serious after that. Well, as serious as you can in sixth grade. He'd walk me to class and hug me. He even bought me a silver ring to make our love official. But our steamy love affair was blown to shit at Track and Field Day at school, when Ryan's mom innocently went up to my mom and beamed about how cute it was that we were "going" together. "Where the hell are they going?" my mom screamed at her. "Courtney doesn't have a boyfriend!" She made such an embarrassing scene that Ryan dumped me.

After that debacle, my mom instituted a new rule: I wouldn't be allowed to date until I was sixteen. As I raged through puberty, she refused to let me shave my legs and armpits, or pluck my eyebrows, which resulted in the lovely nickname Unibrow. Already taller than most of the boys, I was gangly, awkward, and really hairy (thanks Italian heritage!). I was as flat as a pancake chest-wise and wore baggy T-shirts from Target every day. Though I had inherited a lot of my mom's fierce personality, I had not been blessed with her ample bosom. So, in addition to Unibrow, I was also dubbed Brick Wall by the meanest boys on my bus. I didn't really care. I loved boys, even the mean ones.

I always got along so much better with boys than girls. I did have a best girlfriend I'd known since kindergarten, Sara. Looking back, the circumstances of how we met would foreshadow my relationship with her—and women in general—for the rest of my life. Sara came from one of the richest families in the area. Her dad was a famous doctor in Arizona. My family was pretty poor when I was young. We couldn't always keep up with our super rich neighbors. There were a couple times I had to drop out of dance or gymnastics classes because we couldn't afford the dues. Instead of bringing a cool lunch box filled with delicious sandwiches and Capri Suns, I ate the $2 lunch provided at school (in grade school my sister Amy even worked in the cafeteria like Marley's mom on *Glee*). Oh, how I longed for an individual bag of potato chips, a luxury in my eyes! From an early age, I always tried to make extra money doing whatever I could: my dad would pay us a penny for each grapefruit we picked up in the yard, we ran lemonade stands, we pawned knickknacks, and once I even tried to sell leaves off of our mulberry tree. I was distraught that nobody would buy one, until my neighbor pointed out that she had plenty in her own yard.

Before I met Sara, I wasn't even aware of how poor we were. But the day I met her in kindergarten, she took out her shiny, new, gigantic box of Crayolas, the one with the sharpener in the back and fifty magical colors, like atomic tangerine, and it became crystal clear. My mom had sent me to school with a couple of broken crayons from Garcia's Mexican restaurant. Since Sara had a beautiful bounty, I innocently asked to borrow one. "No," she sniffed condescendingly. In that moment, I got a life lesson in both class warfare and cattiness. Naturally, I made her my best friend.

I was also a cheerleader in junior high and then again in my sophomore year of high school, but the sorority vibe of it just wasn't my thing. The girls were always complaining about something trivial, or talking about their feelings. I hated the whole fake Kumbaya vibe, when these girls were ripping each other to shreds behind their backs. I did have a close group of girlfriends growing up, but they were mostly jocks, not your typical girly girls. In the end, I really loved hanging with the guys. Less drama and fewer complications.

I tried to skirt around my mom's ban on boys, but her plan was extremely successful in one very important way. I had been raised to be a gigantic prude: I was completely naïve about sex and totally inexperienced. After my epic make out session with Ryan in sixth grade, I didn't so much as kiss a guy again for another five (!) years. For my first two years of high school, while my girlfriends were hooking up and learning about sex and their bodies, I was still innocently passing notes to the boys I liked. Even though they flirted back, that was the extent of their investment in me because they knew moving forward would just mean blue-ball city. I wasn't allowed to go to dances with boys, so I had to go stag with a group of girls freshman and sophomore year.

Nobody was having sex with me—and nobody was even talking about it with me. Not my mom, not my sister, and not even my best friend, Sara, who had taken a virginity pact with me, even though she was dating a guy who became a star Major League Baseball player. I actually looked up sex in the dictionary once just to figure out what it was. *Merriam-Webster* was not very helpful.

All this sexual repression was starting to make me really curious, and really hot and bothered. I had a TV in my room and, around age fifteen, I suddenly started noticing that when half-naked people hooked up on *Baywatch* I'd get super horny (Jeremy Jackson, people, *not* David Hasselhoff). But it was a particularly steamy make out session between Joshua Jackson and Michelle Williams on *Dawson's Creek* one summer evening that sent me over the edge. After I turned off the TV, I couldn't sleep. I'd heard my friends joking about "flicking the bean" and it was like an animal instinct kicked in. I put my hand down south and went to town. I felt amazing and then suddenly, uncontrollably, I let out a moan so loud I worried I'd woken up everyone in the house, maybe even cute little Dallas next door. I snuck to the bathroom, totally blushing, but thankfully I was in the clear. Apparently nobody heard me.

Emboldened by my erotic discovery, I masturbated every night for the next—well forever. For a little visual stimulation, I started taping (it was still VHS back then) a montage of the dirtiest scenes I could find on *Baywatch,* love scenes between James Van Der Beek and Katie Holmes in *Dawson's Creek,* and a few Lifetime movies. I was convinced everyone knew I was a filthy degenerate. I was paddling the pink canoe so much my hand was getting cramped. *There's got to be an easier way to do this without getting carpal tunnel syndrome,* I thought. Though science was never my strong suit, I had a eureka moment in the bathtub. Like so many industrious women before me, I realized the water stream out of the faucet could do the job. Needless to say, Calgon took me away—a lot.

So, in a few short years I'd gone from Ryan's sixth-grade alien kisses to making myself have multiple orgasms. It was quite an achievement, if I do say so myself. I'd give myself an A for effort *and* execution.

This is probably as good a time as any to mention that I was not getting As for anything else, except maybe gym class. I was practically flunking out of high school. School and I just never meshed. I cried so hard the very first day of kindergarten, like shoulder-heaving sobs, that I got sent home. I ended up getting held back that year. I was put into "developmental kindergarten" because I was "emotionally immature." My attendance in school from then on was spotty, bordering on truant. Bored, easily distracted, and possibly dyslexic, I went to the nurse's office anytime I couldn't deal with a teacher or student, or wanted to avoid a quiz on my archnemesis, the times table. The nurse would roll her eyes when I walked in pointing to a random spot on my body complaining of a phantom ailment.

But the thing was my mom was always happy to come get me. I think she was bored, too. Before she met my dad, she'd opened a successful pottery-painting shop in the mall. But after having kids she sold the store and became a stay-at-home mom. Alone all day and desperate for company, she'd scoop me up from school and we'd sit together all afternoon watching *All My Children* and *Maury*.

My early absences didn't help my future success in school. My parents wanted to test me for dyslexia but my teacher told them I was "perfectly average." She said I may not excel in school but that I was a "social butterfly" and that would help me succeed in life. By high school, I was getting mostly Ds and forging my dad's signature on my report cards. I probably set a record for summer school classes needed to graduate. I was embarrassed about my grades and tried really hard to hide them from my friends. It didn't help that my sister Rachel was a brainiac and would constantly call me stupid. "I got the brains and Court got the beauty" was her mantra. It always bothered me because I knew I was smarter than my grades made it seem. I was just totally lost when it came to school. Unlike a lot of kids, I had no clue what I wanted to be when I grew up. I didn't even think I *could* be anything because I was so bad at school.

One time, after getting frustrated studying, I sat on the patio with my dad and cried. "You'll be okay," he'd say. "You can always be a model." I thought he was just being nice and cried harder. With my flat chest, baggy boy clothes, and broken nose—courtesy of a kick to the face from my sister's handstand in fourth grade—I never really felt that attractive. Puberty wasn't very kind to me.

Frustrated sexually and academically (who am I kidding, I didn't give a shit about school back then), I felt like a big loser. But I was desperate to be in love, like all of those couples I watched on TV. It came to a turning point during the summer before senior year when I finally turned eighteen. Sara invited me to her family's lake house in Michigan, where, after sharing several cigarettes (remember, this is the daughter of a doctor), she confessed that she'd been lying to me. She wasn't a virgin. She and her boyfriend had been boinking for the last two years! Feeling envious and like a lame goody-goody, I vowed right then in my mind that as soon as I got back to Arizona, I was going to ho it up like it'd never been ho'd before. Enough was enough already! But first I needed some tutoring, because I was miles behind my classmates and, apparently, that little horndog Sara.

I decided that my kissing instructor would be Ryan, who I'd never stopped liking but who had moved on to girls who were more experienced. I started dragging him into corners and bathrooms at parties. He had greatly improved his make out skills and happily showed me the ropes. As word got out that I was shedding my nun's habit, my other guy friends started making ethically questionable moves on me. Ryan's best friend, Cole, threw him under the bus and told me that Ryan didn't like me anymore. Because Cole looked like a blond Adonis I chose to believe him (I always had a thing for blonds, excluding David Hasselhoff). Plus, I was a sexually liberated woman now; I couldn't belong to just one man.

I was ready to go to the next level with Cole, so I asked him to teach me how to give a blow job. He quickly and eagerly agreed to be my mentor. One night, we snuck onto a golf course and he instructed me how to use my already cramped hand, and how not to use my teeth. The golf course became our go-to spot for many future fellatio-fests. I understand why Tiger Woods liked to sink his balls in so many holes. Golf isn't boring. It's sexy!

On the way home from one of my dates with Cole, I pulled up to a stoplight, lost in thought. A truck with two guys in it backed up to check me out. I glanced over and the driver was a blond, blue-eyed surfer boy. And, at this point in my life, he was the best-looking guy I'd ever seen. He was God's gift to women and the world. It was love at first sight.

"Hey, where ya going?" he said.

"Home?" I answered coyly.

"We're going to P. F. Chang's. Wanna come?"

"What school do you go to?" I asked.

"Camelback."

Camelback was on the wrong side of the tracks in Scottsdale.

"What are you doing all the way over here?"

"Where do *you* go?" he said, kind of offended.

"Arcadia."

"Of course, that's where all the pretty girls go."

With that, he peeled off into the night and I worried I'd never see him again. Instead, I kept running into this same guy all over town at parties, the gym, and the Fashion Square mall. I found out his name was Chris, star of the Camelback basketball team, originally from Maui. Once, at the gym, I left him one of my signature notes with my number and this message on his windshield: "You're the hottie with the body!" He called me but said he had a girlfriend and the note got him in big trouble. I told him when they were over to get back to me. I may have become a guy magnet that summer, but I certainly was no home wrecker.

Once I mastered the art of the BJ, I was ready for actual sex. The weekend before senior year started, I found the perfect guy to deflower me at a pool party. Jono was a year older and worked at Costco. His mom died when he was younger, he was estranged from his dad, and he lived with a classmate's family. Jono was shy, quiet, and kind of sad and mysterious. I'd never seen him out before this night. Thinking he'd be gentle and discreet, I made him my mark. After everyone went inside, I asked him if he wanted to go swimming.

"I don't have a swimsuit," he said.

"Let's go skinny-dipping," I answered bravely without really thinking it through carefully.

Number one: I was still very self-conscious about my flat chest.

Number two: I had an absolutely gigantic bush. Nobody ever told me or taught me how to shave down there.

Luckily, Jono didn't notice or care. We peeled off our clothes, me covering my nonexistent boobs, and got in the pool naked.

"Hey, I've always had a crush on you," I purred.

"Really? I've never seen you before," he deadpanned.

Before I could get insulted, he pushed me up against the side of the pool and started making out with me. Then he fingered me. I think. Nobody had ever done it to me before so I wasn't sure what was happening. After that, there was some bouncing up and down. Whatever was happening felt good but I stopped him.

We exchanged numbers and after he left I went inside to dish with my girlfriends.

"I think I just had sex!"

"You think?"

"What do you mean you think?"

"Are you sore?"

"Yeah?"

"Then you had sex!"

The drought was officially over. I was no longer a virgin. As senior year commenced, I skipped school about nineteen times to have afternoon delights with Jono between his shifts at Costco. At the same time, Chris had broken up with his girlfriend and we started dating, too, but not going all the way. He even got me a part-time job at Abercrombie and Fitch at the Fashion Square mall, where I folded a shit-ton of shirts and fought off our college-girl coworkers who tried to steal Chris away from me.

Jono was my sad-eyed fuck buddy, but I was totally infatuated with Chris. Chris wasn't so infatuated with my relationship with Jono or my gigantic bush. After he put his hand down my pants during the movie *Shrek,* he made a stinkface, said "Whoa!" and requested that I tame the beast.

But Jono liked the big bush and didn't want me to shave.

What was a girl to do?

I stole my dad's razor, popped a fresh blade in, and did a hatchet job somewhere in the middle.

Though my dad was okay with Chris and dubbed him Cuddles after spotting him for the gazillionth time draped all over me on our couch watching movies, my mom did not like Chris and told me he was "shady." In case you were wondering, my mom was still not talking to me about sex. She avoided the conversation at all costs and had a "no boys allowed in my room" policy. I think she assumed I was staying out of trouble, or just couldn't bear to hear the truth. I knew she would murder me if she found out I was having sex.

KEEPING IT REAL

Hey there *Bachelor* fans. I've asked my family, friends, and your favorite members of Bachelor Nation to offer up tips, tricks, advice on life, love, and reality TV! Be on the lookout for insider info, confessions, and blind items as my journey to love unfolds. Let's kick it off with the woman whose advice means the most—my mom.

My Mom on Men

In addition to "men are scum," Sherry Robertson has many more pearls of wisdom:

- Never marry a man with an ass smaller than yours.
- Never marry a guy who lets you pick up the check.
- Never marry a man with a pageboy haircut.
- Learn to love football if you want to see your husband.

- Do not wear strong perfume. Men hate that.
- Nothing good ever happens between the hours of 10:00 P.M. and 6:00 A.M.
- Marry someone with a nice last name (not Horne or Dick).
- Marry someone who loves you more than you love him.
- Never marry a man with intentions of changing him.
- You have your whole life to let a man screw it up.

Chris hated Jono but I was unwilling to end my sexual liaison because I was learning so much and finally feeling confident and sexy. It all blew up in my face on Valentine's Day. I got both of them boxers with little hearts on them from the Gap. But Chris was over it—and me. I got an urgent call from my sister Rachel, a hostess at Z'Tejas Southwestern Grill in the mall, who snitched that Chris was there with a leggy soccer player named Brandy.

I was shattered. Heartbroken for the first time in my life, I sobbed for days, listened to Coldplay's "Yellow" on repeat, and tried unsuccessfully to console myself in Jono's sad arms. Chris was the most popular guy at his school and he liked *me,* Unibrow Robertson. The popular guys at my school avoided me like Paula Deen at a Jay-Z concert. My mom, of course, ordered me to "snap out of it," but I was so overcome with grief, I started giving away my shifts at A&F because I couldn't face Chris or bear to bump into him with Brandy.

I also wanted Chris to miss me.

A month later, he found an excuse to call me. The store had put up flyers announcing that they were looking for a fresh new face for the Abercrombie and Fitch brand. They encouraged employees to apply.

"I think you're perfect for this," Chris said. "You should enter."

I had never seriously thought about being a model, with my bad haircut, pepperoni face from pimples, and giant slouching shoulders. I imagined how proud Chris would be if I won—my face plastered on the side of the A&F shopping bag—so I decided to go for it. How could he resist me if I was a famous model?

I had one week to get into tip-top shape. First, I went on a crash diet: instead of eating McDonald's cheeseburgers and Taco Bell chalupas, I only ate Cheez-Its from the vending machine. Then I started running like a cheetah at the gym. I even woke up in the middle of the night and sprinted around the block a few times.

When I felt my pale body was ready to be photographed, I enlisted my dad to take pictures of me lounging on a blow-up raft in a pool wearing a light blue bikini. I also posed on a white patio chair and, after shyly practicing my smile in the mirror, did some close-ups of my face. After my dad got the pictures developed at a one-hour photo my mom acted as photo editor and chose her favorite shots. Then we mailed the packet off into the abyss.

About a week later, I was studying at my friend Emily's house (that's a lie, actually she was writing a paper for me) when my cell phone rang. It was an Ohio number.

"Hi, this is John from Abercrombie and Fitch."

I almost fainted. John Urbano was the creative director at A&F.

"I'm calling to see if you'd like to travel with us to the British Virgin Islands for a week to shoot our next marketing campaign."

"Are you sure?" I squealed. "Are you really picking me?"

After assuring me he was serious, he asked if I had a passport (I didn't) and informed me that I'd be making $1,200 per day. I made $5.25 an hour working in the A&F store.

After we hung up, I told Emily I had to go and sped home as fast as I could. I waited for our six o'clock dinner to start, then sprang the news on my parents over a bowl of spaghetti.

"I have exciting news," I started. "But before I tell you, you have to promise to really hear me out. This is something I'd really love to do."

"Out with it!" my mom barked.

As I announced that I had won the A&F contest, my dad had tears in his eyes. I could tell that even my mom, who was never easily impressed, was blown away. For the first time in my life, I felt like I had made my parents proud.

A week later, during my high school's spring break week, I was on a red-eye flight alone to the British Virgin Islands. I went despite the objections of Jono, who was furious I was leaving and worried I'd be naked 24/7 with hot male models. "I can't believe you'd take your clothes off for money," he ranted manipulatively. As I looked down at the passport necklace my dad bought me, I realized I'd never been away from my family for a week. I'd never been out of the country. I hoped I wasn't about to be sold into sex slavery or have my organs stolen.

"It's time to toughen up," I told myself.

Then I turned on my Discman and played Vanessa Carlton's "A Thousand Miles" over and over until I drifted off to sleep.

2

CATWALKING & STARFUCKING

"Oh my Lord, this isn't going to work."

The makeup artist on my very first professional A&F shoot was deeply concerned about the pubic line of my white bikini, which had unruly and unseemly brown hairs poking out. After giving me a razor and sending me off to the bathroom with instructions about how to properly shave my nether region, she also mercifully gave me a professional eyebrow waxing.

After she finished, I looked in the mirror. For the first time in my life, I felt good about myself. I wasn't Unibrow or Pepperoni Face or Stupid.

I was pretty.

My newfound confidence helped me get through what I can only describe as an extremely awkward week of learning how to be a model by trial and error. I fidgeted way too much and had no idea how to pose, but the crew was patient and supportive of me and I earned the nickname Mini, because they thought I looked like a mini May Anderson. I was a "favorite" of the photographer and he used me a lot in the different setups, which included a beautiful sailboat, pristine beaches, and lots of fake, closed-mouth kisses with the male models. I was still such a good girl (thanks, Mom) that when my fellow mannequins went out to party every night in BVI, I stayed in the five-star hotel by myself, though I did chain-smoke cigarettes. I didn't care. I was living the life on someone else's dime. I thought, *I could die tomorrow and be happy.*

Jono had made me paranoid and petrified that I'd have to be naked the whole time, but it wasn't until the last day that I was first asked to strip down.

"Do you mind?" the photographer asked.

I took off my top and all my insecurities about being Brick Wall evaporated. I felt liberated about my body as I stood in the Caribbean Sea and whipped my wet hair back and forth. Naturally, when these in-store promotional photos came out, they'd only used the shots of us naked on the last day.

Jono dumped me.

But I wasn't that heartbroken because I was rich! The first thing I splurged on was three pugs—Emma, Bubba, and Phoebe—one for me, one for my sister Rachel, and one for my BFF, Sara. I blew seven hundred bucks on puppies without batting an eye.

My inaugural shoot in BVI went so well that two weeks later I was asked to fly to Philadelphia to model A&F's fall back-to-school catalog with legendary photographer Bruce Weber, who also shot famous campaigns for Ralph Lauren, *Vogue,* and Revlon. I immediately believed I was headed for supermodel stardom.

When I arrived in Philly, it was 180 degrees different from my super chill tropical paradise shoot. Bruce, known for his provocative, controversial style, had flown in forty of the hottest young models from New York, Miami, and L.A. The girls were super cliquey and peppered me with condescending questions about my modeling experience, or lack thereof.

"Wait, you work in the store?" one asked snottily. "What do you do there?"

"I ring up people on the cash register?" I answered meekly.

I was intimidated and kept to myself, which wasn't a problem because nobody was interested in talking to me anyway. Bruce would come by and watch the models mingling with one another, looking for chemistry. He noticed that I was a pariah in the group and didn't use me much.

I was booked for five days for an astounding $2,000 per day, but on the third day I made a crucial mistake. A photo assistant asked if I would get naked, even though it was freezing outside and it was a back-to-school *clothing* catalog for *teenagers*.

This time I decided to take a stand. It suddenly hit me that the principal of my school could see these photographs. "No, I'm not comfortable with that," I said, proud of myself.

The next day, I got back to my hotel room and found a cold, formal note on my pillow, informing me that I was no longer needed on the shoot. Confused and wondering what I'd done wrong, I eventually realized that if you say no to nakedness, especially with Bruce Weber, you're pretty much dunzo in the modeling business. None of the shots I'd done the few days before made it into the catalog.

It didn't matter. I had a newfound confidence and sense of purpose. I was also kind of a mini celebrity at my school and even got a little ink in the local paper. Even though I almost wasn't allowed to walk at graduation because I had so many absences, the student council asked me to give a speech during commencement.

"Abercrombie!" my fellow students yelled as I spoke.

I had arrived.

AFTER I GRADUATED from high school, I quit my job at A&F after signing with the Ford modeling agency, which was conveniently located just down the street from my house. I rented an apartment with my friends Sara and Emily, studied graphic design at Scottsdale Community College, but ended up dropping out. My modeling career was taking off and I was working like a fiend, booking local catalogs and magazine editorial for clients who did their shoots in the desert.

Chris popped up in my life again—something that would happen over and over for the next decade. He was being really supportive of my modeling career so we started dating. And we finally had sex and it was miiiind-blooooowing (say it like Oprah). Our first time was in a shower. Apparently, for some reason, I have a thing about doin' it in the water. There must be a Masters and Johnson study somewhere that says you try to re-create the time you lost your virginity.

A year after winning the A&F contest, I'd done all the modeling work I could do in Scottsdale. The town just wasn't big enough for my budding career anymore, so I decided it was time to make a big move. I packed up what little crap I had, and drove to L.A. with another girlfriend and model friend named Michelle. Chris was supposed to help me move but totally flaked. I was definitely sad to leave him, yet one of my mom's incessant mottos kept playing in my head on a loop: "Never let a man screw up your life." Chris had given up a deal to play basketball overseas because he didn't want to leave me. But I couldn't stay in Arizona just for him.

In L.A., Michelle and I got a starter apartment on Sierra Bonita, right off Sunset Boulevard, and booked go-sees together for every modeling agency in Hollywood. Within two days I had five offers for representation, but not from the L.A. branch of Ford. They said I was too short after measuring me under 5'9". Clueless about how to pick a new agency, I signed with Nous Model Management because they were on Robertson Boulevard. I thought it was a good omen because of my last name and because the office was on the same street as the Ivy, a famous restaurant where the paparazzi snapped stars eating chopped salads.

Good omens aside, we got off to a rocky start. Despite my initial refusal to disrobe for living legend Bruce Weber, the Picasso of photography, my old agency Ford in Scottsdale got me another chance to be in his next A&F catalog. Nous was unhappy that my former agency was still booking me, but I couldn't pass up the opportunity. This time the shoot was in Rome and I was getting paid $2,000 per day for thirteen days for a total of $26,000!

I guess I finally learned my times table.

Before I left, I made a vow to myself to say yes to any request, no matter how crazy or R-rated. My new philosophy paid off. As soon as I was asked, I immediately answered, "Yes, I'll get naked." About forty male and female models were flown to Rome and slowly, one by one, I saw every naïve soul who dared to say no get sent home.

Now, I'm not sure if Bruce Weber was inspired by Roman orgies or what, but I spent eleven of the thirteen days totally naked, out in the open, in the busy streets of Rome. I don't even know if it was legal or if we had permits, but nobody stopped our massive mobile production, which included five photo assistants, a dozen hair and makeup artists, stylists, and, of course, the Boom Box Guy, whose sole job was to carry a radio on his shoulder in order to play classical ambient music as loud as possible.

I was paired up the entire time with a blond, blue-eyed German boy named Sasha, who had a gigantic boner the whole shoot. Even though we didn't originally have any chemistry, eleven days of his rock-hard penis in my pelvis, butt, and face as we frolicked nude in a bathtub, a waterfall, next to a statue, and in a castle, brought us closer together. At this point, I was basically single because Chris and I were having trouble doing the long-distance thing between Scottsdale and L.A. So one night, I invited Sasha to my room for a massage. Before I kneaded his beautiful back, I asked him if he had a girlfriend. When he said yes, I kicked him out. It was at that moment that I decided I'd never bang another woman's boyfriend. Believe it or not, I'm a big believer in karma.

The shoot in Rome was a game changer for my career, even though every photograph was "burned" or destroyed because conservative and religious groups threatened to boycott A&F over Bruce's sexually explicit pictures, which they believed were obscene and child pornography.

With Bruce Weber on my résumé, I started working immediately when I got back, though I didn't get the best assignments and the castings were few and far between. After months of mediocre jobs, I defected to L.A. Models, where I remained for the next eight years, mentored by my agent and mother stand-in Mamie Indig.

My career blew up at L.A. Models. I started booking gigs and traveling all over the world for big name brands like Izod, Nautica, Mervyns, Diet Coke, Rip Curl, and Target, and I shot my first commercial for Old Navy. I did a runway show with Cindy Crawford and an ad for Jessica Simpson's hair extensions right after she and first husband, Nick Lachey, split. Jessica was very sweet but very sad. She spent most of the day holed up in her candle-lit dressing room, drinking carrot juice, and blasting Sinéad O'Connor's "Nothing Compares 2 U." I was working with the best photographers, including a Roxy campaign with Peggy Sirota at Pismo Beach. But I didn't know how to surf so I got sent home early. They wanted to focus on the surfer girls they sponsored. The awesome part about my job? When they send you packing, they still have to pay up. So I still got my fee: $3,000 per day for three days = $9,000.

As exciting as my new life was, it was a huge adjustment. I was so lonely when I first moved to L.A. that I'd wander around the Grove mall by myself and bump up against strangers just to have human contact. I also had a hell of a lot to learn, like how to deal with constant rejection and stressed-out photographers who had no patience for my inexperience. On one Nordstrom shoot in Seattle, I wasn't moving the right way and was totally bawled out. "You're just a squirrel trying to get a nut!" a mean photographer screamed.

I also was a terrible runway walker, and during a Swarovski event I ruined the entire show when I walked too fast and threw the timing off with the music. I also had a wardrobe malfunction where my nipple was entirely exposed. I looked like a deer caught in the headlights.

Some clients, like online shopping sites or big department stores, are basically sweatshops for models. They have you model their entire collections in one day, basically a hundred outfits nonstop for six hours. It's exhausting. I'd even get rashes from taking the cheap fabrics on and off so quickly. And just when you thought you were done, they'd wheel in another rack of clothes to shoot. When you're young and just starting out, they know you won't say no.

I also couldn't say no when my agency shipped me off to New Zealand and Australia for two months and then to New York City to meet with clients. I had to live in a cramped, mouse-infested "model apartment," that was really just two small rooms with bunk beds. My roommates were several models, who washed their undies in the sink and were so promiscuous they brought home guys in the middle of the day and banged them in the bathroom, while I sat in the living room two feet away watching *All My Children*.

My roommates weren't the only crazy models I worked with. I definitely witnessed my fair share of pukers, and heard stories of girls who wanted to stay skinny so badly they swallowed cotton balls. I hated throwing up so I never was in danger of having an eating disorder. I did try Victoria "Posh" Beckham's 1,200-calorie diet once. But I had no energy afterward so I ditched it. Of course, it was intimidating being surrounded by the most gorgeous women in the world. Sometimes I felt like I was playing a part. I'd see how a successful model dressed and go to H&M and try to re-create her look. There were a few catty girls out there, but I held my own and made really great friendships that last to this day. Yes, modeling can be competitive but there's also a huge sense of camaraderie among us.

KEEPING IT REAL

My Modeling Tips

FOR THE NEWBIES

1. Keep a nude thong, nude strapless bikini, and heels in your car at all times in case of a last-minute casting.
2. Never leave your portfolio in your car. It could melt or be stolen. It's your livelihood!
3. Always be early for castings.
4. Always hang up the clothes you modeled. Clients hate when models leave samples on the floor.
5. Always eat lunch with the clients. They may hire you again if you're a nice person!
6. Stay off your phone. You're paid to be focused.
7. Save all receipts. Your clothes, makeup, haircuts, gas are all write-offs.
8. After you book your first job, treat yourself to something nice, then save, save, save the rest! It's feast or famine in this industry. You never know when your next job will be.
9. Be nice to everyone. It's a small biz and you will work with the same stylists and photographers over and over again.
10. Don't brag. You may be a model today, but who knows about tomorrow.

FOR THE WANNABES

1. The gym is your office and part of your job. Get healthy.
2. Stop drinking soda. It bloats you.
3. Take care of your skin. Get lots of sleep and get regular facials.
4. You need test shots, as many as you can. Find an up-and-coming photographer on Facebook. But never sign anything until a lawyer or a new agent looks it over.
5. Study fashion magazines not only for style and beauty trends, but also to see which companies are using models as opposed to celebrities.
6. Take constructive criticism. If someone wants you to change your hair color, be less buff, lose weight, do it.
7. Don't post unflattering or partying photos on social media. You're only as good as your last photo.
8. Practice your looks in the mirror.
9. Take an on-camera commercial workshop.
10. Tyra is right. Learn to smize (smile with your eyes)!

So here I was, in my early twenties, living on my own and making up to $25,000 per week. Nobody had ever talked to me about managing my money so I started splurging on shoes and $500 Louis Vuitton Speedy bags. Who had time for a savings account? Desperate to make friends, I spent my nights out at Hollywood's hottest clubs, like the Concorde, Cabana Club, and LAX. I had no problem getting in, even when I was underage. The promoters wanted young models to dance on their tables, drink their booze for free, and flirt with their boldface clientele, like Justin Timberlake and Brody Jenner. Bob Saget, David Spade, Spencer Pratt, and Matthew Perry were also club fixtures at the time, and, though I steered clear, I was amazed at how many women threw themselves at them.

One of my new best friends was Matthew, a rich-kid model whose claim to fame was making out with Britney Spears in her *Toxic* video and dating C-list actresses like Minnie Driver and Selma Blair. Matt knew everybody in the nightlife scene and I spent countless hours at the Chateau Marmont with him and his connected friends doing the cliché Hollywood thing.

Through all of this partying, I will say this: I never did drugs and I never had a one-night stand. Matt was always trying to pimp me out to his friends in the rare moments I was single, but it was just never my style. I did have sex one time with a male model friend, who shall remain nameless, but his penis was so insanely small (like the size of a baby carrot stick) that it turned me off from casual hookups pretty much forever.

At this point in my life, I'd done some growing up when it came to men and relationships. No more golf course BJs, thank you very much. I took pride in not being a ho and truly wanted to save some things for the person I'd marry. In all of my years being a prude, and then getting close to my guy friends, I'd pick their brains about what they wanted in a wife. They all said the same thing: if a girl sleeps with me on the first night, she's not the one. They also didn't want to throw their hotdog down a hallway, if you know what I mean.

At that time, I thought Chris's hotdog would be in my hallway for the rest of my life. I really did think we'd eventually get married one day. Even though we were five hundred miles away from each other, and officially "keeping our options open," we texted constantly and I'd always call him when I got home at night, no matter what time, because my neighborhood was so sketchy. Bums would sleep in the bushes right outside my ground-floor window, and on hot summer nights I could hear them snoring and rolling over.

Naturally, the more time we spent away from each other, the more we drifted apart. Chris didn't drink, he was a straight arrow, and he didn't like the whole fake Hollywood lifestyle. He was a small-town boy at heart. Once, when he visited me in L.A., I wanted to take him to a club, but he was so nervous he threw up in the cab on the way there. Even though I was quite lonely my first few years in L.A., I wasn't a small-town girl anymore. In fact, my life was changing so fast it was impossible for Chris to keep up.

Case in point: One day we decided to get burgers at the In-N-Out on Sunset. I needed cash, so I pulled my car over to get money from an ATM. As Chris watched me from the passenger seat, a black Escalade drove by, slammed on the brakes, and then backed up. A guy jumped out and started running over to me frantically.

"CAN I GET YOUR NUMBER?" he screamed. "DO YOU HAVE A BOYFRIEND?"

When he got up to me, he was so beautiful he took my breath away. He had jet-black hair, thick dark eyebrows, and gorgeous green eyes. He looked sort of familiar, but I couldn't figure out who he was.

"Yeah, he's in the car," I said, pointing to Chris, who was staring back at us unhappily.

"Oh," the guy said, dejected.

"Maybe we'll run into each other again," I offered.

"Doubt it," he said with major attitude. Then he swaggered back to his SUV like a brat and peeled out.

When I got back to the car, Chris was very grumpy. "What was that about? What did you say to him?"

"I told him I had a boyfriend, silly!" I said sweetly, though inside I couldn't shake off what had just happened. Chris knew me better than anyone. He could tell I was a little giddy from the encounter.

About four months later, my mom called me during one of her afternoon TV marathons. "Turn on *Oprah*. She has the most beautiful man I've ever seen on."

I turned on the TV and there was the gorgeous, green-eyed guy from the Escalade. It was Jesse Metcalfe, the hunky gardener on the new hit show *Desperate Housewives*.

"Oh my God, I met him! He hit on me at an ATM!"

"That's the kind of guy you should be with," my mom declared. Even though she hated men, she was an avid reader of Danielle Steel novels and shallowly appreciated good-looking guys, especially if they were tall, dark, and handsome. Her favorite was Antonio Banderas.

Mom's least favorite man was still Chris. Her wish for us to split up finally came true one week before the Academy Awards in 2004. Increasingly insecure about my success and unable to deal with the distance and lack of regular sex, Chris broke up with me before I could break up with him. I was really upset, but also finally ready to move on. He hated when I went out so, of course, I decided to go out on Oscar night, the biggest event of the year in Hollywood.

Even though I personally didn't know anybody important, my friend Michelle and I got into one of the most exclusive A-list parties at a multi-million-dollar mansion transformed into a club in the Hollywood Hills. The party promoter asked my agency to round up a bunch of models—no plus ones and no guys allowed, no exceptions—and they shuttled us up to the house in a party bus with blacked-out windows so we couldn't see the top secret location. Once inside the gates, we were released into the party like chum.

As soon as I walked in, I immediately spotted Leonardo DiCaprio and Vince Vaughn. A gourmet chef flipped pancakes, and made fried chicken and waffles for anyone who didn't have to starve themselves to fit into their tuxes and skintight dresses anymore. Feeling overwhelmed, I decided to go outside for a smoke by myself. It was chilly so I was shivering in my little black dress and hugging my arms close to my body.

Suddenly, a tuxedo jacket was draped over my shoulders.

"Looks like you need this."

I turned around and stared directly into the gorgeous green eyes of Adrian Grenier. *Entourage* hadn't aired yet but I recognized him from the teen movie *Drive Me Crazy* with Melissa Joan Hart.

After thanking him, we got into a good conversation about our mutual loneliness in L.A. He'd moved here from Queens and was struggling because he felt like he had no real friends. Adrian was really genuine and warm, and in old-school gentlemanly fashion asked, "Can I take you to dinner?"

We exchanged numbers, he left the party, and I went back inside, looking for Michelle. I found her standing at the bar with, drum roll please, Jesse Metcalfe. *Desperate Housewives* was now a huge hit and he was a huge star.

"Hi. Do you still have a boyfriend?" he asked me aggressively as soon as I walked up.

I couldn't believe that he remembered me from our encounter at the ATM, but I remained calm. "No," I answered. "We broke up a week ago. Are you single?" I needed to know; it's the first thing I always asked a guy. I don't care who he is.

"Yeah. I want to take you out sometime."

I wrote my number on a napkin and gave it to him. As he walked away smirking, I thought, *He's definitely going to lose that.*

The next day I got a text from Adrian, who made good on that dinner invite. I said yes, but truthfully I wasn't excited about it. I really wished it'd been Jesse. I called my mom to tell her I'd run into her celebrity crush at the party and she went bananas. She was more excited than I'd ever heard her in my life. I told her to calm down because I hadn't heard from him and probably never would.

Adrian picked me up that night in the new eco-green car that was all the rage, his "Pry-ous," as he called it, and we went to a hole-in-the-wall sushi place on Highland and Franklin. He knew everybody in there and introduced me to the sushi chefs. He performed a napkin trick where he folded it and dropped it in front of his face and made different funny faces. I'm sure I wasn't the first woman to see this particular trick, but it still charmed me.

As charming as Adrian was, I didn't feel a spark with him. After dinner, we sat in his Pry-ous as it rained. I could tell he wanted to make a move, but to make it less enticing I complained that I was sore from a workout. "Let's go get massages!" he said. "Right now!"

I politely declined. I thought it was a little too intimate for a first date, and he drove me home. He tried to kiss me when he dropped me off but I turned and gave him the cheek. I knew this guy could get ass all day long. I wasn't going to be just another notch. No way. As expected, because I wasn't interested, Adrian pursued me on and off for the next six years! I blew him off a lot, and he sexted me a lot. We did hook up twice but we never had actual sex. I wouldn't let him, which drove him even crazier. "I can make you feel like a queen if you let me," he would say. He had the biggest penis I'd ever seen—and the biggest bush! Even though we had that in common, it just was never meant to be. "You're the one girl I can't get," he'd say to me.

One of the reasons Adrian couldn't get me was because Jesse called two days after he did and asked me out. I was so excited. I put on what I considered my sexiest outfit—a Trina Turk dress, which I got at her outlet after modeling for her, and nude heels. I was so attracted to Jesse, but it didn't go well. He wined and dined me at Italian restaurant Ago, but he was really rude, talking on his phone almost the entire night. It was awkward and we didn't have much to talk about. The conversations we *did* have were really generic. Plus, he's not the easiest guy to talk to. He's actually quite aggressive and challenging. I felt like he had a giant chip on his shoulder the whole night.

I was pretty sure there wouldn't be a second date, but not long after our disastrous night out he called me up and invited me to a dinner at Katana with his friends. This setting, one where he could drink a lot and let his huge personality shine at the head of a table, was more in his wheelhouse. We got pretty handsy that night. We went on a third date, sushi again. I was shocked to see his mom there along with his group of friends. I sat next to her and she was so nice. I thought it was sweet that he brought her along.

Two weeks after we met, we still hadn't had sex. Jesse was being a good boy. He wanted to wait, but I couldn't anymore. I invited him back to my place one afternoon after we went to a movie. He picked me up, carried me inside, and threw me on the bed. I wish I could say that we were the greatest lovers since Christian Grey and Ana

Steele. But I can't lie. The sex was pretty average. Jesse needed a lot of reassurance.

Regardless, the sex was good enough that I wanted more. For the next month, Jesse and I spent every night together at his house. He was working long hours on *Desperate Housewives*, but we were having a lot of fun and he seemed to be letting his guard down with me. I felt like Kate Bosworth in *Win a Date with Tad Hamilton!* But the fairy-tale romance hit a snag when I got an overnight modeling assignment in Arizona. Jesse drove me to the airport, said he would miss me and to send photos of myself (camera phones were just starting to be a thing).

"Don't have sex with your ex," he joked about Chris.

Chris who? I didn't even call him when I went home. That's how cuckoo I was for Jesse, who, as requested, received several sexy pics of me on that trip. The next night, dutifully back in Jesse's bed, I waited for him to finish brushing his teeth. I pulled the comforter back so he could climb into bed, but when the corner flipped up, a pair of pink lace panties flung out onto the mattress.

They weren't mine. They were way too ugly and trashy.

"What the fuck?" I cried.

Jesse came into the doorway and I flung the stanky-ass undies at him. They slid across the hardwood floor and landed right in front of his feet.

"I'm leaving," I said as calmly as I could.

"Let me explain!" he said in a panic.

It was the first time in my life I had been cheated on (that I knew of). I felt like I was going to throw up. I started to call a cab because he had picked me up from the airport and I didn't have my car.

"I was gone *one* night, Jesse."

To my surprise, instead of denying it, he came right out and admitted his betrayal and apologized.

"I messed up," he pleaded. "I went out and my ex came home with me." I didn't even know he had an ex.

Jesse wouldn't let me take a cab home so he drove me to my apartment and I gave him the silent treatment. After I slammed the car door and ran inside, the first thing I did was call Chris and tell him I missed him.

Four nights later, he flew to L.A. and we were back together.

When I was a kid, I'd gone years without even so much as touching a boy. But once I started dating guys, I became one of those girls who couldn't be alone. It was like I was petrified of having another dry spell. My motto from that point on: "The best way to get over a guy is to get under another one." It wasn't healthy, but it's what I did. I was a serial rebounder.

So while Chris and I tried to make it work long distance again, Jesse refused to let me go. He drove by my apartment, sometimes when I was walking hand-in-hand with Chris. He showed up at my gym at times he knew I'd be there. One time, I called him out on it. "I like to drive by hoping to get to see you," he admitted shamelessly.

His persistence paid off and by the summer I'd ditched Chris again and Jesse and I were as hot and heavy as Elaine Benes and the saxophone player. At first, it was a dream again. Jesse bought me expensive diamond necklaces and spoiled me with lobster dinners. We drove down to a resort in La Jolla, where the valets called me Mrs. Metcalfe, and he showed me off at paparazzi hotspot the Ivy. He even met my family in Newport Beach and played Ping-Pong with my dad and drank beers with my mesmerized mom. She actually refused to get a new cell phone for almost ten years because she didn't want to lose her prized pictures of Jesse. Jesse even invited me to be his date at the Emmys. I got dolled up in a Mark Zunino gown and had my hair done by Frankie Payne, stylist for Kim Kardashian and Eva Longoria, and Jesse and I walked the red carpet holding hands.

I often felt like Cinderella when I was with Jesse, but over the next four years, the pumpkin slowly rotted. I'd bounce back and forth between Jesse and Chris like a pinball machine. Chris was a little lost, but my soul mate and my rock. Jesse was exciting and passionate, but a total mess. He liked that I grounded him, but deep down we both knew I wasn't wild enough for him. He was stubborn and really possessive. If he thought I was even slightly flirting with a guy in public, he'd put his arms around me and squeeze just a little too tight.

Jesse was also, by his own admission, an alcoholic and an addict. He never did drugs in front of me but he was always disappearing into bathrooms when we were out. He would also disappear for days at a time. When he was coming down, he'd feel like an ass and be super depressed. Jesse's addictions spiraled out of control after he left *Desperate Housewives* at the peak of his fame. He went into rehab—and in and out of my life. It pained me to see him struggling to stay sober, so I tried not to drink in front of him and to be a positive influence. But he kept falling off the wagon, going MIA, and dating other women. One was a serious relationship with Nadine Coyle, from the Brit band Girls Aloud. After they broke up, for some reason he appeared on the show *LA Ink* to get a tattoo of her naked, holding his bloody heart, on his arm. I could tell that he was in a really bad place.

As much as I liked Jesse, I never felt like I could trust him. Our relationship made me totally paranoid and I turned into that awful girl who resorts to snooping. One night we were going to a Jason Mraz concert and he forgot to print out the tickets. I overheard him tell a friend his password so he could print the tickets and made a mental note. The next day, I broke into his e-mail and discovered he was having a full-on, intimate relationship with a girl in London. He called her "baby," which really bothered me because he never called me that. I also broke into one of his social media accounts and found evidence that he was flirting with random, extremely trashy girls.

I called to ream him out and, as usual, he owned up to everything. I broke up with him again. And again. And again. Over the course of our six-year fling, we were really never together for more than two months at a time.

After bouncing back and forth between two polar opposite guys for years, Chris finally moved out to L.A. in 2007 and into my new apartment by the beach in Marina del Rey. For the first time in our long, rocky relationship, we were a real couple trying to do the whole domestic bliss thing. I was jetting off to modeling assignments, like Nautica and Hearts on Fire, and he got a job at the Ralph Lauren store on Rodeo Drive. We flew to Maui and had sex on the beach. We were always love machines, doing it up to four times a day. Our chemistry was off the charts.

Our physical connection could only go so far though. Emotionally, we were growing away from each other. After so many years apart, living totally different lives, we didn't have much in common anymore. I was living a busy, urban lifestyle and Chris wasn't into it. I also wanted a boob job and he wasn't into that either. I'd always been self-conscious about being a brick wall and truly believe I lost out on some sexier modeling assignments because of my flat chest. I'd done the water bra and used chicken cutlets to enhance my chest, but for me it wasn't enough. Chris was adamant: he did not want me to get breast implants.

He'd also started a strict new raw food diet. I'd been a meat-and-potatoes kind of girl up until then, so the new diet turned me off. But for him I gave it a go. For the next three years I was a strict vegan, and only ate raw foods.

As it turns out, Chris wasn't that into me anymore either. He flat-out told me he wasn't sure if he believed in marriage. And making matters worse, I found a "cons list"—that's right, there were no pros, just cons—he'd made about me and actually carried around in his wallet. It included character flaws such as:

Watches too much TV at night

This was true. I enjoy my downtime and being a lazy-ass couch potato is one of the ways I've unwound since my days ditching school to hang with my mom. It was during this time with Chris that I first started watching one of my guilty pleasures, *The Bachelor*. I forced him to watch with me so I could see which girls he found attractive. I would also talk about *The Bachelor* on the phone with my sister Rachel, who was such a big fan she held regular viewing parties for her friends. Also on the con list:

Smokes

Guilty.

Eats meat

Because of Chris, I became vegan/vegetarian as much as I could. But I never liked taking meat and fish out of my diet completely. He wanted his kids to be 100 percent raw. He didn't even want them to drink milk.

My mom

It's true she could be unsupportive and not very nice. Chris may have disliked my mom, but she turned out to be spot-on about him. He was kind of shady. One day, after I came back from a modeling assignment, I found flirty e-mails from a former coworker he accidentally left up on my computer and a long black hair in our shower.

AFTER A YEAR and a half of living together, I kicked Chris out and moved to Santa Monica. He ended up moving to Idaho to work in a raw food restaurant. With Chris's objections out of the way, I bought myself an $8,000 boob job. I got the smallest upgrade possible, from a full B to a small C, so they'd look completely natural. I absolutely love them and would highly recommend implants to any woman who doesn't like being flat chested and wants to feel sexier. So there.

I wish I could say at this point that I decided to be alone to work on myself and figure out why I was attracted to guys with questionable character and/or addiction issues. But old habits die hard.

Within a week after the breakup, I was back at the Chateau Marmont carousing with my model friend Matt. One night at dinner, Matt sat me across from his friend Gerry, a.k.a. Scottish actor Gerard Butler, whose abs had starred in *300*, but was better known to a lass like me for his cheesy romantic comedy *P.S. I Love You*. In fact, Gerry wasn't eating that night. He was on a liquid diet, because he had to film a love scene with Katherine Heigl for his next rom-com, *The Ugly Truth*. I didn't need to read *Us Weekly* to know that Gerry's bad-boy reputation preceded him. He flirted mercilessly with me, looking deep into my soul like a champion snake oil salesman. He was impossibly handsome and completely hypnotizing, but I forced myself not to jump his bones right then and there.

The next day, Gerry texted me in the middle of the day. He was at the Viceroy hotel in Santa Monica and wanted me to come over. I was torn. I had a callback for another commercial for Old Navy. I desperately wanted to blow it off but after an internal argument with myself, realized I'd possibly be giving up about $20,000 just to spend a few hours with a horny movie star who would try to bone me then instantly avoid me like the plague. So, like a good girl, I went to the callback.

I didn't get the job, but I was so glad I went. The day after that I had lunch with a model girlfriend, who told a wonderful little story about how the handsome movie star Gerard Butler had hit on her at the gym that morning and wouldn't take no for an answer, even when she said she was married.

See, I *could* make good decisions when it came to men. Except for when I couldn't. Another night at Chateau, Matt tried to entice me with another setup. "He's a big agent at CAA," Matt said. "You might really like him." Jim Toth was thirty-eight, about thirteen years older than me, and ready for marriage and babies, the whole nine yards. I wasn't, because I had just dumped Chris, but Jim was funny and smart, and we really hit it off. So when he asked for my number, I gave it to him.

Sure enough, he texted and asked me out for sushi. (What is it with these guys and sushi? It's so L.A.!) We had a really nice time but it was clear to me that we were in different places in our lives and he was too old for me. After our date, he texted me a lot, but I kept blowing him off. Eventually, he called me out on it and I decided to be honest with him. "I'm not ready to date right now," I admitted. After graciously saying he understood, he stopped contacting me completely. The next time I heard about Jim, he'd become Mrs. Reese Witherspoon.

He wouldn't be the only good guy I let get away. I also briefly dated Jamie Linden, the adorable screenwriter of *10 Years* and *Dear John,* who last time I checked, was very seriously dating *New Girl* star Zooey Deschanel.

Instead of dating Jim or Jamie, who were rich, handsome, and talented, whose arms did I run to? A washed-up model friend named Dylan who was scraping by with short-term gigs as a cameraman on reality shows like *Undercover Boss*. Oh, and selling the medical marijuana he grew in his apartment (he was a licensed pot dealer). Dylan was the exact opposite of Chris, which is why I stupidly gravitated to him. He was a man's man, someone who liked drinking and eating meat.

Only two weeks after Chris left, Dylan was on my couch as much as the throw pillows. And for the next year, I thought we were actually quite happy. My career exploded during this time so I was gone a ton. Tragically, my beloved agent, Mamie, at L.A. Models was diagnosed with breast cancer, and a week before she passed away, she took me to lunch and basically ordered me to switch to the Ford agency in L.A. "Don't tell anyone I said that," she whispered naughtily.

After Mamie died, nobody else at L.A. Models remembered to submit me for castings, so I listened to her advice, and signed with Steve Miller at Ford. He had booked me on the Rome A&F shoot in Arizona and had also made the move to L.A. Signing with him was a smart decision: I landed my first US magazine cover for *Fitness* and a bunch of lucrative TV commercials, like Jim Beam, Caesars Palace, and Clarisonic, which was a $35,000 payday alone. My face was also plastered on the front of a Clairol hair dye box, which was very exciting considering my classmates nominated me for Best Hair way back in eighth grade. I also flew to New York once a month to shoot catalogs, which was my bread and butter, and even did a photo shoot with Conan O'Brien, who was on *People*'s Most Beautiful list that year. He was so humble and asked me if I did anything wild and crazy the night before. He said he wanted to live vicariously because he was an ol' married guy.

I was also constantly getting what I called mailbox money, unexpected residual and royalty checks that appeared every time one of my commercials aired. I was loaded and loved spoiling Dylan, who was always anxiously awaiting his own mailbox money—unemployment checks. I made him gourmet dinners, homemade tamales, Ina Garten's meatloaf—and took him on a crazy-expensive trip to Maui, where I rented a stunning three-bedroom beach house.

I must have been so busy that I was ignoring all of the red flags that were right in front of my eyes:

1. Dylan was sponging off of me and eating all the food in my refrigerator.
2. He drank like a fish. When he wasn't working, he'd ride his bike to all of the beach bars, his own little daily pub crawl, and get smashed.
3. Our sex life was awful. Not sure if it was all the booze or what, but we rarely had sex. One of the few times we did, he stopped in the middle because, as he put it, "I just got tired."
4. I was gaining weight. Dylan was so slothy it rubbed off on me (luckily I got the *Fitness* cover before this happened). My agent Steve asked me to lose a few pounds, so I started taking four-mile walks back and forth to Venice Beach. On one of these walks, I bumped into Cavan Clark, a wild and woolly photographer, who

shot me for Charlotte Russe in San Francisco years before. He had a gorgeous house on the strand and invited me up to his porch to chat sometimes.

5. Dylan flat-out told me he didn't believe in marriage. He was the second long-term boyfriend to do so.

Even though we had absolutely no future together, about a year and a half into the relationship, I made two gigantic mistakes. First, I allowed Dylan to take pictures of me naked in the bathtub, which I had innocently gone into one night when I was sick with the flu. Second, I found a cute little house to rent in Mar Vista and we moved in together. Two months into it, when rent was due, Dylan told me he could only contribute $200 of our $2,700 rent.

God, the guy was a total loser! I dumped his ass, paid to put his shit in storage, and thankfully managed to wiggle out of the lease. I moved into my own little house in Santa Monica, mentally exhausted and totally down with love. The first night in my new home, I got drunk by myself and wallowed in misery about my disastrous romantic history. I turned on the TV and *The Bachelor* was on. Brad Womack's second season had recently started and it wasn't clear yet that he would turn out to be one of the biggest dicks in the history of the show. At this point, he had humbly apologized for picking neither girl in his first incarnation as the Bachelor and was enthusiastically and sincerely looking for real love and a wife. He was being so romantic and chivalrous, unlike Dylan.

During one of those commercial breaks, when host Chris Harrison asked, "If you'd like to be on the next *Bachelor* . . ." my ears perked up. Impulsively, I got my laptop, logged on to ABC.com, and applied.

The generic questionnaire took about ten minutes to fill out. I uploaded three of my favorite modeling pictures and wrote a short essay, explaining that it was hard finding love in L.A., that I'd dated actors and models, had my heart broken, and worked my ass off. But after being told by my last two boyfriends that they didn't believe in marriage, I was a hopeless romantic looking for someone who did believe in making a lifetime commitment.

When I pressed SEND, it felt no different, no more possible, than signing up for one of those "Win a free iPad!" contests.

I didn't expect to ever hear anything back.

KEEPING IT REAL

How to Get Noticed in the Application

- Send in your best photo. Cut to the chase and save producers time by wearing a bikini in the photo.
- Be heartbroken. A good breakup story, in which you've been dumped cruelly and callously, helps your chances.
- But be ready for love. Nobody wants to date a sad sack. Say you've recovered and are looking for the real thing.
- Show off your romantic side. Tell stories about the most romantic thing you've ever done. But don't lie. They will eventually figure that out.
- Toss around some clichés. They really like it when you say you want a good story to tell your grandkids someday, or that life is better spent when shared.
- Don't beg. That's unattractive.

I was single again, but not for long. The serial rebounder strikes again! The day after I shot the e-mail off into the *Bachelor* abyss, I ran into Cavan on one of my fat-burning power walks through Venice. He asked me out, and I said yes, even though he was moving back to San Francisco and wasn't really my type. He was bald and kind of overweight, but had a sexy swagger. His confidence was off the charts and he was really funny. We got some fish tacos at James' Beach, made almost famous in the movie *I Love You, Man,* and I was instantly smitten. What can I say? After being burned by Dylan, Cavan was refreshing, a real man: he was independent, hardworking, and a true gentleman.

When it rains it pours. Within two days of that first date, I got an e-mail from a producer on *The Bachelor,* asking if I would come in to meet them at their production office on Bundy and Olympic, which was conveniently located just down the street from my new house. I was totally surprised. I was so certain I'd never hear back I'd already forgotten that I'd sent the e-mail. I didn't respond right away. I went on date number two with Cavan first, and he was so charming, I confessed right on the spot that I liked him. After his eye twitched a little, he said he really liked me, too. And just like that, I had an insta-boyfriend and a response for *The Bachelor* producer. I thanked her for reaching out, but informed her I'd met someone and that I'd be back in touch if anything changed.

Of course, it did change. I quickly realized that at thirty-five, Cavan was a little too old for me. I was twenty-seven at this point. Plus my crazy, nonstop love life was also starting to get a little old. And with Cavan in San Francisco, I was back in an annoying long-distance relationship.

Because I was often home alone, my sister Rachel came to visit me a lot. She unapologetically liked to watch TV, just like me, and we got really into the new season of *The Bachelorette* together. Ashley Hebert was the lucky girl looking for love this time and Rachel asked me which guy I liked best.

"Ben," I said without hesitation. I thought the sweet wine maker from Sonoma was so cute and almost sad. I loved his long hair. He kind of reminded me of my first boyfriend, Jono. On one episode Ben got to ride mopeds with Ashley through the streets of Taiwan and I was actually a little jealous.

Four months into my relationship with Cavan, I started to pull away. The more I watched *The Bachelorette,* the more I realized that Cavan wasn't the right man for me. I wanted a guy more like Ben. As I lost interest in Cavan, he started to lose his cool. He got really possessive and obsessive and would text me constantly when I was out. The final straw came when I went to a Victoria's Secret party and he barraged me with a dozen messages. I couldn't deal anymore and broke up with him. After it was over, he'd call me crying and bombard my landline fifty times in a row.

Only weeks later Jesse popped back up in my life, "bumping into me" at my gym, curiously right after I changed my Facebook status back to "single."

"Well, well, well," I said. "Look who's here."

"I was hoping I'd see you," he admitted shamelessly, like he always did. He said he'd lost my phone number after a jealous girlfriend deleted all the female contacts in his phone.

"Oh no, not again!" the gym's juice-bar girl cried, rolling her eyes. She'd seen this all before.

And darn it if she wasn't right. Jesse and I fell right back into it. This time, he seemed different. Instead of partying, we strolled through the Century City mall together, ate at Pink Taco, and he even went to see chick flicks like *Sex and the City 2* with me. But sadly, a leopard never really changes its spots. One weekend I went out of town, to Arizona again for the love of God, and Jesse called me and said he was in Palm Springs for a boys' weekend playing golf. He was heading back to L.A. and wanted to take me to dinner as soon as I returned home. It was so sweet of him to check in, right? Wrong.

He wasn't even in Palm Springs! At the same time Jesse called me, I got a text from a friend, who'd spotted him in Venice Beach with a girl. I Google imaged Jesse and pictures instantly popped up on TMZ.com of him straddling some chick in a park. "This is PDL—public display of lust!" the caption read. "Jesse Metcalfe reminded us of his existence by tongue-wrestling this skyscraper of a blonde at Venice Beach. The couple had a roll in the green that left Jesse feeling a little too sexy for his shirt, apparently."

That was the final straw. All three of the men I considered the loves of my life had used me and/or betrayed me. None of them—not Chris, not Dylan, not Jesse—had any intention of ever marrying me. And I wouldn't have wanted to marry any of them anyway. They all had major character flaws.

Were there *any* nice guys on the planet who actually wanted to get married?

Ben Flajnik. I felt strangely connected to him. By this point in *The Bachelorette* season it was obvious to me that Ashley was more in love with J. P. Rosenbaum and would probably end up with him. The tabloids were already saying that J. P. won and that Ben might be the next Bachelor.

After being heartbroken about Jesse for about ten minutes, I decided I wanted revenge. I went back into my e-mail inbox and found the address for the producer of *The Bachelor.* I knew the show would start shooting really soon after *The Bachelorette* finale, so I wrote and said I hoped it wasn't too late, but I was single again.

A producer wrote me right back: "Can you come in tomorrow?"

KEEPING IT REAL

How to Throw the Best Viewing Party

by Rachel Robertson

As an ultimate fan of the *Bachelor* and *Bachelorette* franchise (I have watched every episode since the show's inception), one of my favorite things to do during the season is to get my girlfriends together and watch the show. Here are my top five tips for throwing the *most dramatic* viewing party in *Bachelor/Bachelorette* history.

1. **Nicknames Are Key** Especially early on, it is hard to tell the contestants apart and remember who is who. I recommend you and your friends come up with little nicknames or phrases for each person that remind you of what they do (free spirit, cruise ship entertainer, I'm a model!), what was unique about them (horse girl, girl with two kids, guy on the skateboard), or when necessary, notable fashion mistakes (too spray-tanned girl, bad-weave girl, guy with the ascot).

2. **Create Some Friendly Competition** I recommend a drinking game in which each person drinks at certain words (rose, drama, house, date, love) or when certain inevitable things happen (like when a contestant suddenly seems to realize that he or she is not the only person dating the Bachelor/Bachelorette and gets upset—hello, don't these people know what the show is about before they go on it?). Another idea is creating a bracket and getting some friendly wagers going on who will go home on a certain episode or who the ultimate winner will be!

3. **Set Some Ground Rules** With a room full of women, it is quite possible someone will want to talk throughout the entire show. I had to set some ground rules with my friends, especially when Courtney was on. Example: no talking between commercial breaks, unless we paused the show! Another boundary to decide on is whether or not you want to hear spoilers. Like it or not, and accurate or not, Reality Steve is out there and some people may want to tell you exactly what he says happened. I personally prefer the element of surprise, as it makes the whole experience more interesting.

4. **Roses, Hot Tubs, and Some Other Ambience Ideas** While you don't want to creep out your friends by creating a Fantasy Suite, it is fun to incorporate some Bachelor-related decorations or settings into your viewing party. When Courtney was on the show, my girlfriends and I created a foam board where we had pictures of each of the girls and we would remove them one by one as they were sent home. Or you can never have too many roses or bottles of champagne at a viewing party. And, of course, if you can host a viewing party in a hot tub, all the more power to you, girl!

5. **Use Your DVR to Your Advantage** I can't tell you how many times we have watched the preview for upcoming episodes of *The Bachelor,* and particularly the final episode, in slow motion, with frequent rewinds. It is incredibly fun to try to piece together the tiny details to predict who is getting the final rose, and who will be crying in the back of the limo.

3

MALIBU BARBIES & BEN

My hunch was right. On August 1, 2011, Ashley chose J. P. instead of Ben as her future husband in the season finale of *The Bachelorette*. I genuinely felt bad for Ben, who was furious and embarrassed after Ashley let him get down on one knee to propose, only to lift him back up by the elbow and reject him. I wondered if he'd ever recover from such a humiliating and cruel public dumping. The rumor was that the show's fans desperately wanted him to be the next Bachelor, but he was so pissed about being humiliated he was playing hard to get with the producers. Nothing official had been announced yet, not even on the "After the Final Rose" show, when he faced Ashley graciously and stoically.

In my heart, I truly believed Ben would be the next Bachelor and I wanted it to be him. In my very first meeting with the show's producers, they actually asked me who I'd like the next Bachelor to be and I, of course, said "Ben." After having my picture taken, a producer handed me a huge packet and I thought I was in. That was easy! Not so fast. Next, I had to make it through Finals Weekend, which took place just five days after *The Bachelorette* finale aired.

When I showed up to the nondescript hotel, I was told to keep a low profile. Nobody could know that I was there for *The Bachelor.* As soon as I arrived I was escorted from my car and then whisked straight to my own room by a producer. If a random guest asked what all the commotion was about, we were supposed to say, "We're filming a movie!"

Finals Weekend is a twelve-hour audition meant to whittle down the potential dates for *The Bachelor* to about thirty women. But it's also an important test to see who can make it through the intense interview process without cracking, crying, or showing their true (ugly) colors. They shuttle you to various conference and hotel rooms for different parts of the audition. Not once during the entire day did I see another contestant. From the very start, producers want you laser-beam focused on the show. There are absolutely no distractions.

The first leg of the marathon day was a 150-question personality test. After the personality test, which I decided to answer as honestly as possible—as opposed to answering strategically, or what I thought they might want me to answer—I was taken to the show's resident psychologist. I didn't know this at the time, but the curly-haired shrink from Beverly Hills travels with the show and is a permanent fixture on set. I guess she must have thought I was one of the crazy people because she looked over my personality test then peppered me with questions about my drinking habits, asking if I thought I had a problem and if I'd ever had a fight after a night of boozing.

After seeing the psychologist, I shot my very first "scene" on-camera. Now, while most girls may have agonized over their outfit for this monumental occasion, I simply wore jeans and a white T-shirt, a little eyeliner, and threw in my weave. I knew it was going to be a long day so comfort was king. After getting miked up, I was led into a hotel room filled with candles, blue lighting, knickknacks, and a chintzy Chinese wall divider.

I was asked two questions by a lone producer:

1. Will you tell us a little bit about yourself?
2. Who do you want to be the next Bachelor?

I gave a spiel about how I hoped it was Ben because he was a nice, normal guy and I liked his hair because I'd dated some bald eagles (Chris and Cavan). I said he likes wine and I like wine so I think we'd be good together.

"Okay, you're done!" the producer announced. I was shocked it was over so quickly, until he led me through a door into the next room, where—surprise!—the producers were crammed around a big, U-shaped conference table and had just watched my Academy Award–winning performance on closed circuit. Up until this point, I hadn't really been taking it all that seriously. But now I was in it. And I was terrified.

It would have been understandable for anyone in that intimidating situation to start shaking or sweating profusely, or maybe even faint, but my modeling auditions had prepared me for this exact moment. I did my signature double-handed wave and scanned the room, making eye contact with as many people as possible without looking like a phony politician. I sat in a chair in front of the table and was promptly drilled with questions.

"Where are you from?"

"Where do you live?"

"Who have you modeled for?"

"Who do you want to be the Bachelor?"

I told them I was only interested in Ben and if it was going to be any of the other guys from Ashley's season, like Ryan Park or Ames Brown, I wasn't interested.

"What's your personality like?"

After I answered that I thought I was funny and liked making people laugh, I looked to a handsome producer sitting against the wall for a scintilla of support. But he went in for the kill.

"Oh, really? You're funny?" he mocked. "Tell us a joke." I didn't flinch.

"How do you make a handkerchief dance? Put a little boogie in it!" I said, shimmying.

The room totally cracked up and I looked back to the handsome producer. He gave me a private little smile. During the rest of the Q&A, I tried to charm as many producers as possible, asking them questions about themselves and making jokes like "Know any single guys?" before I was ushered out, again doing my signature double-handed wave.

I thought I killed, but back in my lonely hotel room I was only rewarded with a soggy Subway sandwich. I ate it because I was starving. And I had nothing else to do for another two hours.

Next up, I met with a lady private investigator who bombarded me with the most personal questions yet:

"Have you ever gotten a DUI?"

No.

"Have you ever been arrested?"

I took a deep breath and decided to come clean. In sixth grade, Sara and I had stolen Coca-Cola shirts with polar bears on them from Robinsons-May and we got busted. I was banned for life from the department store chain. I thought my mom was going to smack me when she picked me up, but she was surprisingly cool about the whole thing and only grounded me for three months.

The lady PI looked bored.

"Do you have any nude photos?"

Um, yes, I thought, panicking. I had taken hundreds of them. But I didn't tell her the eye-popping number. I just blushed and said my ex had some.

"What's the raciest picture he has?"

"Oh, he would never sell those."

"Are you sure?"

"Yes, definitely," I said, not totally convinced.

"Do you have a sex tape?"

"Yes." I had at least three. In fact, one was with an ex, who told me after I broke up with him that he couldn't stop watching it. I said that was really creepy and to delete it immediately. He promised he would. (Foreshadow alert #1!)

"Do you have any enemies?"

"Not that I know of." (Foreshadow alert #2!)

After the inquisition was finished, I had to get my blood drawn to make sure I didn't have any STDs.

She wanted to know if I was on the pill. I'd been on the pill since I was sixteen years old. My mom actually took me to get them, if you can believe it, but it was to help cure my pepperoni pimple face, definitely not an endorsement to engage in sexual activity.

After the blood test, the day was finally over. Many of the women had flown in from faraway places like LaFollette, Tennessee, or Kissimmee, Florida, so they stayed overnight in the hotel. But since I only lived a few miles away, I drove home, exhausted and in shock. *Wow, what was that?* I thought.

As soon as I made it through my front door, I walked to my toilet and puked. I wasn't sure what it was. After I threw up, I sat on my bathroom floor stressed out and confused. My body was literally having an adverse reaction to all of this.

I must have done okay because two days later I got a call from a casting producer and was told I passed Finals Weekend and officially chosen to be on *The Bachelor.* I was sent a gigantic, inch-thick contract and told to sign it and drop it off at the production offices as soon as possible. Instead of being thrilled, I felt a sense of dread. I just couldn't commit. For the next two weeks, I blew off their frantic calls and e-mails as I agonized whether or not to be on the show. I talked to my sister, who, of course, as a huge fan of *The Bachelor* said to go for it. I talked to my dad, who was really excited and thought it was a great idea. Even my agent, Steve, wasn't worried about the temporary hiatus from the modeling world. "I don't think it will help your career, but it won't hurt it," he told me. (Foreshadow alert #3!) I scoured Ben's Twitter looking for signs that he was "the one" and still I couldn't decide. I made a pro and con list, which included:

• PROS •	• CONS •
Falling in love	Heart smashed into pieces
Making new friends	Catfights
Travel	Isolation, lack of privacy
Fairy-tale ending	Humiliated on national television

Only two people were totally negative about the show. My best guy friend, Matt, didn't think I should do it. And, not surprisingly, my mom was vehemently against me going on the show. My sister had shown her the Hometown Date episode from Ashley's season and my mom thought Ben wasn't my type, and she was leery of his mom, Barbara.

"You don't need a television show to get dates, Courtney," she scolded. I think she was still holding out hope for Jesse and me to make it work. "Do you even want to get married? You're not ready to settle down. It's not a good idea."

My mom had a point. I was confused.

On August 21, I called a producer and asked her to scratch me off the list. "Listen," she said. "You owe it to yourself to at least meet the guy." When I was still unsure, she told me to take two more days to think about it. But I'd made up my mind. After I officially pulled out, my dad sent me an e-mail with the subject line "A Well-Made Decision."

"Bug," he wrote, addressing me by my nickname, "I would like to compliment you for how you reached your decision on the *Bachelor* program. You thought about it from every angle and bounced it off your trusted friends. You came to a very sensible decision, one that is right for you. Time to move forward with new projects . . . try to nail down the Fruit of the Loom job. Why should a girl who made $32,000 for one photo shoot last August take two months out of her career and lose all control on how her image is used on national television?"

I felt like a huge weight had been lifted from my shoulders, but at the same time, over the next week I felt lonelier than ever before. Unattached for the first time in forever, I fell back into my old habits. I called Chris, even though we hadn't spoken in two years.

He'd opened his own raw food restaurant in Florida and was doing really well. He immediately booked me a ticket to visit Labor Day weekend.

I decided to go, even though I knew if my mom found out she would disown me. I was still unsure that I'd made the right decision about *The Bachelor.* I wanted to see if there was anything left with Chris and if a weekend with him would settle my mind once and for all.

But it was the same old story. Though he told me he loved me and we still had amazing physical chemistry, there was something important missing. In a last-ditch effort, I tested Chris one more time: I told him I was considering going on *The Bachelor.* Instead of begging me not to, he was supportive and said it would be fun for me. After, we went swimming in the ocean, and even though his perfectly lean, raw-food-sculpted body glistened in the sun, I had a sinking feeling. I knew this would be the last time I ever saw him.

As soon as I got back to L.A., I e-mailed the producer again and said I'd made the wrong decision. I told her that I wanted to be on the show and was ready for an amazing love story, if they'd still have me. This was something I had to do for myself and I couldn't turn it down for Chris, my mom and dad, or anyone.

"We were so disappointed, we took your pictures off the wall," the producer said. "We've already picked all the girls."

After a long pause, she told me to bring in my contract right away.

The next morning, over a cup of coffee, I flew through the monster document, initialing every lower right-hand corner, without even opening the pages all the way. I dropped off the contract and gave the producer a hug. She gave me a packing list that said to be prepared for all seasons.

It was official. I was going on *The Bachelor,* one of the most iconic shows in the history of television. I was going to meet Ben Flajnik. I only had a little over a week until I had to report to a hotel in Westlake Village, the holding pen until the infamous limo ride to the mansion in Malibu. Holy crap, I had a lot to do.

First, I found a model friend who agreed to rent my spare bedroom while I was away (I'd started being smarter about my money). It would be the first time I'd had a female roommate since I moved to L.A. ten years prior. I gave my sister Rachel all my account information and my modeling contacts so she could manage my bills and my career while I was away. Ironically, one of the last shoots I did before I left was for Kay Jewelers' Neil Lane engagement ring collection. I was a fake bride with a fake husband for the day.

Second, I got my wardrobe ready. I counted out the possible rose ceremonies and borrowed five dresses from Rachel, even though we're not the same size, and two from another model friend named Carrie. I didn't buy anything new. Here's why: When I was dating Jesse I nearly went broke buying new designer stuff. I felt so much pressure to always look good when we went out, just in case he was photographed by paparazzi, but I never got my own style right. I'd try to match his look, but it was just plain bad. Jesse was in an Affliction phase and I was wearing cringe-worthy outfits like denim skirts, Jack Daniel's T-shirts, and cowboy boots. Perez Hilton was all over my ass, no matter how hard I tried to look good. Once, when I made the unfortunate decision to wear a leopard-print tube dress with purple heels, Perez scribbled on my face with his poisonous white pen, "Butt ugly!" I refused to spend my life savings on clothes ever again. The other reason I didn't go on a big shopping spree was that I was superstitious. I thought if I bought all new dresses I'd be sent home the first night. The only new thing I bought for the show was a journal.

Third, I sowed my oats. To be honest, I had a premonition that I would be engaged to Ben and he might be the last man I'd ever make the sex with. So for the first time in my life, I was a tiny bit promiscuous the week before I left. I had one more rendezvous with Adrian, who was living in the penthouse of the W Hotel on Sunset. After we hooked up, he showed me an eco-friendly website he was working on and we had a long conversation about an article in the *New York Times* discussing Dan Savage's "monogamish" philosophy. Adrian actually had a girlfriend at the time, but it was okay, he said, because they were in an open relationship. I tried not to judge. Then I told him about going on *The Bachelor,* the most monogamous thing on the planet and, to his credit, he didn't judge.

I also had a hot hookup with a gorgeous model/actor friend of mine, who I'd met on a Lucky jeans shoot a couple years before. The photographer wanted us to kiss, but he refused because he had a girlfriend. I never forgot that. I was so impressed with his devotion. Now that we were both single, he took me on what started out as an innocent day date, a walk on the beach and lunch at the Library Alehouse in Santa Monica. Then he came over to my house to watch TV. He left around 5:00 P.M., but texted me ten minutes after he left that traffic was a nightmare and he was coming back to wait it out (which if intentional was a brilliant scheme, especially in L.A.). I'd taken a shower—I always think it's sexy to have long, wet hair—and, pretty much as soon as he walked in, we jumped into bed. I let him leave without telling him about *The Bachelor.* I just told him I might be gone for a little while.

I didn't tell Cavan either. Our breakup was still pretty fresh and I thought it would crush him. I also decided not to tell Dylan, even though we were on pretty good terms and he'd recently fixed my screen door. Not being up-front with him would come back to bite me in the ass.

I did tell Chris, who I could tell was disappointed, but he didn't or couldn't tell me not to go. I decided to text Jesse, since he was a celebrity and could be linked to me in the tabloids. His career was heating up again; he'd been offered a starring role on the revived TV show *Dallas*. He immediately called and warned me that it was a bad idea because the girls on the show were "dorks." When I told him it was too late and that I was committed, he moaned, "Fuuuck this guy is going to pick you." Jesse asked to come over, but I said no. He wanted to meet up before I left but we never did.

I was ready to be Ben's girl.

ON SEPTEMBER 14, producers came to my house and shot my "package" for the show, a short video about my life. They filmed me sipping coffee at Urth Caffe, riding my bike to my favorite farmer's market to pick out flowers, and making a salad in my kitchen, after they spruced up the background. I talked for hours about heartbreak and wanting to find true love and what I liked about Ben. It would have gone a lot faster if I didn't live next to the Santa Monica airport. The planes kept messing up the sound.

The night before I left, I lay in bed thinking about Ben. It suddenly hit me that if he did propose, I may have to move to San Francisco. I'd be willing to do that. I also thought about the twenty-four other women and how I hoped to make at least one or two new lifelong friends. But I also made two promises to myself:

1. Don't let my temper get the best of me.

I'm a Cancer and my mood can flare up quickly if I'm not careful.

2. No fights on-camera.

I was nervous about being snookered into a lot of deep group conversations with the other women. As I mentioned earlier, I'm not big on sitting around talking about my feelings. That part of the show would definitely be a challenge.

I'm not going to lie. I did have a strategy going in. I can be effectively manipulative. My goal was to win the girls over, even if I didn't like them, and make friends with everyone. I admit I can be picky with what type of girls I get close with. I always say it's like dating. You have to play a little hard to get with girlfriends, just like with a guy. You can't get jealous and you can't be too readily available all the time. It's almost exactly like Paul Rudd and Jason Segel in *I Love You, Man*.

And if I liked Ben, my plan was to win him over with my emotional and nurturing nature, another big Cancer quality. You can stop laughing now.

Finally, the big day arrived. On Saturday, September 17, at 1:00 P.M., a town car arrived at my house and I began my *Bachelor* journey. I brought the two suitcases I was told I was allowed to bring, and only later I found out that some of the girls brought five. One bag was full of summer stuff, and one covered fall. I brought plenty of bikinis for hot tubbin' and a lot of accessories, like beanies and scarves, which could add a pop of color to the basics I'd packed. I had one small makeup bag—eyeliner, concealer, and bronzer were my staples—because I was told we'd get help from a makeup artist. And last but not least, I threw in my favorite lingerie, just in case. I packed perfectly. Though if I had to do it over again, I would've taken my vibrator.

KEEPING IT REAL

The Perfect Packing List

by Jaclyn Swartz

When I first got the call that I would be on *The Bachelor,* my first question was, "What the hell do I pack?" (Well, after "who is going to dye my hair and paint my nails?"—so, really the third question.) I was so excited to show off my killer wardrobe that I knew would be juxtaposed with at least seventeen Hooters waitresses and ~~NBA~~ dancers. The rules are very clear in that you are only allowed to bring two checked bags, but since I was *sure* I was getting to hometown dates (ha!), I brought seven.

About $550 dollars in baggage fees later, I am giving you a list of the crucial things to pack:

1. Ten Rose Ceremony Dresses (at least). Night One dresses are the most important. *Go short!* Show some leg, you prudes.

2. Bring the sequins, but leave your glue-gunned plastic crystal pageant dresses at home. One Jamie Otis was enough.

3. Fake lashes. I didn't bring these because I literally didn't know how to do makeup before I went on this show. Big mistake, *huge!*

4. 1,000 bikinis. You will end up wearing these in freezing cold tundras while ice skating and performing weird plays. So stock up.

5. Light jackets that are fitted and casual-cute. It gets cold at night on dates (when you aren't in your bikini)—and I would never be caught dead in a cardigan.

6. Accessories, accessories, accessories. Chances are, a top you bring will look like another girl's top. So don't you want to win at this game and accessorize your look? Toodles, loser: I got my one-on-one!

7. Sunglasses. Just kidding. You aren't allowed to wear these on-camera. But don't worry: if you are on this show, you won't need these to hide your ugly face. Chances are, you're pretty—so congrats!

8. Hair products and hair tools up the wazoo. Come prepared, but if you bring mousse for crunchy curls, I will definitely be making fun of you. A lot.

The entire ride I was on my cell phone, knowing that very soon it would be gone indefinitely. I called my sister and she cried. I texted Jesse and he wrote back simply, "I'll always have your back." And finally, I called Chris. We didn't have much to say to each other.

"Think of me," he managed to eke out. "Don't get engaged."

If Chris had asked me in that moment not to do the show, I probably would've dramatically stopped the car and hopped out, like Tom Cruise should have done in *Vanilla Sky*. But I guess he didn't want to hold me back. Chris, not Tom Cruise.

When the limo pulled up to the hotel, not one but two production assistants (PAs) came down to get me. They brought me straight to my room and took away my phone. My room was really depressing. It overlooked an air conditioning vent and had absolutely no light. I asked if there was another one available because I'd be isolated there for the next two days and would go stir-crazy. We were allowed to watch pay-per-view movies, but there was nothing else to do. No phone, nothing to read, no music. Sure enough they moved me to a nicer room overlooking a courtyard.

I sat by the window and stared at a big tree for what felt like an eternity, welling up and overwhelmed by emotion. I snapped out of it when a parade of producers, one by one, started knocking on my door to introduce themselves. There were so many of them I couldn't keep track of their names or figure out who was the most important. A few I recognized from Finals Weekend, like the handsome guy, others not so much. I didn't know it at the time, but there were more than twenty-five girls at the hotel that day.

The next thirty-six hours were a whirlwind, and yet, I still never saw another contestant. I taped a segment for *Access Hollywood,* showing how I perfectly packed my suitcases for the show (thank God I'd skipped the vibrator). I did the photo shoot for the headshot that would accompany my bio on the ABC website and would be framed for Ben to gaze at before Rose Ceremonies. Producers asked me how I was going to introduce myself to Ben. The audience absolutely loves it when the girls do something unique or wacky when they first meet the Bachelor, like only wearing a wine barrel or challenging him to arm wrestling or something. I was adamant though—no song and dance routine for me. I wanted to be myself.

They also freaked out a bit about my outfit, a little black dress, because it was "too boring." But I loved the Dolce and Gabbana dress I'd chosen. I'd bought it for $100 at Nordstrom Rack's Last Chance clearance sale a few years ago and, even though it had a broken strap, it fit me like a glove. To win them over, I tried it on for them and they saw firsthand why it was a good choice. My dress finally got the official seal of approval from the show's stylist, Cary, who made the rounds to all of the ladies' rooms to dig through their suitcases and see what he was working with. "Love! Saw it on the runway" he said when it was my turn.

And then it was D-Day: at sunset we'd head to the mansion. A makeup artist had been scheduled to meet me really early in the morning, but my face would have melted by the time I met Ben. So I was relieved when the producers moved my time slot back to later in the day. Being strategic, I also wanted to be first or last out of the limo. I knew from modeling that the women in the middle chunk of an audition were usually forgotten. I wanted to be special. Amazingly, I found out that I would be last of all twenty-five women to exit the limo.

In the morning, I did a green mud mask. Later—after my makeup was done and my weave was joojed up and petrified with a can of hair spray—I sat in my room waiting anxiously for the sun to go down. I drank a glass of red wine and ate a salmon salad. I wanted to be full because I knew it was going to be a long night. To kill time, I watched a wedding in the courtyard and practiced what I was going to say to Ben. After writing a bunch of one-liners down in my journal, I scratched them out, worried that I'd look like a nerd if I said any of them. I decided to go with a simple, "Hi, my name is Courtney" and then wing it from there.

By 7:00 P.M. I was so mind-numbingly bored and restless, it was a miracle to be escorted down to the lobby, where I finally met my limo mates, three grown women all dressed like they were going to senior prom and wearing enough makeup to rival the stars of *RuPaul's Drag Race*. I was the only brunette and the only one not hammered already. The very first girl I met was Monica Spannbauer, a loud, brassy blonde with an incredibly annoying laugh. She was actually snorting. The other two girls in my limo were the unbelievably named Amber Bacon and Anna Snowball. One was a maternity nurse, the other was, well, I forgot. Neither of these women made it past the first night.

Despite an immediate disdain for them, I was ready to throw myself into this experience headfirst. I couldn't wait to get into that limo and head to the legendary mansion. I couldn't wait to meet my man.

As we drove slowly through Malibu, Monica, Bacon, and Anna Snowball all pounded champagne, "woo'd" at the top of their lungs, and toasted Ben. "Benny boo boo . . . boo boo boo!" they screamed, referencing the chick flick *How to Lose a Guy in 10 Days*. I looked to the lone producer in the car for help, but he just shrugged. Surrendering to the madness, I poured a glass of champagne, even though I don't like it much, and threw in a few "woos" myself.

When the limo pulled up to the mansion, one of the girls shouted out, "Oh my God, it *is* Ben!"

Duh.

I was done paying attention to the other women. There he was, standing there alone, looking so handsome and tall—enough. (My biggest fear was that he'd be shorter than me.) As soon as I saw Ben I *wanted* him. I could see that his hands were clenched, a sign of nerves, and my nurturing side immediately kicked in. I also had major butterflies; I wondered if going last was a huge mistake. He already looked exhausted. And had he already met someone he really liked? I'd have to wait until these buffoons stumbled out of the limo before I could suss it out.

Monica, wearing a long purple gown, was up first. She was a total dud. She said she missed her dog. And that was the highlight.

Anna Snowball—I'm sorry, she has the kind of name where you always have to call her the whole thing—was so smashed she walked right past Ben trying to be all sexy and mysterious. But she just looked lost.

Of the three, Amber had the most personality. I didn't say it was a good personality. She told Ben she was the "Baconator" and asked him if he wanted a taste. He kissed her hand and told her she was delicious. I had a hard time watching this go down because I was already uncomfortable with the idea of any other women touching or kissing Ben.

Finally, it was my turn. I got out of the limo as gracefully as possible and locked eyes with Ben. There were instant sparks.

"Hey, cutie pie," I said as I walked over, completely forgetting my script and remembering not to hunch my shoulders. "You come here often?"

Ben was smiling from ear to ear and I gave him a hug. "I watched last season and I have to admit I have the biggest crush on you."

"Thanks," he said bashfully.

"I love your hair," I said, reaching out to push it out of his eyes. "I'm a hair girl."

"Is that what you do for a living?"

"No, I'm a model."

"Oh, nice," he said. (Lie #1: Ben did not think it was nice, but all in good time.)

There was actually more to our first conversation that never aired. After asking me where I was from, Ben's next question flummoxed me.

"What school did you go to?"

Yet another ominous foreshadow (I'll stop counting now). I'd always struggled in school and believe I may be dyslexic. I'd finished some community college, but stopped when my modeling career demanded all of my time. Thrown off, I answered, "Oh, I didn't." I wasn't planning on mentioning that I was a model the first night, but now it was out of my control.

As I walked away, Ben said, stunned, "Now *that* was a pretty girl."

When the show aired, I noticed that the arrival order had changed. Lindzi Cox appeared last, showing up on a giant rented horse named Levi. Levi needed to get in and out as fast as possible so Lindzi, in reality, had gone earlier. In the episode, I was in the middle of the pack.

KEEPING IT REAL

Actual Rejected Greetings for Ben from My Journal

- "God, you're adorable!"
- "I have this feeling I might be your girl."
- "I love wine."
- "I'm in it to win it!"
- "I think this is the beginning of a beautiful friendship."
- "I love long walks on the beach, red wine, and boys with long, dark hair named Ben."
- "I really want the first impression rose. You won't be disappointed. Trust me."
- "The search is over . . ."

- "If you need saving in there, I'm your girl. Just give me a look and I'll scoop you up and swoop in."
- "Let me give you a good squeeze!"

I was giddy from my first encounter with Ben, but as soon as I walked into the mansion, it hit me that for the last few hours the women had not only been boozing it up, but more important, they'd been bonding without me. It got eerily quiet and twenty-three sets of eyes burned through me (Lindzi, metaphorically still on her high horse, actually refused to look at me). Then I heard somewhere in the crowd:

"Oh God, that's not fair! A model?"

Nope, this was not going the way I'd planned at all.

"Hi guys!" I chirped, trying to be friendly, even though as I scanned the room, I was shocked at how average this motley crew of women seemed. Ben walked in not long after I did and gave a welcome speech that kind of blew me away. He was so well-spoken and really cute. We locked eyes and smiled at each other right then, but I'd have to wait a long time for my turn to talk to him, as the other ladies shoulder checked each other like toothless hockey players to get his attention. So, while Ben made his way through the lot of us, I tried to make some early alliances.

I walked over to Kacie "B" Boguskie, from Tennessee, and complimented her dress. She pretended she didn't hear me. "What do you do?" I asked so loud that it was impossible to ignore me.

"I'm not going to tell you that," she sniped.

So much for Southern hospitality.

Samantha Levey, a tiny little pageant queen from Pittsburgh, asked me about *my* dress. I made the mistake of being honest. I told her it was Dolce and Gabbana but didn't have time to clarify that it was busted and marked down before she cut me off and sneered, "Oooh, Dolce and Gabbana!" like I was some sort of big shot.

I'm all about first impressions and I hadn't received very many warm welcomes so far. I hadn't planned on drinking a lot, but I needed a lot more liquid courage if I were going to make it through this night. I got a glass of red wine at the bar, which was fully stocked with every drink imaginable. A few of the girls bellied up to the bar a lot more than the others. Jenna Burke, a blogger known as the Over-Analyst, was drowning her sorrows after her awkward introduction with Ben. (She misquoted his poignant statement to Ashley Hebert: "Things don't end, unless they end badly." She said, "Good things end badly.") Elyse Myers, a personal trainer with a bangin' body, and Jaclyn Swartz, an ad account manager from NYC, were both partying like they were on *Jersey Shore*.

It was obvious to me that some of these women weren't going to make it very far on the show. Emily O'Brien, a stringy-haired Ph.D. candidate studying epidemiology, kept giving out hand sanitizer and talking about sexually transmitted diseases. She and Kacie B were talking major shit about Brittney Schreiner, a woman who'd brought her grandma to meet Ben, making her an early target and an outcast. As everyone else joined in on their shit-talking, not even really behind anyone's back, Brittney gravitated toward me, the other pariah. Her granny left thirty minutes after she'd arrived. I guess it was past her bedtime.

Not a single person asked me one question about myself or had a real conversation with me. I felt like nobody made an effort to get to know me. It was confusing because I was trying to engage with all of them. I realized this was not a normal situation. It was definitely a competition.

In an effort to hog maximum TV time, Monica, from my limo, started rolling around on a couch with a "VIP cocktail waitress" named Blakeley Shea. She couldn't make up a more distinguished, fake job title like everyone else does? How about hospitality executive? "You're in my life forever," Monica cooed to Blakeley. They didn't look like lesbians; they looked like fools. Plus, the next day they got into a fight and hated each other the rest of their time on the show.

They weren't the only ones desperate for airtime. Epidemiology Emily did a really lame white-girl rap, Nicki Sterling started a line dancing lesson in the living room, and Shawn Reynolds played soccer with Ben out in the driveway. When all the girls stampeded out of the house like elephants to join in, I hung back. I didn't want to look like a stage five clinger already.

I picked out the women in the house who I thought Ben would like best: Lindzi, the horse girl, would go far for sure. Line dancing Nicki, a bubbly dental hygienist with an ass like Kim Kardashian, definitely had a shot. Two gorgeous blondes, Casey Shteamer and Rachel Truehart, a tomboy with a nose piercing, seemed shoe-ins. At one point in the evening Casey and I bonded in the one bathroom that all the women shared. (You can only imagine how filthy it was.) I helped her recurl her hair and we became fast friends. *Phew,* I thought. *At least one girl here likes me!*

I finally got my first private one-on-one with Ben two hours after the party started. He took my hand and led me as far away from the house as possible, which made me feel special. But when we sat down I got a little tongue-tied. Being myself in front of the cameras with the whole crew watching was hard at first. The crowd threw my game off. I kept licking my lips like a snake and playing with my hair. My voice went up three octaves and I sounded like a nervous schoolgirl.

Ben and I had a short yet intimate conversation. We talked about our connection to Arizona. He actually grew up in Tucson and once owned a house in Scottsdale. While Ben talked, I sized him up to see if I was attracted to him. I definitely was. I did pick up on that sadness I'd seen on Ashley Hebert's season and I instantly felt myself caring about him. It's like something innate came over me to nurture him and—I can't believe I'm saying this—*love* him. I will say he seemed very serious and I did worry that he was a little boring. I had an urge to tickle him and loosen him up a bit. He also blinked a lot and had a hard time holding my gaze. I wondered if he had trouble with intimacy.

Even though we had instant chemistry, he gave Lindzi, who had already changed outfits like Beyoncé at the Grammys, the highly coveted first impression rose. I was slightly jealous of her rose, but also a little relieved. It's a double-edged sword. Whoever gets it may be safe until the next Rose Ceremony, but they are automatically hated and tortured by the other girls. I didn't need to be hated any more than I already was. After my chat with Ben, I immediately did my first on-camera confessional called an ITM (In the Moment). I could feel myself swaying and, being a little drunk, I belligerently said about Lindzi, "Screw you and the horse you rode in on!" Oops.

We still had hours to go until the Rose Ceremony, while Ben talked to every single woman. My feet were killing me. I asked a producer if I could soak them in the infamous hot tub, but they said no because it wasn't turned on yet. So I walked into the kitchen and grabbed a couple carrots and snap peas from a scavenged veggie plate and dipped them into the room-temperature ranch dressing. I grabbed a bottle of water. I was cutting myself off, no more booze.

It was a smart move because the more the other women drank, the more bananas it got in there. The biggest fight was between

Monica, the queen of the mean girls, and poor drunk Jenna, who didn't stand a chance against her bullying. Ben was clueless that this catfight was going down. If you rewatch the episodes, you won't see me engaging in any of the drama that night. I never stood in a group of gossiping girls. I stayed out of the toxicity and negativity by sneaking out for a cigarette.

Okay, I wasn't totally innocent. I did try to have a little fun at some of the girls' expense. At one point Ben came over and sat with me; Shira Astrof, a thin blonde from L.A.; and Nicki "the tush" from Texas. After Ben asked where they were from, I joked, "Let me guess. You're an actress and you're a Republican!" Even though I was being a brat, Ben laughed. I was right on both, by the way.

Around 2:00 A.M., we finally met the host, Chris Harrison, for the very first time. He appeared out of thin air to announce that the party was over and the Rose Ceremony would begin soon. It was cool to see him in person after watching him on TV for twelve years. He was pretty cute. But Chris, who wore a shiny gold Tiffany Love Knot wedding ring, didn't talk to any of the girls. He was a total pro. He nailed his speech for the camera and disappeared with Ben to sort through our headshots like a game of Hot or Not.

I knew Ben liked me. We kept locking eyes, and I was already starting to fall for him. I know it may seem cuckoo that I could have real feelings for a complete stranger within eight hours of meeting him, but I did! Seeing Ben at the Rose Ceremony just fueled my fire. We got a late start because a drunk and distraught Jenna locked herself in the bathroom and refused to come out. By the time a producer coaxed her out we all looked like hookers at the end of a shift—a mess of drooping makeup, limp hair, and wrinkled dresses. Regardless, we were lined up for the group shot that would appear in every celeb rag and website in America. Then we were prepared for Ben's first firing line.

Though I was 99.9 percent certain I'd get a rose, there was a nagging possibility that I could be rejected, humiliated on national television, and sent packing. As Ben started calling names, I noticed that he paused dramatically in between each one and had a routine of sorts. He made a concerned face, looked up, then left, then right. I wondered if he did it on purpose so when the show aired they'd have time to stick in shots of the yet unchosen swallowing nervously, shooting daggers at each other, or holding back tears.

Luckily, Ben didn't torture me too much and called my name in the middle of the pack. When he asked if I'd accept his rose, I purposefully answered, "I do." It was clear Ben couldn't remember all of the other women's names, but I know he remembered mine because he kept staring at me between rose handouts and smiling. Suddenly twenty-four sets of eyes burned through me and a target was staple gunned onto my back.

I didn't care, because I already knew Ben was my guy.

4

WHINE & ROSES

The first Rose Ceremony lasted well into the night and seven unlucky girls got the heave-ho. The sun was coming up and roosters were literally crowing outside. Exhausted and hung-over, my seventeen new best friends and I went back to the hotel to recoup. We were allowed to sleep until the middle of the afternoon, but then we had to put on our stinky, rumpled clothes from the night before to do recaps. I was so tired I didn't even put any makeup on. And that's when we got the bad news: a producer informed us that the makeup artist was only provided to us for the first night. From now on, we were on our own. I was okay with this announcement, because I'd learned how to put on makeup for high-definition TV cameras back when I'd modeled in commercials. But this was a potential nightmare for everyone else, especially Blakeley, who had a tendency to cake it on; Lindzi, who had permanent eyeliner tattoos; and for the girls who slept in their makeup.

I thought about the first night: it was totally surreal. And Ben made some surreal choices. He kept Jenna, even though she basically had a mental breakdown in the bathroom. He kept mean Monica, who admitted to a few of the girls she thought Ben was ugly. And he kept Emily, who talked incessantly about heart disease. I wasn't sure how I felt about his taste in women, but decided to give him the benefit of the doubt. He was under a lot of pressure, too.

The next day, we drove out to Malibu, thinking we were moving into the mansion. As we mingled in the kitchen, Chris Harrison appeared from nowhere. The women turned on like a light switch and pounced on him. He introduced himself individually to each of us and I tried to be as normal as possible. The others, especially Kacie B, were busy kissing his ass, maybe hoping he'd put in a good word with Ben or, more likely, hoping he was imagining them as the next Bachelorette in case this didn't work out.

Chris walked us out to the lawn to film a segment. He announced that this season would be different from seasons past: we'd be leaving the mansion immediately and traveling with Ben all over the world. For our first destination shoot we were heading up to Sonoma, where Ben ran his winery. Contrary to popular belief, Ben didn't *own* a winery. He grows his own grapes on an already existing winery, like renting office space. But many of the women, including myself, were under the assumption that Ben was the second coming of Kendall-Jackson.

After the expected squealing and jumping, we flew up to San Francisco and piled into vintage white convertible Rolls-Royces, dividing ourselves into already forming cliques. I gravitated toward raspy-voiced partier Jaclyn Swartz, my hair-curling buddy Casey Shteamer, and beautiful blonde Rachel Truehart. Kacie B, Nicki, Monica, pageant queen Samantha, and Emily were forming their own Pink Ladies' gang. Blakeley, who at thirty-four was a senior citizen in *Bachelor* years, and Lindzi, who rarely spoke to anyone, were lone wolves. The rest, frankly, were floaters, not really a blip on the radar. I kind of missed Anna Snowball. At least I remembered her name.

KEEPING IT REAL

How to Get Noticed by the Tabloids

The key to becoming a *Bachelor* star and getting a lot of ink right off the bat is having a back story. Give them something to write about! Even if it's bad!

- Release a mug shot.

  But only if your hair looks good in it.

- Overcome adversity or tragedy.

  AshLee Frazier was an orphan. Sarah Herron only had one arm. Car accidents, diabetes, and dumped at the altar all work, too.

- Have a weird job.

  Shawntel Newton didn't even come close to getting the guy after two tries but because she ran a funeral home, she nabbed magazine spreads and even got a book deal.

- Be sexually ambiguous.

  Many former contestants have been dogged by gay rumors. Keep everyone guessing; it adds to the fun.

- Flaunt your virginity.

  Sluts are a dime a dozen. The girls and guys who get the most buzz are the born-agains like Sean Lowe or the never-haves like Ryan Hoag or Corrie Adamson.

- Have fangs.

  I think that speaks for itself.

We arrived at a gorgeous rented house overlooking a vineyard and Ben greeted us at the door. Immediately the women took off to find their bedrooms. A gift bag was waiting for each girl—actually a Guess rolling suitcase. It was filled with swag, including bikinis, skinny jean leggings, CC Skye bracelets, and skin care and tanning products. Lindzi was a big fan of the bronzer and her hands were often stained bright orange. Go ahead and YouTube it.

Unlike the others, I didn't run around the house like a chicken with my head cut off. I strolled into the kitchen by myself to check out the fridge. I was thrilled: it was packed with real, healthy food. I felt like I hadn't eaten a proper meal in days and I was starving. Even more thrilling, Ben walked into the kitchen and we were by ourselves for the first time. He told me that the first thing he did on Ashley's season was check out the fridge, too. He grabbed a bottle of wine and, as we chatted and flirted, word spread like wildfire that he was alone with me. By the time he popped the cork, everyone—the other women, producers, cameras—swarmed us like bees.

The first date card was announced on the lawn at dusk. As we gathered around Ben, the sun setting behind us, he kept eyeballing me, not so inconspicuously. "Oh my God," my new pal Casey whispered. "He likes you!" I tried to brush it off, but later Casey told me that it was at that exact moment she and some of the other girls checked out. I was unpleasantly surprised when Ben told Kacie B she got the first one-on-one. I already found her grating. I sort of didn't care though, because I was tired from traveling and Kacie B would only be getting a short evening date. I held out hope that I'd get the longer all-day, one-on-one date in Sonoma.

When Kacie B was getting ready for her date in the hall bathroom, I walked by and told her that she looked beautiful and to have fun. After she left with Ben, the rest of the girls made the first of our many family dinners and ate together out on the patio. When we weren't in hotels, we were left on our own to cook meals. Monica, who had already designated herself the group's resident astrologer, also offered to be chef. She made a giant salad, throwing in tons of meat and cheese without asking anyone if they were vegan or vegetarian. At this point, I wasn't eating dairy, or chicken, so I had to make my own dinner. Even though it was a small thing, this seemed to alienate me from the group. They thought my diet was "weird" even though Kacie B was gluten free and back then nobody knew what the heck that was yet. I thought they'd all be judgmental about my smoking, so I decided to keep that a secret for as long as possible.

After dinner, the producers gathered us all in the living room so we could film the group date card scene. There was a knock on the door; the card was read aloud. Names were rattled off. I wasn't one of them—meaning it was fairly certain I'd get the last private date with Ben on this leg of the trip. I was so excited, but so exhausted. I desperately wanted to go to bed, but instead we answered a bunch of questions like, "What do you think the date will be tomorrow?" Or "What do you think Ben and Kacie B are doing right now?" Nobody was saying anything interesting. I piped up with a few sassy comments just to get myself out of there.

After the crew packed up and left us alone in the house, I had an intense urge to run away. Nobody was there to stop me. All I needed was my wallet and I could run like a gazelle through the vineyard into town, find a pay phone to call a cab, and escape to the airport.

Instead, I just went to bed. Or tried to. I quickly realized there was no such thing as a good night's sleep on this journey. The big partiers (Blakeley, Jaclyn, Monica, Elyse, and more) stayed up late drinking bottles of local wine, playing cards, and cackling—most likely about Monica's inaccurate, totally amateur astrology readings.

I was assigned a double bed with Nicki, a complete stranger. "I guess it's you and me, Texas!" I joked to her. Registered nurse Jamie Otis got shoved into the corner of our room on an air mattress, which made a fart noise every time she moved. I got about three hours of sleep.

At the ass-crack of dawn a producer gently woke me up and I dragged myself out of bed. Throughout the entire process, I never knew what day or time it was because I forgot to bring a watch. Huge mistake. I was totally disoriented. It took me a minute to figure out where I was and what the heck I was doing there. Then the house exploded in chaos. It was the first time we all had to get ready at the same time, in the same place.

I shuffled into the kitchen to get coffee. Some women were making breakfast. Elyse's specialty—bagels with peanut butter and bananas—was quite popular. Others were making themselves mimosas. A couple sat on the counter gossiping about Kacie B's date last night. I wanted to avoid overhearing anything that would bum me out, so I left to get ready for my day's activities. While the other women went on their first group date I had plans that included lying out by the pool, napping, and sneaking in some exercise by walking up and down the driveway. The driveway was as far as we were allowed to stray from the house.

At this point in the trip, there were still a lot of girls, but I could go days without seeing someone. For example, I rarely crossed paths with Jennifer Fritsch, an accountant from Oklahoma, because she was on the group date and slept in a room far away from me upstairs. When I was hanging out, she might have been doing an interview and vice versa. Roommates tended to be stuck together and have a similar schedule. Which could be good or bad. Whoever roomed with Blakeley would have been frustrated because she spent an eternity in front of the mirror primping. Whoever roomed with Lindzi may have gotten old-fashioned advice like "Ladies don't chew gum." I got to know Nicki pretty well in Sonoma since we were sleeping together and I found her to be a worrywart and insecure. She was always so nervous she'd be sent home.

In all fairness to Nicki, everybody may have been extra uptight because, TMI alert, nobody was pooping. Whether it was the traveling, the lack of privacy, or girls fearing that Ben might find out they actually go number two, stomach issues were messing up our mojo.

Even worse than the constipation epidemic was Kacie B buzzing around, glowing about her date the night before. She and Ben had twirled a baton and watched home movies together. It sounded like a total snooze-fest, but she boasted that it was the best, most romantic date she'd ever been on. And on and on. Okay, we got it. Someone asked Kacie B if she kissed Ben and she said coyly, "I'm not going to say!"

Amping up an already anxiety-filled morning was the unknown: Who would Ben pick to take on the second one-on-one date? And who would get absolutely nothing?

When ten of the girls left for their group date, which involved putting on a play for a bunch of kids, I was relieved to have a little peace. The worst of the Pink Ladies—Emily, Monica, Samantha—were out of my hair and I got a temporary reprieve from being the biggest target in the house. During the night pool/hot tub portion of the group date, the bikini-clad mob turned on Blakeley after she and Ben made out in the pool. They went extra nutty after Blakeley nabbed the one rose that was up for grabs and guaranteed her safety for the week. "She's so blatantly fake and overtly sexual!" Samantha the pageant queen cried about the VIP cocktail waitress. "I hate her!"

While all this drama was going on, I was back at the ranch with the rest of the girls, including the insufferable Kacie B, who was still gloating about her date with Ben. Late that night, the doorbell rang and she answered the door to retrieve and recite the one-on-one date card for the next day. "Courtney," she read, her lip curling in disgust. "Let's spin the bottle."

I decided to rub it in, just like she'd been doing all day.

"How'd that taste coming out of your mouth?" I joked, quoting my favorite movie *The Blind Side*.

There was a stunned silence in the room. *The Blind Side*? Anyone? Bueller?

"How'd that taste coming out of your mouth?" I repeated.

"Like vinegar," Kacie B shot back, shooting me pointy daggers from her furious eyes.

Oh, this time she had a comeback! She gets the joke!

Not so much. Sandra Bullock got an Oscar for that line but I got the wrath of twenty humorless women. I apologized to Kacie B, but the damage was done. The next day, while I was on my date with Ben, Kacie B ran around the house retelling the story to anyone who would listen, adding in what a bad person I was. On a scale of wonderful to horrible, I was back to being worse than Blakeley, quite an accomplishment considering she'd been called a "slut" and "horse-face" by several of the girls during the group date. (I, myself, had not yet called Blakeley "Horsey." That came later and never aired.)

Ben, of course, was oblivious to my scarlet letter in the house and I wanted to keep it that way. So when we drove off to have our private date, a picnic down by the Russian River in Sonoma, I made sure sparks flew as soon as possible. I wore little white shorts with sexy brown cowboy boots, even though I'm self-conscious about my legs and it was actually kind of cold out. I put his adorable Jack Russell terrier, Scotch, in my lap—dog people love it when you show affection for their best friends—and suavely put my hand on his thigh. We drove together for about twenty minutes so the producers could get some overhead helicopter panoramas and a few shots of us chatting in the vintage convertible truck (always convertibles on this show!).

Ben and I held hands and talked naturally without any cameras in our faces. We discovered that we had a few things in common: our favorite snack was power bars, which we both pulled out at the same time, and our favorite band was Mariachi El Bronx. He had his iPod with him (apparently, the Bachelor is *not* cut off from the world) and he played our favorite song, "Sleepwalking":

Electrify the night
Follow the moon
Islands don't dream
Of cities like you

I had goose bumps listening to it with Ben. I wanted to kiss him so badly. We didn't. Instead, we had a conversation about kissing. We decided we wouldn't make out a lot on-camera because we didn't want to gross the viewers, and our mothers, out.

KEEPING IT REAL

Ten Fun Facts About Flajnik's Follicles

The biggest controversy on season 16 of *The Bachelor* wasn't my big mouth. It was Ben's hair! You either love it or hate it. There's really no gray hair-ea. Test your knowledge about Ben's lovely locks with this extremely challenging quiz.

TRUE OR FALSE?

1. Ben flat ironed his hair on *The Bachelor.*
2. Ben hides a receding hairline with his long locks.
3. Ben colors his hair.
4. Ben owns a hairdryer.
5. Ben uses Moroccan oil for ultimate sheen.
6. Ben has worn his hair in a ponytail.
7. A Twitter account called BachelorBenHair was created during the show.
8. Ben has split ends.
9. Humidity wreaks havoc on Ben's hair.
10. Ben owns scrunchies in several colors.

Answer key: 1. T; 2. T; 3. F; 4. T; 5. F; 6. T; 7. T; 8. F; 9. T; 10. F

When we arrived at the redwood forest Ben's dog, Scotch, took off running. Ben was totally panicked and I felt so bad for him. Luckily Scotch was found, so we could relax and have a good time. Or try to relax. It was still hard for me to let my guard down with fifteen random people standing around staring as we tried to talk intimately. I spoke quietly, my voice going up a few octaves, hoping everyone wouldn't hear what I was saying to Ben. Which was silly because we were miked up almost all the time.

We had a picnic by the water and shared our first kisses on-camera. It was very natural and it just kind of happened. It was a textbook first kiss, soft and sweet. There was room for improvement, but it felt really comfortable.

For part two of the date, I switched into a gray sweater, scarf, and the free leggings I'd gotten in my swag bag. We climbed up on a tractor and drove into Ben's favorite local vineyard for a romantic dinner. I use the word "dinner" lightly. No one really eats the delicious gourmet food they place right under your nose because nobody wants to be seen talking with their mouths full.

We made out a little more at dinner, but our kisses were so quick that producers jokingly shouted at us to keep them going longer. When we refused, they gave us our first nickname as a couple—the Pecking Pirates.

It was definitely the best date I'd ever been on in my life and I wanted to savor every moment of it. But a couple of things Ben said during dinner raised red flags. Like, he asked me how I was getting along with the other girls. How did he know drama was going on already? The other thing that concerned me was when Ben reminisced about his glory days of staying up and partying all night. He claimed he was ready for the next phase of his life, settling down and marriage, but I wasn't so sure. I worried Ben might be immature. And that the other girls were already talking about me.

Of course, I pushed those red flags out of my mind because Ben gave me a pink Core Balance band bracelet. He always wore a white one so when he pulled a pink one out of his backpack for me, it was a sure sign in my mind that I was his favorite.

At the end of the night, which was freezing, he gave me his coat to wear and we sat in a swing talking, kissing, and cuddling. "This is the best first date I've ever been on," I said. "Me, too," he replied.

They separated us for our final interviews, and then we left in separate cars.

The next morning, I woke up happy, thinking about Ben. *This could work*, I thought. It could be him and me at the end: Ben Flajnik could be my husband. After Nicki rolled her rump out of our shared bed, I secretly wrote Ben one of my signature love notes in my journal, ripped the page out, and folded it. Tonight was the cocktail party and Rose Ceremony and even though Ben had given me a rose on our date and I was safe for the week, I wanted him to know how I felt.

The other women, who were very envious of my new bracelet, had an entire day to get ready for the party. It was too much idle time. Some, like Jaclyn, Elyse, and Jenna, had stayed up late drinking bottles and bottles of wine while I was on my date. To cure their hangovers, they hair of the dogged it and started drinking mimosas early. Others, ahem Blakeley, used the entire time to get ready. I'm not kidding. She hogged one of the bathrooms for three hours. Her intense beauty rituals and bad manners just gave Kacie B and her former couch lover, Monica, an excuse to talk shit about her nonstop. Not that Blakeley didn't deserve it. I noticed that she was super bossy and high maintenance with the PAs, ordering them to get her drinks and food. Maybe because she was a VIP cocktail waitress she wanted someone to wait on her for a change. I don't know. For someone who probably earned a living on tips, Blakeley was also surprisingly lazy. Once, as I walked by her room, she called my name out. I poked my head in the door and found her sitting on the floor putting (more) makeup on.

"Hey, what's up?" I asked. Maybe we were going to bury the hatchet.

"Can you close my door?" she answered, completely seriously.

"Sure," I said, and then slammed it as hard as I could. Maybe not.

Nobody really asked me about my date with Ben, which was rude, but also totally fine. I didn't want to confide in them anyway. So I put on my best poker face. I wanted to play it a little cooler than Kacie B, who was flying around the house sweating rainbows. We get it. You're in a good mood. Nicki must've had a sixth sense that my date went well (maybe we bonded subconsciously in bed?) so she was snappy with me all day. I overheard her whining that I shouldn't be allowed to have any one-on-one time with Ben at the cocktail party because it wasn't fair to everyone else.

At least Samantha, the little Chihuahua always running her mouth, had the cojones to insult me to my face. She was constantly harshing on me, about everything from being so tall to my diet. "There's Courtney the model eating another salad!" she'd sneer as I ate. Samantha wasn't as tough as she looked though. She could dish it out, but she sure couldn't take it. Once, when I told her to leave me alone or I'd "dropkick" her, she ran to her room crying. She was so upset she was late to a cocktail party.

By the time we all headed to the cocktail party in Sonoma, half of the girls were hammered and/or on the verge of hysteria. I threw on a white lace dress I'd borrowed from my sister and prepared myself for the inevitable shitshow. Nicki and Rachel were really nervous, and the few women who didn't get any date with Ben that week were practically catatonic. Nicki even asked the group, "What's the plan tonight? Who thinks that people who had dates shouldn't get time tonight? Courtney shouldn't have any more time with Ben."

"I don't think there should be rules," I said, defending myself. I didn't want anyone telling me when I could, and couldn't, talk to Ben.

Later, Nicki apologized for being snappy toward me. I didn't want the girls to hate me so I stayed away from Ben as long as possible. I also didn't want him to think I was being aloof, so I asked a producer to pass along my note. I also whistled at Ben like a construction worker whenever he walked by. (I did this throughout the show and it would end up being one of our inside jokes.) Despite trying to respect the girls' wishes that I keep a low profile, I needed to have a one-on-one chat, so I interrupted Lindzi, whose face was now as orange as a construction cone from all of the free bronzer. I apologized to both of them, but Lindzi didn't seem to care. She made stinkfaces here and there, but for the most part, to her credit, she'd stayed out of the drama so far.

Ben read my note out loud on-camera. I was mortified, but should have known better. Nothing was private on this show. On the cover I'd written: Rose are red/Violets are blue/I like you a lot/I hope you do, too. As he read the inside I cringed even more:

> Dear Ben,
> Thanks for the nice date last night. I woke up feeling happy and wanted to write you a love note. I could see you being my husband. There I said it. It's out there . . .

Lucky for me, the note never made it on the air. There was way too much other juicy f'd up drama swirling around us that night.

Even though the party only lasted ninety minutes this time, it was a disaster. We could tell how many girls were being sent home because we counted the roses on the platter. It made everyone nutty. Blakeley followed Ben around like a stalker, as the Pink Ladies continued their verbal assaults on her character (calling her "jugs" and a "bitch"). When Ben gingerly told Blakeley to give him some space, she ended up crouching in the fetal position in a corner of the luggage room sobbing. Brittney, the girl with the granny, was not adapting to the reality show lifestyle at all and angrily pushed a camera out of her face. Jenna Burke flipped out again and passed out drunk in a bed.

Rumor had it that our cast was the drunkest the producers had ever seen. Which is not surprising, considering our beloved Bachelor's livelihood was based on alcohol. There were times at our cocktail parties when they actually had to close the bar because they didn't want everyone wasted and throwing up. I heard that the cast of conservative Jake Pavelka's season spent more money on their food budget than on booze. "I don't think any of us ever got drunk," one of the girls on that season told me. "We were like grandmas. We'd sit and talk and have tea." Same with born-again virgin Sean Lowe's conservative cast of characters.

I hated doing interviews, but while all of this insanity was going down, I was happy to be pulled away. I was escorted down to a barn in the vineyard, which the crew had converted into a mini studio. While the camera and sound guys set up for my ITM (or TMIs, as the girls had now dubbed them), I sipped a glass of red wine as a producer put on Adele's song "Someone Like You." I felt so comfortable and I just wanted to make the crew happy. I wanted to make them laugh. I wanted them to like me.

KEEPING IT REAL

Cheers to the Clichés!

Watching *The Bachelor* or *The Bachelorette* at home and want your own cocktail party booze-fest? Drink anytime someone says:

1. I didn't come here to make friends.
2. We have a strong connection.
3. I feel like my wall is up.
4. [Insert name] threw me under the bus.
5. The words "journey" or "process."
6. [Insert name] isn't here for the right reasons.
7. I came here to find love.
8. I could be going home tonight.
9. I'm falling in love with more than one woman.
10. This is the hardest decision I've ever made in my life.
11. I can be myself around him/her.
12. I have to trust my heart.
13. At the end of the day . . .
14. I just don't see him with her.
15. You haven't seen the last of me.

I would end up making their jobs a little too easy. I didn't say anything too outrageous that night, just that it was "a war out there." But soon I would get a little too comfortable with the crew and insert my foot in my mouth a lot. Very soon.

When I went back to the house for the Rose Ceremony, Blakeley was still being bullied by the Pink Ladies. As Ben handed out roses I couldn't help but be a little cocky. I knew he liked me.

This wasn't going to be that hard.

I'd just sit back and watch all of these self-sabotaging cuckoo birds implode.

5

BUFFETS & BREAKDOWNS

We weren't even that far into the journey, and yet everyone, now sixteen of us, were already going a little stir-crazy, especially me. Emily talking incessantly about her mind-numbing job in epidemiology was like nails on a chalkboard. Rachel and Nicki were terrified they were going home every moment of every day. Kacie B took it upon herself to be "Julie McCoy, cruise director" of the group. She'd lead sing-alongs on bus and car rides and pose irritating ethical questions, like the ones you'd find in a Scruples board game, to jumpstart conversations. Shut up already!

By the time we got to our next destination, San Francisco, a lot of the girls were emotional and on edge. The first night we were given our own rooms at the historic Fairmont Hotel, but didn't leave them. We got to order in anything our little hearts desired from room service, but there was no television. I felt like I was being groomed. With absolutely nothing else to do, I journaled for two hours. Even though the girls were annoying, I was relieved when we took over the entire penthouse and the presidential suite as a group. It was better than being in solitary confinement. And we got to pick our own roommates. I chose my new friends, Casey and Rachel, the hot blonde, unaware that she snored like a freight train.

Most of us, in our normal lives, worked out a lot. I consider it part of my job back in L.A. Going without regular exercise was starting to make us testy (though Kacie B was always chipper, probably because she'd somehow hid weights and a jump rope under her bed). We tried to schedule what we called Yard Time wherever and whenever we could. We'd even resorted to doing laps of the driveway back in Sonoma. Thankfully, there was a real gym at the Fairmont. Once, I saw Jaclyn headed to the gym carrying a workout water bottle filled with vodka. "I'm only gonna burn like ten calories," she slurred. "But I can't wait to watch TV!"

The hotel was beautiful, but I had cabin fever. San Francisco was intense for me, especially knowing that I wouldn't have a one-on-one date with Ben because I'd just had one. Plus, my secret smoker cover was totally blown when one of the producers came into the suite and announced, "You can go down to smoke now." Jaclyn and Blakeley overheard this and decided they wanted to smoke, too, which bummed me out because I cherished the private time.

At the Fairmont, Nicki and I bonded while working out together. When we walked into the gym I felt like I was walking on air. I watched the news for the first time in weeks while I ecstatically exercised on the elliptical. The physical release was so intense I may have even cried post-coital-like tears.

As I was working out, I checked out a cute guy who walked in wearing a baseball hat pulled low and black socks with his workout clothes, a look I think is so hot. *Oh shit, it was Ben!* He spotted Nicki and me, walked over, and made small talk. I felt relieved and proud that I was watching the news and not *Maury*. Maybe because he thought I was worldly, he talked to me more than Nicki—something that she definitely noticed and definitely didn't appreciate. He jumped on a machine right behind me and as he worked out, I could see him watching me in the mirror. I was happy I was wearing my Lululemon workout pants, which make every woman's butt look amazing.

The producers knew we needed a special treat to stay happy so they made sure the food was really yummy in San Francisco. We had a catered spread 24/7 at the Fairmont and a lot of the girls took advantage of the endless amounts of food wheeled in. The three down days before the Rose Ceremony were so long and tedious if you didn't get a date that a lot of times we had nothing better to do than stuff our faces. I devoured pastries and eggs for breakfast, giant salads with salmon for lunch, and plates of pasta for dinner. I even saw skinny Rachel eat a whole box of Cheez-Its in one sitting. A couple of the women, who shall remain nameless (Nicki), gained ten to fifteen pounds during taping.

While we all sat around eating and drinking our feelings, Ben gave Emily the worst one-on-one date ever: a terrifying climb to the top of the Bay Bridge. She matched her pink construction helmet with a full-blown panic attack. After burning however many thousands of calories walking up the darn thing, poor Emily probably wouldn't eat on their dinner date. Even though she admitted to Ben the lame fact that an online dating site matched her up with her older brother, she still got a rose and was safe for the week.

From our hotel window, we saw fireworks going off and we knew they were for Ben and Emily. It was like the cannons going off in *The Hunger Games,* except I knew Emily was making out, not being harpooned with a bow and arrow. This whole experience felt eerily similar to *The Hunger Games* so far: we were fighting to the death for Ben.

Picturing Ben kissing Emily made me want to throw up in my mouth a little. It really bothered me. It bothered everyone. Earlier in the day room service staff had wheeled in a fancy silver tray stocked with top-shelf vodka and every Bloody Mary accoutrement known to mankind, so many of the girls were sloshed and belligerent. I don't usually partake in day-drinking—I don't like to drink hard alcohol because I'm such a lightweight—so I didn't really get to bond with the other girls who were day-drinkers.

KEEPING IT REAL

Embrace Your Inner Villain

by Kalon McMahon

Can you name the guys from Emily Maynard's season? Can't remember that many?

- You remember the guy who wins.
- You remember the guy who you *wanted* to win.
- You maybe remember the guy who cried after two weeks of knowing Emily.
- And you remember me—the guy you hated from day one.

If you can tell a good story, people will listen, regardless of which character you play in it. Just don't be boring. Otherwise you just end up a *Bachelor* statistic, and statistics don't get to write books.

"Celebrity," no matter how brief, is not a commodity. It's a vehicle. And if driven correctly, this vehicle will take you wherever you want to go. It opens doors. When you are newsworthy, it becomes much easier to shed light on the things that are important to you. Two years ago I participated in a charity date auction to benefit CAPS (Citizens for Animal Protection). The date consisted of a helicopter ride to my family's ranch for an afternoon of drinking champagne, riding horses, and shooting guns. I sold it for a measly $600. Flash forward to after I was on *The Bachelorette,* virtually the same date sold for $10,000. So the moral of the story is that if I have to be a dick on TV in order to be a better person in real life, sign me up every time.

Fortunately for me, I got the chance to totally redeem myself on *Bachelor Pad 3.* If nothing else, *BPAD3* proved just how fickle the Bachelor Nation and *Bachelor* fans can be. One second I'm being tarred and feathered for calling Emily's daughter "baggage," and then poof, I became America's sweetheart's rebound romance. I mean if Lindzi Cox liked me, I can't be that bad—right?

The more dates Ben had the more connections he was making. The tension between everyone was palpable. Kacie B, who was now rooming with Lindzi, was the ringleader of the girls who didn't like me. They had a big dance party listening to their clock radio, jumping up and down on the bed. When I saw them after, I asked, "Where was my invite?" I was met with crickets.

To kill time and keep the peace I started taking long naps. The other women all complained that I slept all day, but they didn't know that Rachel's buzz saw snoring kept me up all night.

The next day I wasn't on the group date, "skiing" down one of San Fran's steepest streets on fake snow wearing bikinis, which was okay because it terrified me. The downside was that it alienated me even more from the rest of the women. The upside was that Emily and I actually bonded a little in the suite together. She was a lot nicer to me when nobody else was around. She told funny stories about being a nurse, and how people always came into the ER with things stuck in their butts. I confided to her that when Chris and I broke up, it felt like a piece of me died. She then confided in me about the humiliating reason her last serious relationship blew up. Her longtime boyfriend was cheating on her the whole time and proposed to another girl while they were still dating. Ouch.

Besides a few fleeting moments, it absolutely stunk being trapped in the hotel room *again* while eleven of the other women, including my BFF's Casey and Rachel, went on the group date. The only thing that made me feel better about it was that I heard later that Kacie B fell down more than the other girls.

Sure, I had mild cabin fever, but Brittney was totally freaking out. She couldn't handle the show and wanted to go home as soon as possible. I sensed that the producers wanted to let her go too, but that they couldn't let her just waltz out the door with no explanation about why she suddenly disappeared. But Brittney didn't want to waste any more time. She packed her shit up in the free purple swag bag, rolled it right into the night portion of the group date (Rachel got the rose that night, yay!), and told Ben she was outta there. And that was that. She was gone.

Because Brittney bailed, Lindzi got the next one-on-one date by default. It was strange. I don't think anyone ever felt threatened by Lindzi because she was just so goofy, neutral, and corny, always talking about her "shenanigans." As she got ready, Lindzi announced she was going to bring fake plastic poop on her date and prank Ben by putting it on the seat next to him. *Great idea, Lindz,* we all lied. *We're sure he'll love it*. I'm not sure if she ever did it, but their date was pretty Mayberry: they took a trolley tour, ate ice cream, and slow danced at city hall as one of Ben's favorite singers, Matt Nathanson, serenaded them.

Finally, day four in San Francisco arrived. I never thought I'd be so happy to go to a Rose Ceremony. I was bored stiff and restless, on the verge of completely flipping out if I didn't see Ben again soon. I wasn't the only one losing my mind. When we got to the cocktail party, I made a toast to all the girls hoping for a positive, drama-free night, even though I was about to go postal myself. Shortly after my phony Kumbaya moment, I got into a little tiff with Switzerland (Lindzi), calling her out for making one of her classic stinkfaces at Elyse. When I got up to walk away, Emily called me "weird" and said I had a "personality disorder" behind my back.

In the meantime, Ben had been making out with Jennifer within sight of all of us. Sensing I was about to go ballistic, he pulled me away for a private talk. He took me to the most special place in the hotel. We walked through a secret bookshelf in the library to the roof, where JFK had once brought Marilyn Monroe. We kissed in the misty rain and he told me he couldn't stop thinking about me. I told him he was worth this process and I promised I could carry the weight of all the BS going on around us. Then I said we'd make cute babies.

I felt amazing for about four minutes. Then the shit hit the fan. The producers sprung a surprise on us—they invited Shawntel Newton, a reject from Brad Womack's season—to come back on *our* show to try to win Ben's heart. The timing couldn't be worse. We were all already so filled with anxiety, stress, and Cheez-Its. As soon as the foxy funeral director walked into the party, she walked over to talk to Ben and interrupted his chat with Elyse. Incredulous, we all watched and tried to eavesdrop on their conversation, but we couldn't hear what they were saying. When we figured out who she was, everyone completely fell apart. We're talking, crying, cursing, criticizing her thighs. It was ugly.

I was apoplectic—primarily because Shawntel looked like the kind of girl Ben would be into. As soon as I confirmed that they'd known each other before we started taping, I stormed out, declaring that I was leaving the show because I did *not* need to find love like this. I made it down to the front of the hotel, with one of the producers trailing me and asking me to come back.

"We actually have a connection and you just blew it!" I screamed at him with tears rolling down my face.

Eventually I agreed to go back upstairs, but I told the producer that I wanted to call my sister Rachel at the next stop on the trip.

When I returned to the suite, I looked like a wet rat and the other women looked like the walking wounded. Nicki had mascara stains running down her face (ever heard of waterproof?). Erika, the law student who had barely even talked to Ben, was on the verge of collapsing. Jaclyn was screaming that Shawntel was "Dumpster trash." We were emotionally drained and I was devastated for all of us (except for Swiss Family Cox—Lindzi, bless her heart, said she was being "open-minded" about Shawntel).

Yes, for a few short hours, I loved my crazy roommates. They were my temporary dysfunctional family and nobody messes with my temporary dysfunctional family. Vendettas were put on the back burner, for we had a new common enemy. When the producers brought us to the U-shaped couch to hash it out, we all banded together to make Shawntel's life a living hell.

"Why are you here?" Elyse yelled at her. "You don't even know Ben!"

"So now you're a part of us?" Jaclyn taunted.

"Why do you think you deserve to be here more than the girls who already went home?" Rachel implored.

"I think she's uglier in person," Nicki sniffed.

When the Rose Ceremony finally started, the tension was off the charts. A lot of girls were still crying, terrified that Shawntel would steal away a rose that should have been theirs. I refused to look at Ben. If he gave Shawntel a rose, I was done.

Lucky for him, he called my name first.

"Courtney, will you accept this rose?" he asked with a little fear in his eyes.

"I will," I said, shaking. "But tonight was a lot, and I just want you to know that. It was heavy for me. I saw you talking to what's-her-butt and it was not easy."

Ben was stunned that I called him out on-camera, but I was as serious as a heart attack (luckily Emily would know how to treat that). As he rattled off a few other names, it was obvious he was going to intentionally leave the Shawntel decision until the very last rose for full dramatic effect. I refused to look at him again and prepared myself to walk out if she got the last rose.

"I think I'm getting dumped for a girl he's known for three minutes!" Jaclyn yelled.

Then Erika fainted. Twice.

After a couple breaks, Ben decided to send the last three girls—Erika, Jaclyn, and Shawntel—home. I was so busy yelling "sayonara" and cackling at Shawntel that I missed Erika fainting again and Jaclyn locking herself in the bathroom.

The Rose Ceremony was such a circus the next day Ben sent sushi to the hotel room. "Aww, how sweet, he sent me a gift!" Emily beamed, trying to make it seem like it was just for her.

Everyone shot her dirty looks.

"He knows I like raw food," I taunted, then got up and walked away.

And just like that, because of a few pieces of tuna, we were all back to being enemies again.

6

FLY-FISHING & FIGHTING

Kacie B was the first one who figured out how to poo.

But it wouldn't happen until we got to Utah, the next stop on our journey to find love with Ben. The lucky thirteen of us left traipsed through San Francisco International Airport like sister wives. Before our flight, I had to go to the bathroom. When I came out, I spotted Ben sitting in a restaurant, again with his baseball cap pulled down low. We locked eyes and I waved, trying to play it cool.

When we arrived at the ritzy Waldorf Astoria in Park City, I was tipped off to the exact location of the best suite. It was huge, and had a beautiful view and private bathroom with a double shower. I told Casey and Rachel to run there with me to stake our claim as soon as we got to the hotel.

I also cashed in on my call with my sister. I went out on my balcony where nobody could hear.

When I heard my sister's and my dad's voices for the first time in two weeks I got a lump in my throat. I didn't want them to know I was crying, so I told them I was okay and that I really liked Ben, but was having a hard time with the girls. My sister gave me a pep talk and said she read on the spoiler website RealitySteve.com that I'd be going to Puerto Rico, Panama, and Belize next. She said she knew what cities I'd been to so far because I'd charged incidentals on my credit card and she was paying my bills. I promised after that to charge a gift in every airport so they'd always know where I was.

My dad was pretty quiet. I could tell he was trying not to cry.

Before I knew it, the call was over. It wasn't as fulfilling as I'd hoped it would be because I felt bad that I'd worried them. My dad can always hear in my voice how down I am.

A lot of the girls were down, even though we were in a gorgeous mountain town and got to see the city's first beautiful snowfall of the year. Jennifer was sick and kind of being snatchy. Samantha was openly bad-mouthing Ben, saying she knew a mutual friend of his and that Ben was just here to promote his winery. It alarmed me, but I thought maybe she was just being sour grapes because he wasn't that into her.

Even Kacie B was starting to lose it. Her normally indefatigable sunny disposition turned dark as soon as Ben whisked Rachel away in a helicopter for the first one-on-one date in Park City. Her mood improved a tiny bit after she came up with the brilliant idea to take a suppository. Inspired by Kacie B, I put in a request for laxatives, stat, plus earplugs to block out Rachel's foghorn snoring, which was *killing* me. Knowing help was on the way for my stomach issues, I gleefully stuffed my face again with all the locally grown vegan food they'd stocked in our new kitchen.

Producers knew we were on edge so they arranged for us to watch a movie and also took us on a field trip to get our nails done. In the lobby. Desperate for someone new to converse with, I tried to chat up my manicurist, but she shot me down.

As expected, I didn't get another one-on-one date in Utah, but I was thrown into the group date with Nicki, Kacie B, Casey, Lindzi, Blakeley, Jamie, and Samantha. Ben rode up to us on a horse and expert equestrian Lindzi just about creamed herself. I picked Romeo, the slowest, oldest horse. Unfortunately for Lindzi, she got stuck behind me on the trail so she couldn't show off her snazzy riding skills to Ben up ahead. Sorry!

We stopped to go fly-fishing in a river. The rest of the girls tried to catch a trout to impress Ben, but I knew my goal wasn't to catch a fish. My goal was to hook a man. While the other girls socialized with each other, I waded over to Ben to get a private lesson.

I'm sorry to sound like a hater, but the reality is most of the other girls just didn't try hard enough. They could have waded over to Ben, too, flirted and fondled his long rod. But they just rolled over and let me monopolize him. I refuse to apologize for taking advantage of their weak game play.

The only other girl who was super aggressive was Blakeley. Like me, she was punished with cruel insults and cold shoulders by the other women. But Ben rewarded her. During the group date's night session, he made out with her in the pool. (There is always a pool on the group date. Always.) I have to give Blakeley an A for effort, even though it made me physically ill to see Ben putting the same mouth he kissed me with on her mouth. After seeing it firsthand, I did question whether I could ever put my lips on his again.

Grossed out by Blakeley, and then pissed that Kacie B had disappeared with Ben, I sat by myself and sulked while the other girls soaked in the hot tub together. At some point during the night, Ben sent Samantha home. He'd apparently heard about her insults. Plus everyone including him suspected that she had a crush on one of the crew members.

When informed that Samantha left, the Pink Ladies started crying and carrying on. I wanted to lighten the mood, so I joked, "Another one bites the dust!" That went over like a turd in a punchbowl. I just couldn't understand what they were so upset about. Didn't they want the number of women to go *down*? I wished he'd have sent *five* girls home. They were treating this experience like an Outward Bound retreat, not a dating competition. Only nobody would catch each other in a trust fall.

Ben seemed to think the same thing. When he finally pulled me away for a little one-on-one time, he started nagging me that I should get along with the girls. I told him I couldn't really fake it—that I wouldn't be friends with any of these girls in the real world. They had such widely varying and polarizing personalities. He didn't see my side at all. I pressed him about what Samantha had said, that he was only here to promote his winery. Ben seemed shocked and offended. He denied even having mutual friends with her.

The bottom line is that this conversation happened when we were lying in each other's arms, him shirtless and me practically naked in my skimpy bikini. So outweighing our negative conversation was the fact that our bare skin was touching for the first time and it was pretty hot. At the end of our little talk, he went back to the pool, grabbed the only up-for-grabs rose in front of the girls, walked back, and gave it to me. I was safe for the week.

Winning!

Yeah, I know. I stole that from Charlie Sheen. The *Two and a Half Men* star had his breakdown in the months before I left for the show. So his favorite catchphrase was fresh in my brain during my

ITMs, when I was trying to think of witty quips to say. Here's the other thing about my "controversial" interviews: by the time we got to Utah the producers knew I was a loose cannon, especially after a glass of red wine. As time went on, and as it became clear that Ben liked me and I'd be sticking around for a while, I got pulled into confessionals and found myself trying to be a comedian on-camera, doling out increasingly outrageous insults.

After the group date was over, I thought about my conversation with Ben. I was falling for him hard; we clearly had an intense connection. I decided I didn't want to lose him and would try to make a better effort with the girls, even though I felt like a bomb was about to go off.

At the cocktail party before the Rose Ceremony, I complimented Emily on her silvery dress and congratulated Jennifer on the rose she'd received on the other one-on-one date, even though she'd been pissy in general for the last few days. I felt like maybe we could have a breakthrough if I just turned on the charm. Ben walked in, looking so handsome, and made another amazing speech about how it was a difficult situation, but that he was so glad that we were all being open to the process. He made me smile.

During my one-on-one time with Ben, which never made it on-air, I didn't know that Emily was in a stairwell just outside the room we were in. She overheard Ben and I whispering sweet nothings to each other and kissing.

During *her* one-on-one time, which *did* make it on-air, she then slammed me to Ben, saying I was different with him than them (she also said in an ITM that I was like a statue made of marble, beautiful but cold and hard on the inside). He was annoyed and totally shut her down. Few straight guys want to be pulled into a catfight between girls. Just ask any of the *Real Housewives*' husbands. Emily knew she'd messed up, yet when she came back to the living room she picked the totally wrong person—Casey, my BFF—to commiserate with.

"I hate that I jeopardized my time with him to talk about Courtney," Emily whined.

"She's not a fake person," Casey said, standing up for me.

"Are you serious?" Emily shot back.

"I think she's one of the most genuine people here," Casey insisted. "I love her. She's awesome around me."

"She has no friends."

"Obviously that's not true."

"All I've seen is a bitchy, cold, callous, rude demeanor," Emily continued. "And then she's sweet to Ben. She's not sweet. She's actually kind of mean."

"She's sweet to people who are sweet to her," Casey retorted. "Obviously we're not going to see eye to eye on this." Then she got up, walked away, and, of course, told me the whole conversation. I had steam coming out of my ears like Yosemite Sam I was so mad.

It's one thing for the girls to hate on me in the house, but another for Emily to assassinate my character directly to Ben. I could only take so much before I boiled over. Her biggest mistake was assuming I was a doormat, but I had a strong backbone, courtesy of my mother. "I want to rip her head off and verbally assault her," I said in my ITM. I threw the show a bone on this one. Later I regretfully told Casey I wanted to shave Emily's eyebrows off in the middle of the night. I was just kidding but I do wonder what Chris Harrison's promo would say: "The most violent episode in *Bachelor* history!"

KEEPING IT REAL

Reality vs. Realistic

by Ashlee Frazier

The one question that always comes up about *The Bachelor* is: "Is it real?" The truth is . . . yes. Are we asked the same question by producers in five million versions? Yes. Is it staged? No. Here are some key tips for future contestants:

1. Say "hello" and "good morning."
2. Take a quick moment and review your seventh-grade English book. You'll want to know when to properly use your prepositions, pronouns, and verbs.
3. Do be aware of what you say. If you don't say it, it can't be used against you. I'd say by week three and four you've been in the house long enough to get comfortable and people's true characters start to come out.

Tips for future Bachelors and Bachelorettes:

1. If you sleep with the contestant, you will be found out.
2. In key moments, make sure to say the right person's name.
3. Refrain from making any contestant feel they are the One when you still aren't sure yourself.

Knowing World War III was about to start, the producers gathered a bunch of us on the U-shaped couch, which was Kacie B's cue to ask one of her silly Scruple questions.

"How many of you have learned more about yourself in the past two weeks than in the past two years?" she said, raising her own hand first.

A handful of girls raised their hands, too. I did not. Emily was first, which set me off. Should I have raised my hand like a good girl? Probably. But I was so furious about Emily's gossiping I was itching for a fight. Kacie B was offended that I thought she asked a stupid question.

"I think most people who have gone through this process would agree with *you,*" Emily said to Kacie B.

I laughed at Emily.

"What are you laughing at?" she sneered.

"You," I said calmly. "You know why. My guard's up with you. You talked bad about me to Ben tonight."

"What are you talking about?" she lied.

"I'm up on it."

"Courtney, we're not in fifth grade. C'mon, let's be adults."

After I told her that she was the one acting like a child, she again told me I had a personality disorder. Our fight was getting so ugly several of the other girls got up and walked away.

DURING THE ROSE CEREMONY, Ben picked Emily last to teach her a lesson, I guess, and dumped Monica. I was relieved that one of the Pink Ladies was sent packing. She was a huge troublemaker and started a lot of drama behind the scenes. At the same time I was hurt that Ben chose to keep Emily after she insulted me directly to him and said I had a personality disorder.

In the champagne toast right after, Ben announced that we were going to Puerto Rico. He asked all of us if we'd ever been there before and I said that I'd just been there. We all had a normal conversation about it. But here's how it looked on-air:

Ben: "We are headed to the exotic island of Vieques, Puerto Rico!"

Courtney: "I was just there two months ago."

Silent angry stares from the girls, taken out of context.

After the cameras were gone, I was walking down the hallway back to my room when Emily snuck up right behind me.

"You're such a fake bitch, with your fake hair and fake boobs," she whispered menacingly.

Emily had fake boobs, too.

I thought about turning around and smacking her. Instead, I yelled, "You better check yourself, bitch!" suddenly as O.G. as 2 Chainz. "No wonder your boyfriend dumped you!"

It was the meanest thing I'd ever said to anyone in my life.

7

DOODY & DIPPING

When we landed in Vieques, there were still eleven girls left, but only five (me, Nicki, Lindzi, Kacie B, and Jennifer) who I took seriously as a future wife for Ben. I refused to acknowledge that Emily was a contender. My BFF, Casey, was clearly not into Ben, but I had a hunch he was keeping her around just to keep me happy. Rachel was so nervous in front of Ben that they didn't have any real chemistry. Jamie and Elyse had basically morphed into Snooki and Deena. Blakeley was an unknown wild card. And drunk a lot, too.

Honestly, I was getting kind of bored with Ben. Because we hadn't had a real date in weeks, the short bursts of time we'd had together were really just subdued, earnest talks about our relationship, which weren't really that deep. We had ten-minute Hallmark card conversations with weird girls peeping around the corner at us. We were still the Pecking Pirates and his excruciatingly slow, closed-mouth kisses were getting old. I might as well have been kissing Brittney's grandmother.

I was dying to have a little fun and wanted to see if Ben had a spontaneous side. But first, I created a little excitement of my own. On that first afternoon in PR, my Duralax arrived. Hallelujah! At about 3:00 P.M., Casey and I met in my room to take the laxatives. The directions said it'd take about eight hours to kick in.

Later that night producers gathered us on a U-shaper to announce the next day's group date card. Oh *crap*. Literally. I forgot about the group date! If it was something active, and I was on that card, I was in serious trouble. Jennifer read it out loud:

"Diamonds are a girl's best friend."

In the episode, you can see Casey and I look at each other and giggle nervously when our names were called. We prayed that the date would have something to do with jewelry but were mortified to find out we'd be taking a long bus ride, then a little puddle jumper plane to San Juan to play baseball in hundred-degree humidity. This was not good for my hair or my intestines.

That night while we were sleeping, exactly eight hours after we took the laxatives, Casey and I each had our own private nightmares. How can I put this politely? Okay, combine the toilet scene in *Dumb and Dumber* with the wedding dress shop scene in *Bridesmaids* and multiply it by infinity. I was sharing a bed with Rachel when all of a sudden I broke out in a cold sweat and my stomach started gurgling uncontrollably—like a geyser about to blow. I didn't want to gross out Rachel by going in the loo in our room, so I ran like a maniac across the hotel suite with my butt cheeks squeezed to find the most private bathroom. My rear end was making such crazy loud noises I was dying laughing and crying out in pain at the same time. I went back and forth to the bathroom so many times during the night

I kept apologizing to my poor bedmate, Rachel. At least now she knew what it felt like to be kept up all night.

The next morning, when I saw Casey, she just shook her head slowly. No words.

"I think I know what childbirth is like now," I mumbled like a zombie.

As we got ready to play baseball in the sticky, blazing Caribbean sun, I kept dashing off to the bathroom. Every time I went I thought, *There* cannot *be anything else left in there!* But there was. I was terrified that I was going to have an accident in front of Ben diving for a fly ball or running to first base. Once, in junior high, my old boyfriend Ryan was so sick during a baseball game he pooped his *white* pants in center field. He didn't show up to school for three days after that. What if I pooped my shorts on *The Bachelor* in front of 8 million viewers? I'd have to move to Antarctica and live with the penguins.

The long commute turned out to be a godsend because by the time we arrived at the baseball stadium, home of the Carolina Gigantes, everything seemed to be out of my system. Chris Harrison chose Blakeley and me to be team captains, and then we had to pick players schoolyard style. Since we had an odd number, it made sense that Swiss cheeseball Lindzi would play for both teams. I chose Kacie B—she walked like a football player so I assumed she'd be athletic—Casey, and Jamie. Blakeley got Emily, Jennifer, and, last but not least, Rachel. Unfortunately, she just didn't strike me as Sporty Spice. I'm pretty sure if you asked her to haul ass it would take two trips. I felt bad that I didn't pick my friend but I *really* wanted to win. The reward was a team group date with Ben. It may have contributed to the demise of our friendship, which was already on shaky ground. Rachel had been very grouchy from PMS and was starting to pull away from all the girls in the house.

Anyway, there's no crying—or talking about menstruation—in baseball! Game on!

Though Kacie B was bossy, she *was* a great athlete and an excellent draft pick. We got along the best we ever had. She even put eye black on my cheeks so we'd look like real baseball players. Casey was still feeling the laxatives and had to be escorted to the bathroom several times during the game. I played third base on purpose so I could stare at Ben's butt while he pitched. He looked really cute in his uniform.

The game was super close and super competitive, and I was surprised at how athletic Blakeley turned out to be. She kept catching my balls and getting me out. She plowed into me when I was trying to run to second base and elbowed me a few times. But in the end, after Jennifer struck out, we prevailed 10–9. The other team burst into tears and I admit I was not very sympathetic. I believe I called them crybabies? Then, in a follow-up confessional, in which producers asked us to put back on our smelly uniforms and reapply the eye black, Blakeley's all-star performance led me to say, "Who knew strippers could play baseball?" I'll take responsibility for that one. Nobody put a gun to my head and forced me to say it. If you think about it, though, half of the sentence was a huge compliment. She was a terrific ballplayer!

Listen, Blakeley and I didn't hate each other. In fact, we had a really nice conversation in Puerto Rico about her trying to break into modeling when she returned home to North Carolina. I told her she was really pretty and I meant it. She said she'd met with agencies there but had been rejected. I promised to make a few calls for her when this was all over. I never did, but still, I offered and would still do it today.

As soon as the game ended, Kacie B and I were definitely no longer on the same team. We were back to competing for Ben's love. During the group date on the beach, I decided to give Ben a pop quiz to see if he was daring or a total drip.

I whispered to him that I'd love to go skinny-dipping.

"I'll go right now!" he whispered back eagerly, his eyes lighting up.

"No, the girls are watching!" I wouldn't even kiss him in front of them. I sure as hell wasn't going to get naked with him in front of them.

While I was lost in space fantasizing about Ben and me frolicking nude in the sea, he gave Kacie B the rose. My stomach pain may have subsided but my verbal diarrhea was on full blast in my next ITM. Bitter about Kacie B, and thinking about her in the baseball uniform, I blurted out, "She's just like a little girl in a little boy's body." At this point, I didn't know she'd overcome a serious eating disorder. If I did, I would never have said that.

Not my best moment but you have to understand, I hadn't had a one-on-one date with Ben since Sonoma. I'd been stuck in these group dates with women who despised me for weeks and I was frustrated. I knew the rules of the game—I knew the drill—but I was impatient and confused. Could Ben possibly like these other girls? Or was he just going through the motions? I needed to know.

I got one small clue at the end of the group date. Ben confided to me that his one-on-one date with Elyse tomorrow would be "short." Ben's hint seemed like a challenge to me: Feeling like I had nothing to lose, I went to the producers and told them I wanted to set up a secret rendezvous with Ben after his date with Elyse. They loved the idea. They were all for it, and set the wheels in motion for a secret operation dubbed Team Romance.

That night, while Ben was dumping poor Elyse, I took a shower, put on the sexy lingerie I'd brought, and covered it up with a robe from the hotel. As I sat on the couch listening to the girls obliviously answering Scruples questions posed by Kacie B, the front door swung open dramatically and a bellhop yanked Elyse's Guess rolling suitcase into the abyss. I made another bad joke that went over like a lead balloon. "Maybe she got drunk and the Jersey Shore came out!" The girls were shocked but I didn't care. I was about to launch the most epic, diabolical plot right under their noses.

Finally, I got my cue. I went to the stairwell outside of Ben's room. Ben had no idea I was coming. Although in a confessional, I did say "I hope I'm a sight for sore eyes because after the date with Elyse, his eyes are pretty sore!" I actually liked Elyse a lot. She was one of the few who wasn't that mean to me, and she was always giving me great workout tips to make the most of our thirty-minute Yard Time. So I do feel bad about saying that.

So, Ben comes home, I whistle at him, and he sees me sitting there in the stairwell wearing a robe, a mischievous grin, and not much else. I think he was shocked and a little petrified. We grabbed some wine and headed down to the beach. This was the moment of truth. I wanted to make sure Ben was spontaneous and fun. I need to be honest here: I also wanted to check out the equipment. They say it's not the size of the boat; it's the motion of the ocean. But "they" wouldn't have to spend the rest of their lives with a little dinghy. Know what I mean?

"Should I take off my robe?" I teased.

"Are you going full nude?" he asked, not sure if he wanted to hear the answer.

"We can go in our underwear if you want," I said. He could tell I'd think he was wimpy if he wouldn't go full monty.

We stripped down to our birthday suits and ran into the water holding hands. We went out as far as we could, thinking the cameras were far enough away that they couldn't really see us (duh, zoom lens).

So, let's get to the good part. To answer your question, yes, Ben and I did have sex in the ocean. On-camera. It was immediate but it was only for about twenty seconds and, um, it was just the tip. We'd gone too deep (in the water, get your mind out of the gutter), and the current was so strong we couldn't get our footing. We kept getting pulled apart, and waves kept crashing on us and knocking us over.

Ben and I may have made sweet (succinct) love but we also took advantage of not being miked up and had a heartfelt, though brief, conversation that night in the ocean. He told me he was listening to "our song"—"Sleepwalking" by Mariachi El Bronx—over and over and that he thought about me all the time. "I can't believe I feel this way already, so soon," he said.

I told him I couldn't stop thinking about him either, and for the first time I told him, "I like you love you." It was basically a coward's way of saying I liked him so much I was on my way to loving him. We briefly touched on the situation with the girls but I made a point to say I didn't want to talk about them when I was with him. He did hint to me that he didn't like Emily. I was relieved.

We didn't want to get out of the water, but we couldn't stay in there forever. As we waded to the shore, I pointed at Ben's loins and joked, "I could marry that!" After, in my ITM, I wouldn't confirm or deny that we'd done the deed.

When I returned to the hotel, a producer let me blow-dry my hair in her room before I went back to the suite glowing. The girls were in the middle of a wild dance party. My roomies were jumping up and down on couches, going absolutely apeshit to a Justin Timberlake song. It was the first time they'd heard music in weeks and it was like they were possessed.

They had no clue where I'd been and they didn't care. They were euphoric.

Everyone was still on a high the next day, when we were getting ready for the Rose Ceremony. I even had a rare special moment with Nicki. My dress was really wrinkled and I didn't know what to do.

"Kacie B has a mini steamer," she said. "I'll get it for you."

Nicki knew I wouldn't ask Kacie B for a glass of water if I were on fire. She also knew if Kacie B found out she borrowed the steamer for me, it'd cause some drama. But she went out on a limb for me anyway and I thought that was pretty cool. She got the steamer, I ironed my dress as fast as humanly possible, Nicki returned it, and Kacie B never had a clue.

During the cocktail party, the producers gathered us on the couch for a game of twenty questions. Magically Jennifer asked out of the blue if any of us had ever gone skinny-dipping. I raised my hand, quite self-satisfied.

I was also feeling self-satisfied that Ben would finally get rid of Emily because of our talk. Once again, in her one-on-one time, she bad-mouthed me, saying I was "weird." Ben told her to drop it and to tread carefully but the warning fell on deaf ears. I had pushed Emily's buttons so hard she was obsessed with ruining my life. Instead, she was ruining her relationship with Ben. Mwah.

But Emily would get yet another lucky break. Jennifer, unaware that Ben was now completely whipped by me after our dip in the ocean, made the mistake of being the first to tell him during her private time that she loved him, which totally wigged him out.

She got the hook.

By the way, Lindzi got the first rose during the ceremony, which was kind of a slap in the face, considering Ben had had his penis inside of me less than twenty-four hours before.

I cried the entire way to our next destination—Panama.

Oh, I didn't cry because I was upset about Lindzi. I was in pain: my whole body—including my vajayjay—had been bitten by some sort of little water bugs or mosquitoes while I was cavorting in the water with Ben. I was having an allergic reaction, itching like crazy and covered in a huge rash.

I hoped Ben wasn't in this much pain and prayed we wouldn't run into him in the airport. If the girls saw *both of us* looking like giant red tomatoes, there'd be a lot of 'splaining to do.

As soon as we arrived in Central America, a paramedic gave me a shot in the ass and some antihistamine pills and I was cured within twenty seconds. I was relieved. That meant Ben was probably okay, too.

Because I'd been so sick, producers gave me my own room at the exclusive Trump Ocean Club. I was the only one who didn't have to share so I was ecstatic about the privacy—and the clawed bathtub with a privacy curtain around it, smack dab in the middle of the room. I wanted Calgon to take me away, hint hint. After being sexually dormant for the last month, the skinny-dipping incident reignited my libido. *Oh my God, this is definitely happening,* I thought as I stared at the spigot. I tried a few times but failed miserably. I was too paranoid someone would come in and see my shadow through the curtain, my legs in the air.

I also started plotting a way to sneak Ben into my room for secret tryst number two. I was right next to the elevator; he could have snuck in and out so easily. I wasn't planning on more sex. I really just wanted a little affection or a snuggle.

As happy as I was about my luxurious accommodations, I had a complete freak-out when my second bag didn't arrive in Panama and I had absolutely nothing to wear. I had designated the first suitcase for all the clothes I'd already worn a million times and were worn out and dirty, like the H&M maxi dress you saw me in like five hundred times. Doing laundry on this journey was a major operation and hard to organize. You couldn't just do it whenever you needed it. We had to be in a location where it was doable for a PA who didn't have a million other things to do. Then we all had to give them our stinky clothes and they mixed them all together. Blech. And it wasn't like you could borrow clothes from the other girls. Not only were we *all* running out of new options, you couldn't be seen on-camera in something another girl had worn.

KEEPING IT REAL

Casey Shteamer's Best-Dressed Awards

My BFF may not have given a shit about Ben, but she definitely cared about what we were all wearing. Here, the cast's fashion guru (and editor of ImperfectWonder.com) gives out roses for the most gorgeous gowns.

1. I remember seeing Jenna the very first night and thinking, *This girl knows how to dress.* Her white, loose-fitting sequined dress, paired with black strappy heels, could have looked dated if it had been formfitting. This look was ahead of its time, and I love that.
2. Samantha won week two in her LBD. Rarely does a little black dress catch my attention. However, this gown by Pleasure Doing

Business has such great thick material and is structured so well that when I saw it I put it on my "need to have" list.

3. In week three, Jennifer nailed it with her color-blocking red-and-pink number. Ever since I saw Sarah Jessica Parker wearing this combo (perfection in my eyes), I'd filed it away in my mind to re-create her look. Jennifer beat me to it and did it effortlessly.
4. Jaclyn's orange "Women Tell All" Ani Lee dress with the daringly deep V cutout had me at hello. I love things that not everyone is brave enough to wear. It is also fabulously flattering.
5. Courtney's purple Alice and Olivia dress was perfect for her complexion. This flowy, drapey number was sexy without trying. It wasn't skintight, but it still made her look gorgeous—not that she needs any help!

Luckily I didn't have to worry too much about my outfits on this leg because Kacie B got the first one-on-one with Ben, cracking coconuts together on a deserted island. I was going to be wearing traditional garb on the group date—playing soccer and dancing with the natives in the remote Embera Village. They'd never been filmed before and spoke no English.

So, everyone went cuckoo for Cocoa Puffs that I spent that afternoon shimmying and seducing Ben in a see-through bikini top. That's not entirely true. Here's what really happened. When we arrived, soaking wet from riding in a canoe in a torrential downpour, the native women took us in a hut to try on their handmade beaded bikini tops. They did *not* wear bras under their handmade beaded bikini tops and asked us all to take them off. The other girls were prudes and declined. I'm very comfortable being naked from my modeling gigs, plus I didn't want to offend our hostesses, so I happily ditched my bra and wore *two* of the beaded bikini tops.

My fine-feathered frenemies totally overreacted but Ben sure liked it. By the way, he was way more embarrassing than I was in his little loincloth: he was going commando underneath.

Everything in Panama was like a melodramatic telenovela. Kacie B was now bad-mouthing Rachel to anyone who'd listen. She made the mistake of telling me she couldn't stand her and that the other girls started a new drinking game: every time Rachel talked about herself, they had to take a sip. Rachel had been testing my last nerve with her snoring and moodiness, but she'd *always* had my back. I told Rachel what Kacie B said about her, which started a huge fight.

It just wasn't Rachel's week: She and Blakeley got the dreaded two-on-one date with Ben, where one girl gets a rose and one girl gets dumped on the spot. As if this double date weren't awkward enough, they were forced to out-tango each other. You'd think Blakeley would have had the advantage in this dance-off, being a VIP cocktail waitress and all. But there wasn't a pole within miles so Rachel got the rose and Blakeley got rejected.

Sadly, the alliance with my BFF also blew up in Panama. Casey, who rarely had any quality time with Ben and didn't care, couldn't just hang around being my sidekick forever. Somehow, the producers found out that she still had a boyfriend back home in Chicago. Chris Harrison did one of his classic on-camera confrontations and kicked Casey off the show. She cried like a baby. I'm still not really sure why because her interactions with Ben were painfully awkward and miserable for both of them. It all ended well for Casey though. Months later she started dating a handsome producer.

As expected, the Panamanian Rose Ceremony was a shitshow again, especially now that we were down to seven overly emotional women on the verge of nervous breakdowns. Jamie realized if she didn't do something drastic soon she was doomed. She knocked back a few too many drinks, then, in her private time with Ben, straddled him so clumsily that she ripped her dress. She also tried to give him a kissing lesson/instruction manual that went down as one of the least sexy and most humiliating moments in the history of *The Bachelor.*

Once again, Emily was saved by another girl's epic fail. Jamie, stumbling and swaying by the time the Rose Ceremony started, got the heave-ho. Ben gave Emily the last rose again, making her sweat it out until the very last possible second.

I knew Ben was doing that for me and it was a sweet gesture. But by the time we landed on a tropical island in Belize, our next location, I was hanging on to this whole thing by a thread. Despite our quickie in Puerto Rico, I hadn't had an official one-on-one date since Sonoma. I'd been on three lousy group dates and had little private time with him at the Rose Ceremonies, to make sure the other girls didn't get jealous.

I really liked Ben. I was falling for him for sure, but I was also losing sight of why. My feelings were slowly evaporating and I wasn't missing him that much when he wasn't around. Sure, skinny-dipping was fun but Ben hadn't done or said anything to make me feel special since Sonoma. I didn't doubt my feelings for him but the spark was gone. With the Hometown Dates just around the corner, I didn't feel ready to introduce Ben to my family. I didn't feel connected enough to him to do something so intimate, and I knew my mom wouldn't want camera crews in her house if I weren't 1 million percent serious about Ben.

KEEPING IT REAL

Production Lingo

10-1	Contestant has to tinkle
10-2	Contestant needs to go number two
ITM	The "In the Moment" interviews we gave while the action was happening
Dab	There were always a box of tissues next to the interview chair because our foreheads would get shiny, especially in the tropical locations
B Roll	Contemplative shots, walks on the beach, car rides
William	The name we had to call Ben in public
Kate Hilton	Lindzi and my public name during the finale

I just didn't know if Ben was "the one" yet. I felt it was a good time to walk away.

The girls talked about the possibility of bringing Ben home about a billion times on several different couch configurations. I came up with a new strategy: I decided to let everyone and their mother know that if I didn't get one of the three available one-on-one dates with Ben in Belize, I would not accept a rose and would go home.

It was manipulative for sure and it served one major purpose. If the other girls thought I might take myself out of the game, it would get them off my back. We only had one more week together before we'd all go our separate ways and I couldn't wait to never see any of them again.

You know that feeling when you have to go to the bathroom really badly, and when you finally get home, you almost pee your pants at the front door because you're so close you can't hold it anymore? That's what Belize felt like.

I had such a strong hatred for the girls by this point and they hated me back just as passionately. Kacie B held a boot camp on the condo's front lawn and even though they all could see me running up and down the stairs nearby, nobody invited me to join their makeshift exercise class.

I felt so bullied that when Emily got one of the date cards, I broke down on-camera and cried. Turns out that Ben had the worst time on his date with her but I had no way of knowing that then. In my mind, I was starting to believe that he liked her, I was getting played, and I would be humiliated on national television. She wasn't the only problem. Kacie B and Nicki were now declaring like town criers that they were in love with Ben and during their group date, swimming with sharks, ganged up on me and begged him to get rid of me. Rachel, who was also on the date, didn't say anything but she didn't defend me either.

"I'm concerned she's just in this to win it," Kacie B, who had now taken to calling me the Black Widow, told Ben.

"We want you to be conscious about Courtney," Nicki added with faux concern for Ben. "It's what comes out of her mouth. I want you to be happy in the long run. I want you to be with someone who's going to be there for you and give you one hundred and ten percent."

I felt like I was the one swimming with sharks. By the way, Ben must go down in *Bachelor* history for having the most adventurous/least romantic dates. So far, he'd made Emily climb the Bay Bridge, Jennifer spelunk three hundred feet down into a deep dark cave in Utah, Lindzi jump out of a helicopter into the Great Blue Hole in

Belize, and now he was turning Kacie B, Nicki, and Rachel, who was having menstruation issues, into shark bait. It didn't hit me while it was happening but his choice of activities was a major red flag. These were all things Ben wanted to do and it was incredibly selfish and immature. He never took into consideration that some girls might want to look sexy, not sweaty, wet, and/or scared shitless. Patti Stanger, *The Millionaire Matchmaker,* would have ripped him a new one if he arranged any of these asinine dates on her *Bravo* show.

So, my diabolical plan to threaten to leave worked and I did snag the last, best one-on-one date in Belize, a visit to a Mayan temple that dates back to 100 BC. Rachel told me about Kacie B and Nicki's witch-hunt during their date, so when I left for my date, I infamously shouted at them, "Bye! Can't stand you all!" After a short flight in a small plane flown by Jimmy Buffett's personal pilot, Ben and I arrived at the ruins. Of course, the date included a rigorous workout, climbing up a hundred steep stone steps in hundred-degree humidity. Our hair was plastered to our faces and we were dripping in sweat. But the thing is that this was the moment I realized that nothing Ben could do would ever gross me out. We looked absolutely awful, we had BO, and yet I was still so attracted to him and thought he was super sexy (I was hoping he felt the same way about me, especially the next morning when I caught Montezuma's revenge and he came into my hotel room to say hi right after I'd hit the pot for about the hundredth time).

Producers suggested I teach him how to model when we got to the top but I thought that was corny. Instead, we had the most intimate conversation we'd ever had. We talked honestly about how the girls, especially Emily, had been torturing me. I admitted having a hard time not feeling "special" in this setting.

He opened up about his dad dying for the first time. We talked about our past loves, how none of the guys I'd dated wanted to get married. We came up with a baby name, Forrest, in honor of his grandfather Forrest Flajnik. It was also the first time we discussed living together in San Francisco after the show was over.

I could have spent forever with Ben but the night portion of the date didn't last long. We pretended to have dinner when he again brought up getting along with the other girls. I tried not to be offended but he could tell I was getting defensive. We laid in a hammock together for another five, then jumped into a hot tub for the last five.

I didn't really need more time. After this date I had that "aha" epiphany moment. Not only was I ready to take Ben home to meet my family, but I was also ready to admit to myself that I was falling in love with this man. I was 99.9 percent sure he felt the same way about me. And I felt confident we were going to end up getting engaged in a few weeks.

I was the only girl feeling confident in Belize. The other girls were so desperate to bring Ben on a Hometown Date they were losing their minds. Before the Rose Ceremony, Nicki asked, "Does anyone feel safe?"

"I do," I said snottily. "Nicki, you're safe. I'm not worried about you." I shot a smug glance at Emily.

At this point, I was hours away from never having to deal with any of these women again. I just didn't care anymore. But then I kind of felt bad.

"There are plenty of fish in the sea," I added, trying to be helpful. I knew Ben and I would end up together. "Ben's not the only man to have ever existed. The spark is there, or it's not."

Emily and Kacie B were flabbergasted that I was so blunt.

"Did she just say Ben isn't the only fish in the sea?" Emily whispered to Kacie B, hoping that might be the ammunition she needed to finally convince Ben that I wasn't really here for him.

But these girls had no idea how amazing my date with Ben had been. They had no idea we'd gone skinny-dipping and had already sort of had sexual relations. So when he pulled me out of the Rose Ceremony for "a talk" on a bench, they thought their trash-talking finally got through to him and he was kicking me to the curb. They couldn't have been more wrong.

"Before we go further, I just want to make sure you're not going to leave," he said when I got out there.

"I'm not going anywhere," I reassured him. "I think we could be happy together." I paused. "Did you do this to make me feel special?"

"Yeah." He laughed. "I just wanted to spend a little time with you."

I skipped back into the Rose Ceremony, admittedly a bit obnoxiously, beaming. Rachel was eliminated, and I was sad, even though she was so moody lately we'd drifted apart. And last but not least, drum roll please, Ben eliminated Emily. I was over the moon. I rotated away from her so I wouldn't have to give her a hug or handshake good-bye.

"See ya. Wouldn't want to be ya!" I said very childishly.

After the champagne toast with the final four—Lindzi, Nicki, Kacie B, and me—it hit me like Chris Brown. I was *done* living with the other girls! It was over! It was a miracle! I was so proud to have made it through this exhausting, unnatural, emotionally draining process without having my eyes scratched out or my weave yanked out of my head. Barely.

The four of us were immediately split up. We hopped on a ferry and, as each girl got dropped off at her individual hotel dock one by one, I felt the oppressive weight that had been on my wide shoulders lifting. My guard dropped and I finally felt like my old self again.

Nicki was first to be dumped off, then, when Kacie B got off the boat, Lindzi let out a gigantic sigh of relief.

"I thought you guys were besties!" I asked, in disbelief. They had been roommates almost the entire time.

Lindzi shook her head and made her signature stinkface.

"Wow," I marveled. "Yeah, Little Miss Sunshine gets a little bit old." In that moment, I really respected Lindzi for miraculously staying out of the fray for six long weeks. I was blown away by her stamina and her class.

Speaking of being blown away (perfectsegue.com), the next day a scary Category 5 hurricane threatened to hit the island and we all had to be evacuated immediately from Belize. I never saw the other girls but hoped they were making it out safely. Sure, I hated them but I didn't want them to *die*. At 5:00 A.M., I was flown back to civilization by Jimmy Buffett's personal pilot, then hopped another flight back to L.A., where I'd stay until my Hometown Date.

In hindsight, I'm not sure what was more terrifying—escaping the hurricane or the thought of introducing Ben to my mom.

8

I DO'S AND DON'TS

Landing back home in L.A. was a massive shock to the system. It was no longer normal or acceptable to wear bikinis fourteen hours a day, have catfights, or dance in the rain to tribal drums. Fortunately, producers did their best to make the transition easier. For four days I stayed at a luxury hotel right next to the 405 freeway. I ordered in bottles of wine and ate tuna tartare from room service, worked out, and lay around lazily in my robe.

A few days prior, they asked me what I wanted to do with Ben in Scottsdale on my Hometown Date. I knew I'd end up golfing or doing something sporty if I didn't take matters into my own hands. I told them I wanted to take Ben to the Farm at South Mountain, a twelve-acre oasis of lush gardens, pecan trees, and rustic, gourmet restaurants just outside of Phoenix. Ever since I was a little girl, I'd dreamed of getting married under the Farm's ivy-covered canopy in the grove of pecan trees. I took my ex Dylan there once on Valentine's Day, but he didn't think it was romantic. He was totally bored and laughed at me when I told him I wanted to have our wedding there. I cried myself to sleep that night. I'd also done several photo shoots on the property, so taking Ben there was important and sentimental to me. I prayed he wouldn't laugh at me, too.

The producers suggested that I ask Ben to write and exchange fake vows with me at the Farm. I was really uncomfortable with that—it was *so* over the top—but I knew that the fallback might be putting on a pair of hideous plaid knickers, strapping a bag of clubs on my back, and walking eighteen holes at one of Scottsdale's championship golf courses.

I warily agreed to the vow thing. A PA took me shopping in Los Angeles to find a white dress that would subtly resemble a wedding gown. I found it at my favorite boutique in Beverly Hills. It was gorgeous and it only cost $30. We actually ran into Lindzi strolling down Rodeo Drive, but we had to pretend we didn't know each other. Hashtag awkward!

Besides the dress outing, I spent most of that time alone in my hotel room. Bored one day, on a whim I picked up the phone. There was a dial tone! Thrilled and paranoid, I dialed quickly.

First, I checked my voice mail, hoping for a message from Chris begging me not to get engaged. Nope. Nada.

Then I called my dad.

"Hello?" Hearing his voice made me want to weep.

"Hey, it's Bug! I'm calling you illegally!"

"You better not be!"

I heard my mom in the background ask impatiently, "Who is it?"

"It's Bu—" he started to say, and then abruptly stopped himself.

Then he hung up on me.

I didn't know it, but he was riding in a car with a few producers, who were already in Scottsdale setting up my Hometown Date.

They'd already taken my parents out to dinner to explain what was about to go down in their house. On October 31, they'd bring a "small" crew of fifteen to twenty people over to Casa de Niñas, for a total of about eight hours. They instructed them to tell curious neighbors that I was filming a mayonnaise commercial. They told my mom not to worry about cooking any big meals because they would buy some food and set it up (and it would just sit there untouched, but they didn't need to know that).

My mom was not happy about this occupation of her home, but she was especially peeved that her favorite holiday would be ruined. She would have to take down her beloved Halloween decorations and the neighborhood kids wouldn't be allowed to ring the doorbell, yell "trick or treat," and get their handfuls of candy.

When I arrived in Scottsdale, I stayed at a boring hotel three blocks away from my parents' house, while Ben and the crew were put up at the swinging hipster Hotel Valley Ho. It was torture not being able to see my parents and my sister, who were so close, yet so far away.

With little else to do, I focused on writing my fake vows to Ben on the hotel stationery.

I wasn't really ready to tell Ben that I loved him. I definitely was in lust and in like with Ben, but in love? It was starting to feel that way, but it felt rushed. There was so much I still didn't know about him. And I realized that I hadn't really done a good job of digging. I hadn't gotten any real reactions to real-life situations. I hadn't asked simple questions like:

"Are you a Democrat or Republican?"
"What was the longest relationship *you* ever had?"
"In real life, what would be your ideal Saturday activity?"

Mine would be going to a movie or on a hike. I didn't know yet that Ben would prefer to sit in a bar drinking and watching football with ten of his closest buddies.

Anyway, I wrote the vows:

> I'm looking for love, real love. Passionate, consuming, can't live without each other love. To love unconditionally. A partner and a best friend for the rest of my life. When I look at you from across the room I know that your happiness is the key to mine. My one true love. For better or for worse, in sickness and in health. To honor *not* to obey or control. To love, to hold, and to nurture. To love you faithfully and wholeheartedly. I'll give you my hand, my heart, my body. I will trust you, respect you, and encourage you, laugh with you and cry with you. For all of my days. In the famous words of Bob Marley: Ben, I want to love you and treat you right, every day and every night. I hope you know I'm one hundred percent ready for marriage and I'm so happy I found you. I want you to know I'm in love with you.

I was so freaked out about what was about to happen, I tried to lighten it up a little with some reggae lyrics, mon, and a quote from *Sex and the City*. Then I added that I loved Ben at the very bottom of the page, the very last sentence.

Before the big day, we rented a convertible and we went to the Last Chance outlet so I could buy a dress for the next cocktail party/Rose Ceremony back in L.A. I found a gold sequin Alice and Olivia gown with a giraffe print for $24. It was too big and the zipper was broken, but I'd ask Cary, the show's stylist, to help me fix it. That night, I went to dinner at my favorite restaurant, Hillstone.

third-grade perm, 1992.
as all the rage, I swear!

In 1993, the Phoenix Suns played the Chicago Bulls in the NBA Finals. I painted my window to support the home team.

best friend from growing up, Sara (*right*), and me (*left*), 1992.

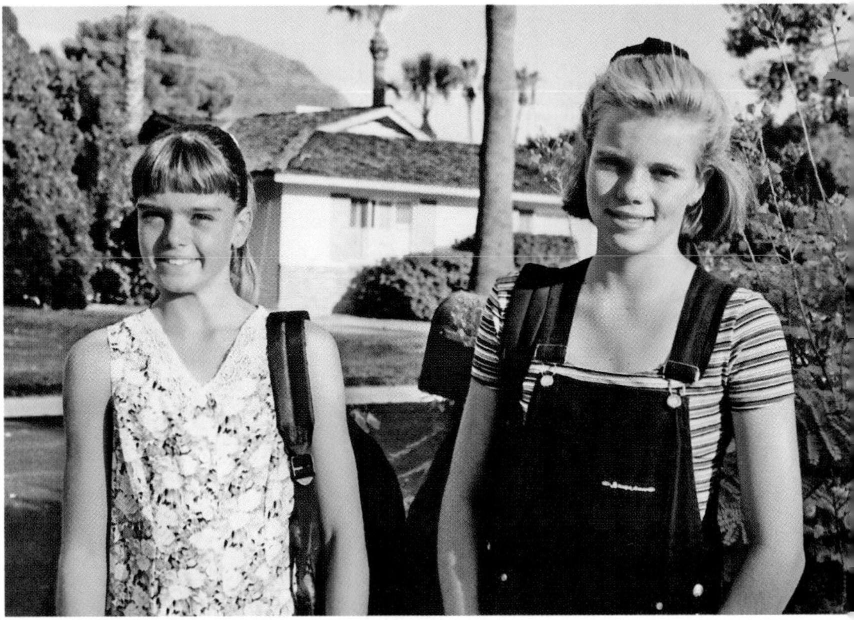

My amazing sister Rachel *(right)* and me *(left)* on our first day of school in 1994. Posing for a first-day snapshot was an annual ritual.

A model in the making—my sixth-grade school photo, 1995. Hello, unibrow.

Mom painted a sign to warn the whole neighborhood that I was fifteen.

hese shots are from my first
odeling job. Abercrombie & Fitch
vited me to shoot on location in
rtola, British Virgin Islands, when
vas a senior in high school, 2002.
hn Urbano)

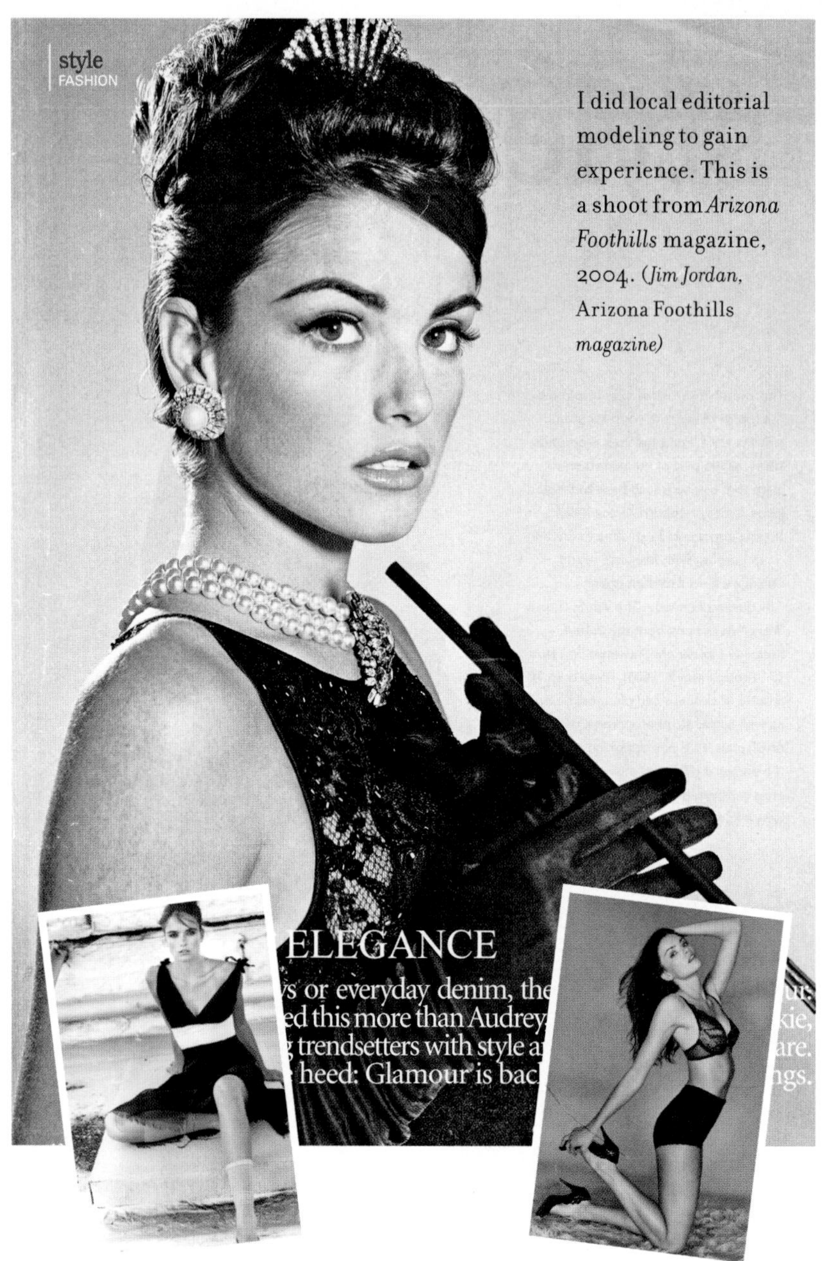

I did local editorial modeling to gain experience. This is a shoot from *Arizona Foothills* magazine, 2004. (*Jim Jordan,* Arizona Foothills *magazine)*

My first test shoot in Los Angeles, 2003. My career started backward—with a big first job at A&F, but no portfolio of work. I needed to build up a book and learn to model professionally.

I took this test shot after signing with Ford Models and getting back in modeling shape.
(Brian Kaminski)

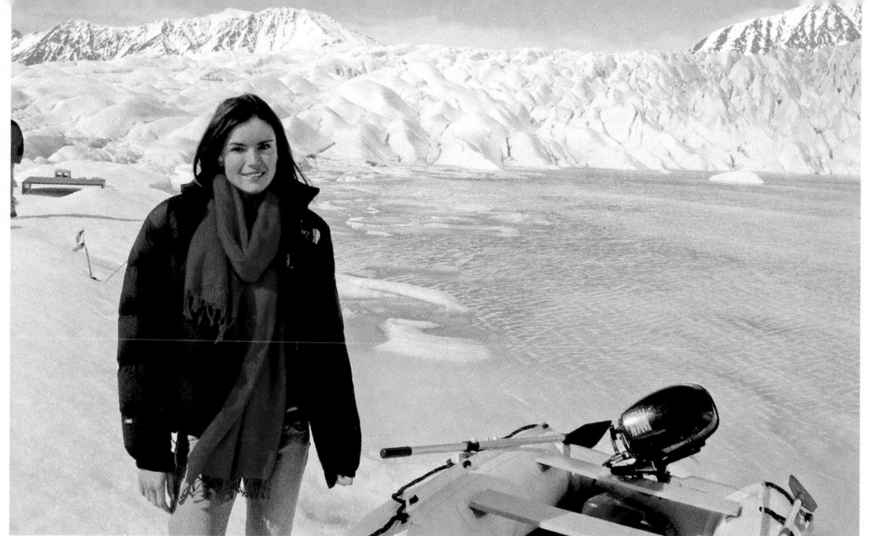

A behind-the-scenes look at a campaign I did for Izod in 2008. We shot on location on a glacier in Alaska.

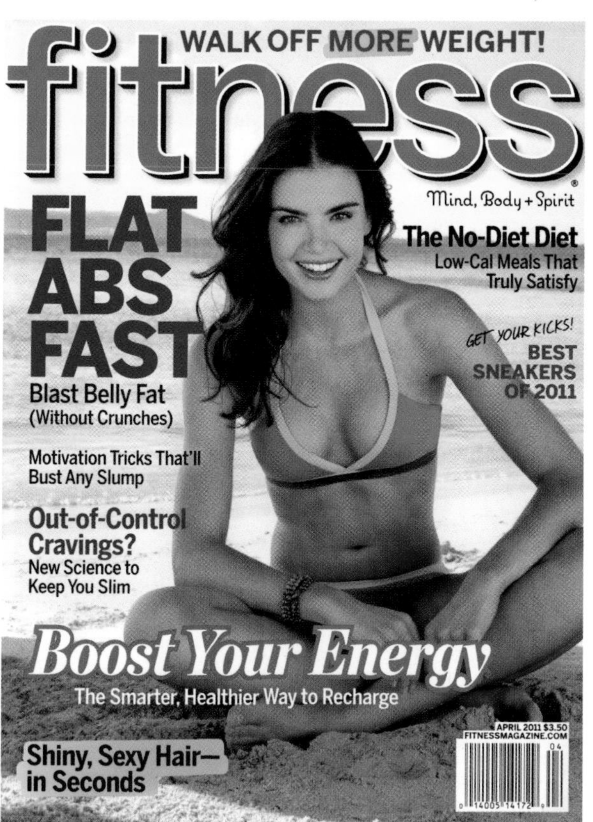

My big cover shoot for the April 2011 issue of *Fitness* magazine. We shot on location in Puerto Rico. Who knew I'd be back there six months later with the *Bachelor* crew? (Fitness *magazine*)

The calm before the storm. My family and me at the Farm at South Mountain, right before my season of *The Bachelor* began airing.

(Left to right:) Me, Rachel Truehart, Casey Shteamer, and Jaclyn Swartz, having lunch around the time we filmed "After the Final Rose."

February 20, 2012

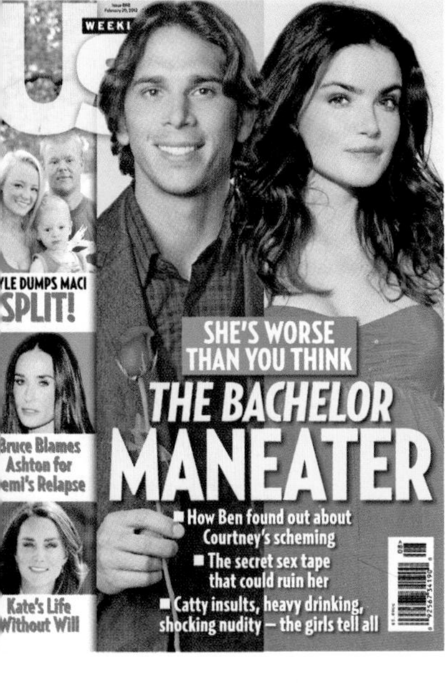

March 5, 2012

March 12, 2012

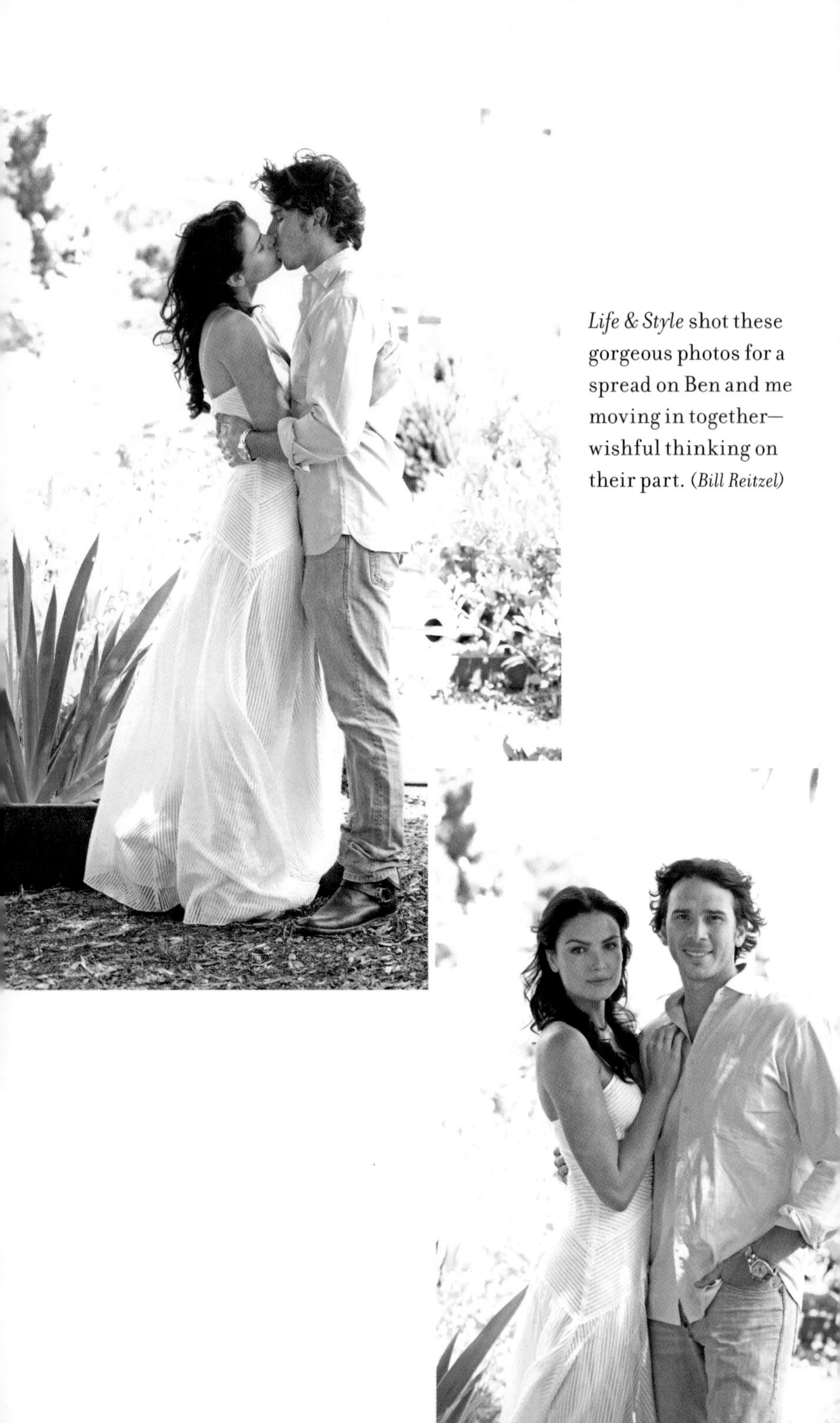

Life & Style shot these gorgeous photos for a spread on Ben and me moving in together—wishful thinking on their part. (*Bill Reitzel*)

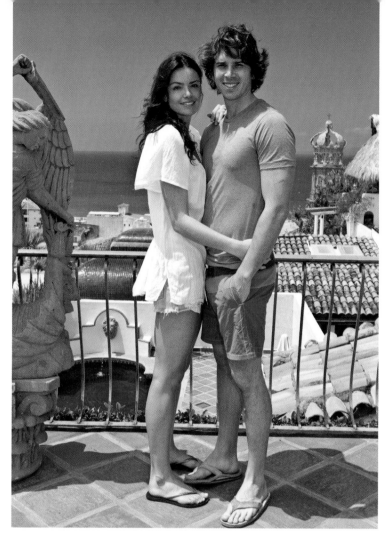

Ben and me in Puerto Vallarta, Mexico, our first trip together after *The Bachelor*. (*Josef Kandoll W*)

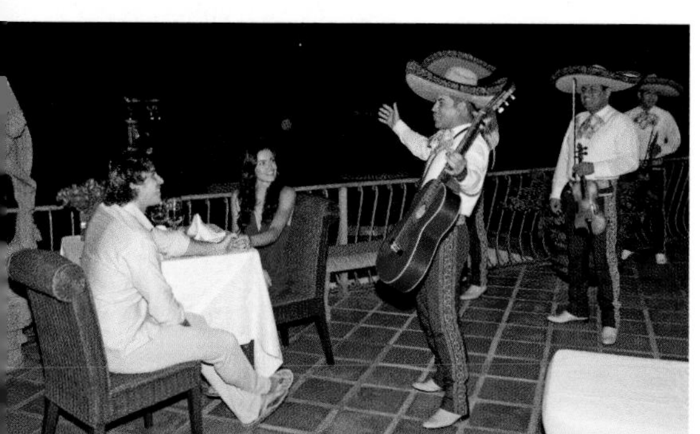

We stayed in the same hotel room that Richard Burton and Liz Taylor used. Foreshadow alert! (*Josef Kandoll W*)

After the show, we spent most of our time together as a couple at Ben's place in San Francisco. My favorite moments with Ben were spent at Baker Beach in the morning. We would both take turns running with Scotch. I took this photo, and had it blown up and framed for Ben's birthday.

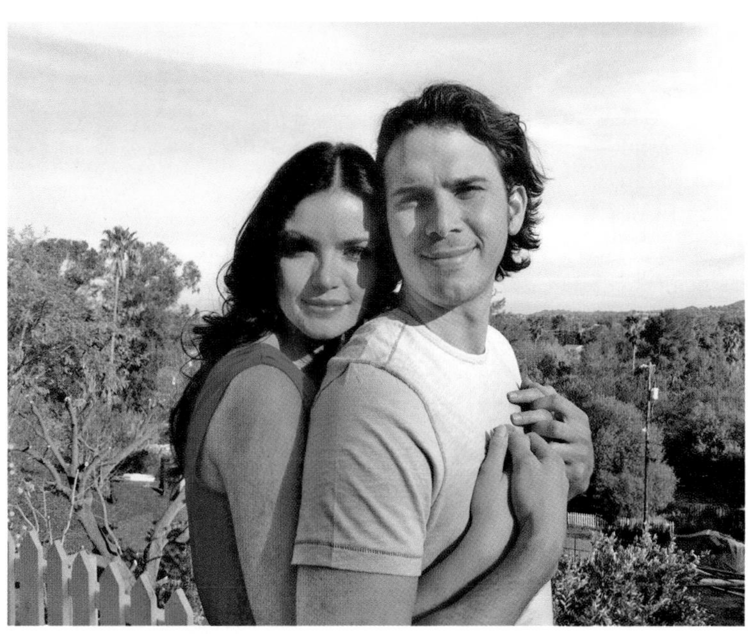

A behind-the-scenes photo from our *People* cover shoot. Me in a pink dress, a rare occasion.

The famous Neil Lane ring up close!

We may have had our ups and downs, but we sure took a pretty picture when things were good. Ben and me at the Fairmont Sonoma Mission Inn & Spa, during my sister's visit to San Francisco.

Relaxing on th grass after a trip with Ben's sister, Julia, to Cowgirl Creamery in San Francisco

Dancing at Pure in Las Vegas. This moment might have been the high point of a trip that ended in tears. *(Erik Kabik)*

On-again, off-again, on-again . . . Here we are day drinking together in Santa Monica.

We took a trip to the East Coast together to see Ben's friend, who played for the Boston Red Sox.

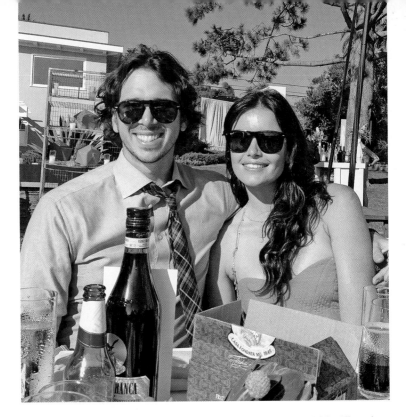

Ben and me, attending a *Bachelor* producer's wedding at Mike Fleiss's spectacular Malibu beach house.

The wedding guest list was a who's who of Bachelor Nation! (*Left to right:*) Me; Emily Maynard; Ali Fedotowsky; and my bestie, Casey Shteamer—all celebrating together.

This is the last photo taken of Ben and me. You can feel the tension.

The Kissing Bandit himself. My chemistry with Arie was off the charts, but it wasn't meant to be.

(Left to right:) My sister Rachel, my dad, and me, shopping for my sister's wedding dress at Kleinfeld. I pulled some strings and arranged for us to appear on an episode of *Say Yes to the Dress* together. After the difficult year I'd put my family through, it was important to put the focus on Rachel and her big day.

My family has always been my rock. They've supported me through everything and they continue to challenge me to be the best person I can be. Here we are together in 2013, celebrating Rachel's wedding day. *(Left to right:)* Me, Rachel, Mom, and Dad. *(JeffplusAmber.com)*

KEEPING IT REAL

Guess Who!

On a Hometown Date, this Bachelor promised the contestant's young brother that he would be back to teach him how to do things like throw a football. When the show ended, and he didn't pick the contestant, the little guy burst into tears and asked if he was the reason why the Bachelor didn't propose.

In the morning, I headed to the Farm to begin my nerve-wracking Hometown Date with Ben. When I got there, I realized they'd hired a legit licensed preacher guy to officiate the "wedding." I was so scared that Ben would flip out and run for the hills. I wouldn't blame him. I wanted this to be fun and lighthearted and now it felt like we were actually getting married! Gulp.

When Ben arrived, he was having a bad hair day. He looked like Francine from those *Arthur* cartoons on PBS, and yet I was still very attracted to him. We had a picnic on the grass. There was an amazing basket of goodies right under our noses, honey and apples fresh from the farm, but, of course, we didn't eat any of it. Not that I could have eaten anyway, my stomach was in knots and I could barely concentrate. I suddenly had a newfound appreciation for how stressful it must be for the Bachelor to set up so many "perfect" dates.

After picnicking, we walked over toward the altar in the pecan tree grove, and Ben commented nervously that it looked like a wedding was being set up. I took a deep breath and mustered the courage to tell Ben the truth. I explained that I picked the Farm because it's where I wanted to get married and that I wanted to exchange pretend vows with him. To my utter relief, he didn't bolt like a runaway bride. He was totally into it. He could see that I was shaking with nerves, and he hugged and comforted me.

I gave him a little book to write his vows and was impressed when he wrote a beautiful message to me off the top of his head, right on the spot. I'd spent hours toiling over mine in my hotel room. Then we stood under the canopy and I declared my love for him before God, some weird preacher dude, and the crew.

Ben didn't flinch when I said I loved him.

Then he read his vows back to me:

> From the moment I saw you, you took my breath away. What I asked myself after our first date was, *Is this too good to be true?* The answer I found in Belize is no, you are incredible. I love how you make me feel when I'm in your presence. You are strong, kind, beautiful, and I find myself falling for you more and more every time I'm with you. You are real and honest and for that I am thankful. A breath of fresh air in a world of uncertainty. I firmly believe in timing and I have always felt that the timing of us has been beyond our control, a sign that I have never felt before. So thank you for believing in me and trusting that we would get to this point after an incredible journey.

Huh, guess he didn't feel he was ready to say *he* loved *me*? Oh well. We exchanged rings made of twine, kissed like the Pecking Pirates we were, and always would be, and prayed that we hadn't just legally tied the knot. (Now that would be the most shocking episode of *The Bachelor* ever, because my mom would kill me right on-camera if I walked in and announced that we eloped.)

After the "wedding," which took approximately thirty minutes, the "reception" was a total bust. I quickly wolfed down a salad at Delux on the way to my parents' house, while Ben enjoyed a gourmet lunch at the Farm.

I was so excited to show Ben my childhood home, but as soon as we walked in, I ditched him in the doorway to give giant hugs—the holding-on-for-dear-life kind—to my dad, mom, and sister.

For what happened next, I'm going to hand over the keypad for an insider's account from a special guest. Take it away, Dad:

"When Courtney and Ben bounded into the living room like two barnyard animals in heat, we finally got to hear about all of the exciting places they'd been visiting. And we saw how happy they were together. It was immediately clear to me that Ben was very infatuated with my daughter. He had already filmed the other three Hometown Dates previously that week and I was not surprised that they saved the best one for last."

Aww, that's sweet!

"I did think it was kind of odd that Ben asked me if I ever went skinny-dipping in our swimming pool."

That *is* weird.

"Then Courtney told me they had gone skinny-dipping in Puerto Rico, but not to worry because it had been shot from a great distance and you could not see much in the moonlight."

Oops. Sorry, TMI.

"Ben and I had a one-on-one discussion in the backyard. I could see he was truly smitten with Courtney and I told him that 'marriage is life's greatest gamble.' I asked him, 'Are you ready to make that bet, Ben?' He answered, 'I'm ready to be in a serious, committed relationship.' "

Hang on, that doesn't sound like marriage to me. That sounds like dating.

"He then told me, 'Rick, I love your daughter.' I chuckled and said, 'You do not have to tell me that. I can see it in your eyes.' He had been struck by the thunderbolt. There was not a doubt in my mind that he would propose to her in Switzerland."

Very well said. Thanks, Dad!

During his visit Ben also had a private chat with my sister, who took away a good first impression after they bonded over *Anchorman*. She jokingly told him, "The jazz flute is for little fairy boys." And he said, "Why don't you go back to your home on Whore Island!" He also talked to my mom, who didn't want to be on-camera but did it for me. Briefly. Because she loves me she forced herself to say, "I like him very much," even though I could tell she wasn't that impressed. She quit halfway through during her final interview with the producers.

She didn't trust Ben either. "I just saw you propose to another girl on TV a few months ago," she drilled him. "How could you be in love with my daughter so soon?"

We all went outside to the patio table. We all had an awkward conversation while Ben and I pawed at each other lovingly. An hour after we got there, it was already over and time to leave.

As we all mingled in the foyer, I tried to get a read on my family.

"Do you like him?" I whispered.

"He told me he loves you," my dad whispered.

"I can tell he's in love," my sister whispered.

The date was over and I had to leave. I was so incredibly sad to leave my family. The next morning, before we left town for the Rose

Ceremony in L.A, I asked my handler to drive us over to my parents' house in the convertible. I could see my dad reading the paper through the window and wondered what it would be like to have a normal life again. I left a box of cookies in the mailbox, honked the horn, and headed back to the land of make-believe.

KEEPING IT REAL

How to Give Your Daughter Away to a Stranger

by Rick Robertson

When Ben called me from Switzerland to ask for Courtney's hand in marriage, I'd only had two hours to get to know him. I had to deduce quickly whether or not he was a lunatic or a murderer. These clues helped:

- His eyes. On the Hometown Date, I could see that he was in love with my daughter and vice versa. I guess it could have been lust, but I chose to ignore that.
- His background. I liked that he had grown up in Tucson and had a strong connection to Arizona.
- His manners. I received a call from a producer asking if I'd be available to speak to Ben on the phone. I knew he wanted to ask my permission to propose to Courtney. He seemed like a good guy and I consider myself a good judge of character.

When everyone got back to L.A., the Rose Ceremony was held at the Regent Beverly Wilshire, a.k.a. the hotel where the movie *Pretty*

Woman was shot and the location of a runway show I did once with Yoko Ono. It was kind of fitting that we were at the *Pretty Woman* hotel. I felt like I had a lot in common with Vivian Ward—not the hooker part, but living in a fairy-tale romance bubble. On some level, even though I hated the claustrophobia and catfights, I knew it was going to be hard to go back to reality after this incredible experience.

I hadn't seen the other three girls in more than a week (well, besides the face-off with Lindzi on Rodeo Drive), so when we were herded into the Rose Ceremony it was jarring. I may have experienced PTSD just seeing Kacie B's face.

We weren't allowed to talk to each other so I had absolutely no clue what had happened on their Hometown Dates. I wouldn't find out until months later that Lindzi opened up to Ben that she'd basically been suicidal after her last breakup. And that Ben really bonded with Nicki's amazing family. Or that Kacie B's ultraconservative father not only didn't drink, but also wouldn't approve of a devilish wine maker living in sin with his daughter before marriage.

It didn't really matter. To be honest, I'd forgotten that they were all still on the show. Ben and I had a huge turning point in Arizona and it really felt like we were dating. It felt like he was my boyfriend. I couldn't imagine that any of them had a better time than Ben and me.

My hunch was confirmed when Ben gave me the first rose—and then eliminated Kacie B. It didn't take a rocket scientist to deduce that Ben, a sophisticated city boy from San Francisco and Kacie B, a country girl from Clarksville, Tennessee, were doomed after the Hometown. She proceeded to have one of the most epic, ugly-cry meltdowns in the history of *The Bachelor* during her exit interview.

And her sunny Southern belle shtick went right out the limo window when she started hurling profanities.

"What the fuck *happened*?" she wailed. "What the *fuck* happened!"

I'd like to say I handled her elimination with grace and compassion, but it just wasn't meant to be. After the Rose Ceremony, I returned to my hotel. I walked into the lobby, carrying my rose, in quite the celebratory mood. As I whooped it up with the hotel staff, who'd become my pals over the last couple weeks as I'd bounced from L.A. to Scottsdale, they subtly shushed me and nodded toward a dark corner of the room. I looked over my shoulder and saw Kacie B, alone, slumped over on a bench sobbing.

Her limo driver had accidentally dropped her off at my hotel.

9

BONING & BABS

Okay, we're finally at the tantalizing, titillating Fantasy Suite portion of my *Bachelor* journey, so I'm going to skip the boring details of our first day date in Switzerland and get right to the good stuff. I mean do you want to hear another story about Ben and me having yet another picnic, or how he spoke fluent German to order us a hunk of cheese in a quaint little shop? I didn't think so.

When we arrived in Interlaken, one of the most gorgeous mountain towns in Switzerland, I was the last of the three ladies to have my overnight date with Ben. I was staying in my own hotel room in a town called Thun, hanging out and getting massages, while Nicki and Lindzi were being handed Fantasy Suite keys to Ben's heart and pants. I honestly wasn't worried about him hooking up with the other girls. In fact, I had encouraged it. While we were skinny-dipping, I told him I was crazy about him, but that if we were indeed going to get engaged, he should sow his oats. I had. I told him to take advantage of being a single man because once we were officially together, I'd be the last woman he'd ever make love to.

"Do *you*," I insisted. "Explore your options."

We made a pact to never talk about his nights with Lindzi and Nicki. But that didn't prevent me from hearing traumatizing stories. After the show ended, one of my cast mates spilled to me that Nicki had a major meltdown because, during pillow talk, Ben informed her that after his dad died he didn't believe in God and was an atheist.

I guess I wasn't the only one who didn't ask the hard questions before it was too late.

Anyway, my turn with Ben finally came about five days after we arrived in Switzerland. Producers arranged for us to stay in a charming little cottage with low ceilings, a roaring fireplace, and a barrel of popcorn. I was grateful because popcorn is my absolute favorite food and I was starving because we couldn't really eat on the day date.

Ten minutes after we were in the cottage, the camera crews, handlers, and producers scrammed, and we were completely alone for the first time ever. We immediately ripped each other's clothes off and had intense, passionate sex on the couch in front of the fire. Producers had left a cell phone for us in case of emergency, but they did not leave us any condoms.

After sexual interlude number two, a sweet, slow lovemaking session in the bedroom, Ben and I lay facing each other, snuggling. We fit really well together.

"I'm madly in love with you," he confessed. "I haven't been able to tell you."

"I am so in love with *you*," I whispered back googly-eyed.

When we weren't doin' it, we drank wine, did some naked hot

tubbing, and listened to Bon Iver on his iPod. We talked about everything.

Our sex was pretty good, but pretty textbook. There was definitely room for improvement. I wanted to see if Ben had a little more adventure in him, so I disappeared into the bathroom and came out wearing another naughty lingerie outfit I remembered to pack. Seeing the sexy black lace skirt with silk ribbons, Ben's tongue practically rolled to the floor like in a cartoon. I could tell he was blown away and worried this might be too much too soon.

He was so nervous he wasn't really sure what to do with me. So I kind of threw him around a little bit, and I'm pretty sure he liked it. We did every position under the sun, but I believe I sealed the deal when we successfully completed the reverse cowgirl.

I'm guessing Kacie B had no clue we'd successfully completed the reverse cowgirl or she may not have flown halfway across the world to Switzerland to inform Ben, yet again, that I was a menace to society and to beg for answers about why she was dumped. When he got back to his room after our steamy night together, Kacie B was there. He was so furious. He immediately sent her back home with her tail between her legs.

KEEPING IT REAL

Banging the Bachelor

Show creator Mike Fleiss once claimed that the Bachelor has sex an average of three times per season. And the action doesn't only go down in the Fantasy Suite. What actually happens sexually between contestants has always been as closely held a secret as the Mafia's omertà—until now! Enjoy these naughty blind items (to protect the innocent and the prude, names have been withheld):

- This Bachelor was so asexual, his extremely hot and bothered Fantasy Suite partner kept filling up his glass with more alcohol every time he tried to hide in the bathroom. The unlucky lady was just trying to loosen up the guy, but it didn't work.
- This Bachelor was so horny he couldn't wait to get to the Fantasy Suites to get laid. On a group date, he snuck away with a contestant for an off-camera hookup. But producers busted them just seconds after they left—and she was already on her knees giving him a BJ! When the producers tried to break them up, they didn't stop and had to be pried apart.
- This *Bachelorette* contestant was such a slimeball he hooked up with an ex at his hotel right before Hometowns!

That night at the final Rose Ceremony, Nicki also got sent home. Nicki said she felt "like a fool" in her limo exit interview, and I can't blame her for thinking that if she did indeed sleep with Ben. I don't doubt that she felt like she had something special with him. I'm sure he told all three of us that he felt a connection. Which annoyed me. If he meant all of the things he'd said to me in the Fantasy Suite, why did he go through with his dates with Lindzi and Nicki? I'd never been a clingy-after-sex kind of person, but now my usual cool-girl demeanor was history. Even though I'd told him to sow his oats, I found myself feeling possessive and jealous; the thought of him having sex with either girl made me sick. Couldn't he just stop this now so nobody got hurt?

Other Bachelors/Bachelorettes had played with the format and sent people home earlier or spared them a public elimination out of the kindness of their hearts.

But Ben was going to see this through to the bitter end. He was a by-the-book kind of guy. He wasn't really into breaking the rules.

After Nicki left—eight long weeks and twenty-four rejected girls later—we had finally reached the final two. Lindzi and me. The entire production moved to the picturesque city of Zermatt and we were put up at the Grand Hotel Zermatterhof under the majestic Matterhorn for the thrilling conclusion of this seemingly never-ending story.

Now that Ben had become acquainted with my vagina, naturally it was time for me to get acquainted with his mother. Barbara Flajnik and her daughter, Julia, flew all the way to Switzerland to interrogate Lindzi and me on-camera. Lindzi went first, which was fine with me because I was kind of terrified to meet Ben's mom. I wasn't alone. Ben was so nervous he spent the entire morning before I met her on the pot. I'd seen Babs on Ashley Hebert's season, during the Hometown Dates, and she seemed snobby and uptight—the polar opposite of my mom. My mom can be tough, too, but she's always the life of the party. To butter up Babs and Julia, I'd bought them gifts—a vintage leather bag for Julia's Vespa and a wine rack shaped like a bicycle for Babs.

I met both of them together and we had pretty painless, idle chit-chat at first. During my private time with Julia, I really liked her. We instantly hit it off, though she made one jab about my vegan diet. I was surprised that, of all things, Ben had told her that about me. I didn't realize that my eating habits might be such a deal breaker.

Before I talked to Babs one-on-one on-camera, we had to wait for the crew to set up the shot.

"Do I look okay?" she asked me nervously.

"Yeah! You look great," I said, reassuring her.

Once the camera turned on, though, Babs went for the jugular on her first question.

"Why didn't you go to college?" she asked condescendingly.

I explained as nicely as possible my stock answer: that I chose modeling and had been supporting myself for the last ten years. I also informed her that I'd gotten my real estate license as a backup plan.

She asked me what I liked about her son, but otherwise our talk was really brief and she seemed very unenthused with me. Then again, I don't think she was enthused about Ben being on the show again and the trip to Switzerland in general. She asked producers to be moved from her hotel, which she called a "dump."

When Ben later asked me how it went with his mom, I simply said, "Really well." I didn't go into detail and didn't rave about meeting her because, honestly, I didn't get a good vibe. I just couldn't picture her being my mother-in-law.

After Babs and Julia left, Lindzi and I had our final dates with Ben. Lindzi went first again, so I had two days to think, plot, and plan. I wanted to give Ben a special gift to remember our romantic, dramatic journey. My handler and I took the train to Zurich, where I knew a renowned artist named Andy Denzler. Andy had once painted my portrait in L.A. and we were friends. We had a wonderful dinner at a vegan restaurant, but in the end, he declined to paint Ben's portrait. The show wouldn't pay for it, I couldn't afford it, and he didn't need the publicity. Like so many past contestants I decided to make the standard "love scrapbook" for Ben. I bought a $100 leather journal and had a local farmer brand the cover with "Past, Present, Future." I pasted copies of cell phone pics the producers had taken along the way and an antique photo of a forest, to remind him of our future child's name.

When our final date arrived we spent the day portion on a terrifying helicopter ride around the Matterhorn. After picnic #532 on the side of the mountain we went sledding, threw snowballs at each other, and wrote our names in the snow (not with Ben's pee-pee). We had a blast.

The vibe during the night portion of our date, however, was a major buzzkill. We filmed it really late, in my hotel room, and it was short. As we lay on my bed, I gave Ben the scrapbook and another love letter I'd written him. He didn't seem that blown away by either. He was acting kind of weird—very quiet and not his normal sweet self—and it made me feel uncomfortable. *Did something change over the last few hours?* I thought. *Did he change his mind about Lindzi?* Could he possibly be in love with her? The thought crossed my mind again that Ben was messing with me the whole time and I would be a laughingstock on television.

KEEPING IT REAL

Five Burning Questions for the Bachelor

Dear future contestants, it's okay to ask the hard questions. Don't be shy. It's only the rest of your life on the line!

1. Have you ever cheated on anyone?
2. What are your spiritual beliefs? (You may want to ask political party, too.)

3. What's your idea of a perfect weekend?
4. Do you have a problem with your partner making more money than you?
5. Do you have a good relationship with your mom?

On the flip side, if he *was* madly in love with me, could he be getting cold feet? I began to wonder if this whole experience was getting too real for him. We were two days away from professing our undying love for each other for eternity and suddenly Ben was very disengaged and detached.

When he walked out the door, I freaked out. I was no longer calm, collected, confident Courtney. I was an absolute wreck. Everyone kept saying that all guys act weird before they propose.

But I realized that we'd never had a very crucial conversation.

I'd never once asked Ben, "Do you *want* to be engaged?"

10

BACK TO REALITY

Welp, if you don't know it by now—or just skimmed over the prologue of this book, how rude—Ben and I were betrothed on November 16, 2011, after he called my dad and asked for my hand in marriage.

After giving his permission, my dad told Ben, "Whatever you do, take care of my Bug." My dad was extremely hesitant; he'd only met the guy one time, for little more than an hour. But what was he supposed to say? "I barely know you. Screw you!" He gave the go-ahead and prayed for the best.

Though I, too, had some reservations and uncertainties about the whole situation, I was thrilled to be Ben's fiancée. I couldn't wait to be his wife and plan our future and family together.

We weren't supposed to tell anyone the big news, and, for a hot minute, Ben wasn't even going to tell his own mother. Logistically, it was kind of impossible to keep the engagement under wraps, so we ended up telling our immediate family members.

And I also told Casey Shteamer. And my best friend from Scottsdale, Sara.

Ben and I only saw each other five times from mid-November until March 12, when the *Bachelor* season finale aired. All five of our Happy Couples ended up in California, where we both lived.

In between the Happy Couples, we could call each other freely, but to avoid hackers we had to set up new e-mail accounts and aliases the day after we left Switzerland. We came up with tootsmcgooterson for Ben and mrstootsmcgooterson for me. The names are really sexy—stemming from his immediate ease passing gas in front of me and my love of bathroom humor.

Our correspondence may not have been as passionate and filled with yearning as *The English Patient* or something, but we were very lovey-dovey in the beginning:

From: mrstootsmcgooterson

To: tootsmcgooterson

I just woke up with the biggest smile on my face. You're always the first thing on my mind. I love it! I'm so happy. That's all ;). Hope you and the prince [Scotch] slept wonderful.

Mrs. T

From: tootsmcgooterson

To: mrstootsmcgooterson

All I think about is how wonderful our life is going to be together. I love you more than life itself.

Mr. T

From: mrstootsmcgooterson

To: tootsmcgooterson

> Aww babe, you just melted me and made my day ;). That's all I think of too. I love you with all my heart!
>
> Mrs. T

Our e-mails and texts to each other were romantic, overflowing with "love you's" and pet names like Monkey Head, Muffin, and Baby Cakes. Early on, Ben often texted me saying that I was the best thing that ever happened to him. "I'm like a 6th grader in love for the first time," he'd gush. But I wouldn't ever call our messages to each other *hot*. We never once engaged in a steamy sexting session or dirty talk, though I did receive an "oh me o my" from Ben once when I texted him that I was naked. But it didn't go any further. Whenever I sent him an X-rated picture, his signature response back was usually "Beep Beep" or "#beepboner." In fact, "Beep Beep" was his response to anything sexy.

In the beginning, Ben made the mistake of frequently commenting on the size of other women's breasts in front of me. "Wow, her boobs are so big!" he'd marvel. When I turned the tables, and started joking about the size of random guys' packages, he finally looked at me and said, "Okay, I got it."

Since I wasn't getting any action electronically, thankfully we didn't have to go very long without seeing each other after filming wrapped. Thanksgiving weekend was Ben's ten-year high school reunion in Tucson, so we made a secret plan to meet up without anyone knowing. I was excited that Ben was willing to break a rule.

I picked Ben up at his friend's house, and we drove back to my sister Rachel's house in Scottsdale. The entire time Ben lay down in the backseat and when we arrived, we pulled into the garage and closed it before he got out of the car. Rachel and her boyfriend, Moe, made themselves scarce so we could be alone for the first time in the United States of America. The first night we played house together. It finally felt like we were a normal couple. We were so comfortable together.

Rachel really liked Ben during our Hometown Date. She thought he was friendly and sincere, but she changed her tune over the course of our first weekend together. Ben wasn't very warm and didn't seem interested in getting to know her at all, even though we were staying in her home. He was distracted, constantly on his phone or laptop, and would rarely pipe up, unless it was to announce the new, increasing number of Twitter followers he had. She thought he was a little self-important, especially when I offered to take Scotch for a walk. He was concerned that his dog would be recognized on my cul-de-sac in the middle-of-nowhere suburbia. The show hadn't even aired yet.

I could tell that Moe, a firefighter, wasn't impressed with Ben either. He thought that Ben was standoffish, spoiled, and a frat boy. It didn't help that Ben had his own hipster language. When Moe explained to Ben that he drove the fire engine, Ben declared, "That's BA," without translating that BA meant "badass." Other examples include using the word "dart" in place of cigarette and "pull the trigger" instead of throwing up. For example, if used in a sentence, it would sound like this: "My love e-mails to Tootsmcgooterson may make you want to pull the trigger."

Ben made a better impression on my dad during Thanksgiving. We went over to my childhood home for the day and they bonded while watching football. But when Sara, my best friend from childhood, came over, he made no effort to get to know her. Granted, the day was already sort of a disaster. My mom was so nervous about hosting Ben that she forgot to turn on the oven after putting the turkey in. By the time we ate the worst Thanksgiving meal ever, it was 8:00 P.M. Ben, who is a self-proclaimed foodie and wannabe chef, admitted, "I almost took a peek, but I didn't want to let the heat out. Fa ra ra ra ra!" he sang, imitating the movie *A Christmas Story*. We all laughed about it, but I could tell he was mortified that our stuffing came from a box and our gravy from a package. In his family, they made everything from scratch.

It was my first inkling that my friend had been right: Ben was a little snobby. I'd find out soon enough that he and his mom had an aversion to bargain or mass-market shopping. "We don't shop at chains," Babs sniffed (I decided not to tell her that most of my wardrobe comes from Target), while Ben stated as fact on numerous occasions that "there are no chains" in his hometown of San Francisco (a quick Google search shows at least three Victoria's Secrets in the metropolitan area alone).

Ben may have been disappointed in the Robertson clan's culinary cornucopia, but my family and my friend Sara were pretty disappointed in him, too. Sara texted that she could tell we were in love, but she was hurt that he didn't make an effort with her. When the weekend ended, Rachel drove me to the airport to go back home to L.A. and didn't mince words.

"Court, I don't know . . ." she started.

My heart sank. My sister's opinion meant the most to me. It really hurt my feelings that she wasn't blown away by Ben.

"I just don't see it," she added sadly.

I made excuses for him—he was tired and nervous—and I tried to put the conversation out of my mind. It might take some time, but they'd all eventually see what I loved so much about him.

The next time I saw Ben again, during an officially sanctioned Happy Couple Weekend right before Christmas, he was swamped and stressed. Not only was he running his winery, but he was also now doing tons of press for *The Bachelor,* which was scheduled to premiere on January 2.

The cast had just been announced so now I had to be extra careful when I met up with him. I took the train from L.A.'s Union Station up to Montecito, California, near Santa Barbara, and a producer picked me up and drove me to meet Ben. Our rented house, located behind a big gate and covered in ivy and Mexican saltillo tile, was just down the road from Oprah's gargantuan estate. Of course, it had a hot tub. Why would you even ask?

We were told that we couldn't leave the property at all, so I was hoping for a romantic shut-in weekend filled with sex and snuggling. The first night we cooked a big meal together, but I quickly realized Ben's almost as bossy as Gordon Ramsay in the kitchen and likes his knife cuts as precise as Morimoto. He made a San Fran classic, cioppino, a spicy fish stew filled with clams, scallops, crab, and shrimp, but I wasn't allowed to help him. I was relegated to salad duty.

While we were cooking, his mom called and I talked to her for the first time since Switzerland. She was really nice and chatty. I'd gotten holiday gifts for Julia and her and she sent me a thank-you card right after Christmas. "I love the scarf you bought for me," she wrote. "Beige is my color. Joe used to call me, 'Queen of Beige.' Isn't that funny? Also, I have one of Ben's new 'Epilogue' bottles of wine in the bicycle you gave me in Switzerland. You are very thoughtful and have an eye for the perfect gifts."

I'd also bought Ben several Christmas gifts—his favorite snack, See's Candies, a charcoal beanie and cashmere socks from Marc Jacobs, and a pickling kit. I also commissioned an artist to draw a picture of his dog, Scotch. He got me the best gift I've ever gotten from any boyfriend—a sparkling diamond band to wear on my right hand until the show could give my engagement ring back to me. I wore it on my left hand, just for me, when I was inside.

While Ben and I ate dinner, listening to our favorite songs by Drake and Bon Iver, there was that comfortable silence between us but something was definitely missing. I felt like we could have connected more and been more intimate. Not that we didn't have a great time. We definitely made love in Montecito and spent most of the days in our PJs, watching movies or *Parks and Recreation* on an iPad in bed. One night, we forced ourselves to get dressed up for dinner like it was a real date. Only we actually ate the food this time and there were fifteen fewer cameramen watching.

It was fun to lounge around, but it was also a lot of alone time, too, and we both went a little stir-crazy cooped up indoors. Ben, again, spent a buttload of time working on his laptop, while I puttered around aimlessly. We weren't allowed to go for a walk or run. My job entailed going to castings, which I couldn't do during these long weekends. Ben also invited his handler over for lunch one afternoon. It wasn't the first time I noticed that Ben needed to be surrounded by "his people," and definitely not the last.

Ben wasn't overly attentive to me when I was right in front of his face, and he was even less so when we were apart. On New Year's Eve, two nights before our big *Bachelor* season premiere, he cohosted the ball drop in Times Square with Jenny McCarthy and Ryan Seacrest, while I stayed home by myself and drank a bottle of wine. I stayed up all night to watch him and he texted me one picture.

We didn't even watch our first episode together. My roommate, Ally, had a viewing party, but it was really awkward watching the show with so many people. They kept talking loudly during it and I just couldn't stand watching myself. Halfway through that first episode, I went into my room and didn't watch another second of my season until more than a year later.

Three days after the show aired, Ben and I had another Happy Couple Weekend at a mansion in Bel Air. We picked the location so he could easily do appearances in Hollywood. I actually felt bad for him. He had so much press to do he was being run ragged.

He had one very early morning interview on Ryan Seacrest's radio show. According to a friend/spy who worked there, the *American Idol* host had a mildly inappropriate conversation with my hubby-to-be after their interview.

"Dude, she's so hot," Ryan allegedly told Ben.

"Yeah, I never thought I could get a girl like that."

Well, he got me but wasn't doing much to keep me. During our Happy Couple Weekend, Ben was gone one entire day and spent much of our other time together on his computer, wearing a Lululemon workout outfit, which was kind of a turnoff. I did have a handler drive me out to one casting, but other than that I found myself sitting by the pool alone most of the weekend. He'd come out to kiss me a few times and thank me for being so understanding.

"Of course, no problem!" I said, trying to be supportive.

Ben did countless phone interviews and watched future episodes of *The Bachelor* with his headphones on, laughing loudly when I said drunkenly in Sonoma, "It's a war out there." He also was tippity-tapping away on his blog for *People.com*. He didn't tell me what he was writing and never asked for my opinion. I had to read it myself online with everyone else after it was published each week. I was none too pleased when Ben confessed that Jennifer was the best kisser in the cast.

Ben also invited a bunch of crew members over for lunch, where I learned that Vienna Girardi and Jake Pavelka also stayed in this house and almost had their cover blown after they accidentally tripped the alarm and the fire department showed up. Later, one of the producers pulled me aside and warned me that it was going to get progressively worse for me. I had no idea what she was talking about.

It was the first time someone from the show hinted that there might be something larger going on, something that I had no control over.

BY THE TIME we got to our third Happy Couple Weekend in Inverness, on a misty oceanside peninsula an hour from San Francisco, the third episode had run. I had officially become the villain of season 16 after I asked Kacie B, "How'd that taste coming out of your mouth?" among other explosive comments and general cockiness.

I wasn't watching the show, but my sister was, and she was getting bombarded with e-mails and tweets from strangers, friends, and distant relatives who crawled out of the woodwork. Rachel, who is a lawyer, was even accosted in the copy room by a coworker demanding to know the scoop about Ben and me. Rachel was already exhausted trying to defend me—and the show had barely started airing.

KEEPING IT REAL

Life After *The Bachelor*

by Graham Bunn

The show is a privilege to be a part of but comes with a cost that many people aren't ready for, myself included. In that you are exactly who the show portrays you to be, just magnified beyond measure. Whether you like it or not, you are forced to see yourself in a blinding light of self-evaluation. You find out a lot about who you are and who you want to be after its airing. Now, granted, you get the experience of insane dates, incredibly beautiful women of past, present, and future cast, this author included, of course. The lessons learned come with the experience of doing the show but what you do with those lessons are sold separately.

Ben was aware that I'd become a lightning rod, but so far he hadn't said a word to me about it. On the way to Inverness, he asked me to stop at Whole Foods, where I blew $1,000 on food for our weekend and groceries for Ben's apartment, including paper towels and "good" olive oil, as he requested. As I shopped, he drank at a bar down the street from our cottage.

The first night Ben invited his sister, Julia, and her boyfriend, Garrett, over for dinner. Julia and I were instant best friends and I loved Garrett. He was warm and captivating, and a really good boyfriend. He treated Julia like a queen.

You know how couples try to out-lovey-dovey each other? Ben was very affectionate that night as we played board games and Uno. He even talked for the first time since filming the show about me moving up to San Francisco. He'd been looking at properties online and showed me a few he liked. "Is it crazy to think about buying a house?" he asked. I was so excited and told him I could go to castings in the city.

All was wonderful, until Ben decided to make steaks for dinner. He was bossy boots in the kitchen again and criticized the way I chopped tomatoes for the salad I was allowed to prepare under heightened supervision. "Are you really going to cut those like that?" he asked. "You eat with your eyes."

At first, his passion for cooking was cute. But now it was starting to annoy me that he thought he was a Michelin star chef and I was his lowly sous chef. As he sliced and diced, he was so in the zone that he ignored everyone. Then when we sat down to eat, he discussed and dissected the meal, bragging how perfectly he charred the steak and criticizing me for putting an entire portobello mushroom on top of my steak without slicing it first. He was mad I ruined his plating.

The next day, Ben's mom came for a visit. I noticed that they bickered a lot and she was hard on him about not spending enough quality time with her. I'd noticed her demeanor toward me had changed drastically since our friendly phone call before the show started airing. I could tell she no longer liked me and couldn't fake it. She seemed very uncomfortable when I was affectionate with Ben, staring at us with a baffled look on her face when we held hands.

"Is this real?" she asked point-blank.

"Yes, Mom," Ben said. "This is real."

Right before Julia and Garrett left, Babs asked me how work was going. I told her that I had to go to New York soon to model for Stein Mart.

"Oh, I can't believe you work for them," she said condescendingly, rolling her eyes.

"Mom!" Ben and Julia scolded.

"Well, they pay me $2,500 a day and I love going to New York."

Babs's comment cut me to the bone. It's really hard to get regular clients in modeling and I was proud to have such a long run and steady income from this bread-and-butter client. I mean would she have preferred Ben brought home a VIP cocktail waitress? Or is being a nanny, like Kacie B, a more suitable career for her son's future wife?

After Julia and Garret left, Ben had to go back to San Fran so I was left alone with Babs for an hour before I went home to L.A. As we sat drinking tea, we had another awkward and confrontational conversation.

"How is your family doing?" she asked.

"My mom isn't happy about what's happening."

"I didn't want Ben to do the show either. Couldn't you find a common bond with the other girls?"

"Those girls were really mean to me."

"Couldn't you have tried harder? Couldn't you have faked it a little bit?"

I wished Ben hadn't left me alone here. I tried to change the subject again. She hadn't asked me much about myself, so I started to talk about my past and my career, to show her how hard I've worked. I wanted to tell her that I'd lived in New Zealand, because I wanted her to be proud of me.

"I've traveled the world . . ." I started to explain, but Babs cut me off.

"You said that on the show. You should never say that. It makes you look bad."

If my mom were here, she would have bitch-slapped this woman. But what came next truly knocked the wind out of me: "I guess you should wait it out and sell the ring. You can split the money."

I WENT BACK to Santa Monica with an awful taste in my mouth—from both Ben's steak and his mother. I loved Ben so much but I wondered how I would survive the rest of my life with Babs as my in-law. It was a serious problem.

Another serious problem with our relationship was that when I wasn't with Ben, I was completely out of sight, out of mind. At the end of January, he left for the Sundance Film Festival in Park City,

Utah, to film a segment with *Extra* host Mario Lopez. As soon as Ben left, he fell off the map and I couldn't reach him. He was barely responding to my texts or calls.

"Sorry muffin," he texted. "Lots of little girlies that want pics."

I went online to look for clues and saw in paparazzi photos that he was Sundance's celebutante. He was carousing all over town wearing a white beanie I'd never seen before. One gossip story claimed that while he was partying at the Bing Bar "multiple" ladies were lining up to meet him and that he definitely wasn't acting like an engaged guy. He'd been attending screenings, going to clubs, picking up mountains of swag, and even hung out with Michael Cera and *Parks and Rec* star Aziz Ansari at a Drake concert. He was having a little too much fun without me and I was furious.

"I'm sorry that you've been so busy. I'm trying to be as understanding as possible," I texted him. "But this is hard. I feel neglected and am unhappy. Call me."

I finally reached him on his cell and chewed him out. I asked where he'd been and what happened to the charcoal beanie I'd bought him for Christmas. He said he lost it somewhere in Park City.

For the first time in our relationship, I warned him that he needed to start making me a priority. Then I hung up on him.

11

PAPS & A SMEAR CAMPAIGN

For the first month after the show premiered, I continued living my normal, pre-*Bachelor* life. I was still modeling for regular clients like Stein Mart and going on frequent castings. The only stories about me that had surfaced in the press were a few small items about me dating Jesse Metcalfe, Adrian Grenier, and Jim Toth. Only one person on the planet knew about Adrian and Jim. I felt really bad that Jim was named, since we'd only been on one date.

Ben wasn't that upset that I'd been with celebrities. We'd come clean about our dating histories in Belize. I also knew that he'd hooked up with *The Client List* star Jennifer Love Hewitt during the short break between *The Bachelorette* and *The Bachelor*, but he admitted to me that she got too clingy after one date. In fact, he dished that she offered him twice as much money as *The Bachelor* offered him to *not* go on the show. He declined. I thought it was kind of funny that right before the show aired, she was photographed looking miserable carrying the book *Why Men Love Bitches*. I joked that it was a jab at me.

Even as negative press started to bubble up, Ben and I were solid and very much in love. I thought. The long distance was really hard. Because he was so busy, we often missed each other's phone calls. When we did connect, we rarely had good conversations. They were always short and strained, and lacked substance. We never lay in bed on the phone for hours, laughing and talking about our future.

The tide started to turn when Ben was invited to be a guest on *The Ellen DeGeneres Show* on January 25. She drilled him and tore into me, to the delight of the audience. "She manipulated you," Ellen proclaimed. "She came off not nice . . . She was just playing you . . . man. You got played." Ben wasn't allowed to say much; only three episodes had aired. But he didn't even try to defend me either. He warned me with a text after the taping: "Probably don't want to watch."

The shit really hit the fan on January 30, when episode 4, "Skinny Dippers Gone Wild," aired and Ben's bare ass was beamed into 8 million homes across America with only a pixilated square for cover. It didn't seem that controversial in the moment, but we grossly underestimated how taboo and rare male nudity is on prime-time network television. (Remember David Caruso's ass shot in the shower on *NYPD Blue*? Me either, that's how long ago it happened.) Plus, Ben just looked so utterly and easily wrapped around my finger on the show. I barely had to bat an eye and he dropped trou, his underpants tossed onto the beach like a hot potato.

"How are we going to get through this?" Ben asked me in a frantic phone call. He was super embarrassed and blaming me for everything, even though he was getting negative press, too. He had been called out for being boring and insensitive to the girls, especially when Kacie B admitted to him that she overcame a serious eating disorder and his response seemed unmoved, uncaring.

I tried to calm him down. I assured him it was going to blow over.

Well, it didn't blow over. It blew up. We were skewered in the press and on social media, with critiques ranging from "Hot and disgusting!" to "Obnoxious and daring!" I was called "a flaming bag of cunt" by one commenter and "topless and bottomless and classless" by Possessionista, the self-described fashion critic of *The Bachelor.* BachelorRant.com ran photos of lanky, disheveled Brit comedian Russell Brand and me, claiming that we were long-lost twins. My favorite headline came from *Business Insider*: "How Courtney the Sex Genius Ruined *The Bachelor* Forever." Someone in Jesse Metcalfe's camp gave off-the-record quotes to a gossip site trivializing our relationship, saying we only dated for a few weeks, that I used him to get famous, and was a "stage five clinger." That really hurt. It's something I feel he never would have said about me. Even to this day, I hope it didn't come from him.

Ellen wasn't the only talk show host hating on me. Kelly Ripa ripped me a new one on her show. I was pretty bummed because I was a huge fan of her on *All My Children.* She imitated me, twirling her hair on her finger like a ditz and pursing her lips like she'd eaten a lemon (in all fairness, I did do those things). She even acted out the skinny-dipping scene with *Harry Potter* star Daniel Radcliffe playing the role of Ben. "You made him sound so sensitive and smart," Kelly marveled.

Many in Bachelor Nation, the unofficial name for the show's alumni, did not have my back. Ben himself said he felt "crappy" after the skinny-dipping incident. Chris Harrison's wife went on the record saying, "I was rooting for Lindzi the whole time." Ashley Spivey, one of many rejected by Brad Womack, called me "the devil" in her blog and ranted, "I would *never* do that on national television. I think it's extremely disrespectful to the other girls." I heard through the grapevine that she also said about me, "I don't know what everyone sees in her. She must have a magic vagina." Ben's best friend from Ashley's season, Constantine Tzortzis, called me "dishonest," an "Ice Princess," and "a mistake."

Original Bachelorette Trista Sutter was particularly vicious, launching tweet-bombs about me from the very beginning like, "As a mother, I can't imagine that Courtney's is even remotely proud of her. Poor choices in actions, words and attitude." She also gave a television interview in which she said she wanted to reach through the television and slap me. This is coming from a forty-one-year-old married woman who apparently has nothing better to do with her life than hurl insults online about a person she's never met. Yep, she's setting a great example for her two children.

A few alums did try to support me. Though Ashley Hebert tattled that I'd "stolen" my fake vows from *Sex and the City*—and her love J. P. called me a "manipulative villain"—she also said, "I'm trying to give her the benefit of the doubt!" A producer contacted me and said Bachelorette Jillian Harris had reached out, offering advice. "If she needs to talk, tell her to call me." Unfortunately, I had no idea who she was. If I had just asked my superfan sister, Rachel, she would have told me how sweet Jillian is and how she stoically survived brutal press about her engagement to alleged cheater Ed Swiderski. Regretfully, I never called her, but I want to thank her now for being one of the few who didn't judge me.

KEEPING IT REAL

Trista's Terrible Tweets

Get a life, Sutter!

JAN. 9: I think the chemistry between Ben and Courtney is obvious. Whether he sees the inconsiderate side of her is yet to be seen.

JAN. 16: Booksmart can be a little boring. Courtney has a point but confused as to whether she's saying she's really stupid or really boring herself.

JAN. 16: I don't care who you've modeled for, rude behavior is not pretty.

JAN. 25: Wonder why [Ben] can't see . . . the alarmingly conceded [sic] Courtney.

JAN. 25: Courtney calls herself confident. I'd say maybe uneducated because what you are is conceded [sic] not confident.

FEB. 6: Think Courtney may need another lesson on meanings of words. Respectful & prude are not the same thing. Clearly u know about neither.

FEB. 6: Seriously Courtney? Shaking ur '1 with nature' breasts 4 the village children? Stay FAR away from Vail & 2 little ones w/last name Sutter.

FEB. 27: That weird magical force that draws Ben to Courtney is manipulation.

MARCH 5: You are incredibly meanspirited.

MARCH 12: Courtney thinks she was just being honest thru the show and honesty hurts. Actually, cruelty hurts. Honesty is something different altogether.

MARCH 12: Truly don't think Courtney knows the difference between right & wrong & how to treat the rest of the human race. Hoped she had learned. Nope.

My ex Chris came to my rescue as well. He was hounded by every media outlet on the planet and his phone was blowing up constantly, but he ignored offers for thousands of dollars from every tabloid. He only gave one free interview to an entertainment website.

Thank God my parents were on a cruise (ironically in Puerto Rico) and missed the skinny-dipping incident. Ben was suddenly MIA up in San Francisco. "All I see is negativity and I'm struggling to know what's real or not," he texted. "Just need time to clear my head."

"That hurts to hear," I responded. "You know me. I thought we were stronger than that. You should let me be there for you to work through this. This is causing damage and the lack of communication is very unhealthy." I'd heard from my show sources that when Ashley Hebert got slammed in the tabloids, J. P. was Super Fiancé, sending her flowers and talking to her on the phone for hours on end to cheer her up.

Since Ben was little help, my sister Rachel flew to L.A. for an emergency visit and, as I drove to the airport to pick her up, I noticed a creepy man following me in his car. I hoped he wasn't a stalker or a deranged *Bachelor* fan. I was terrified.

From the airport Rachel and I drove to Venice Beach to go to First Friday, an outdoor street fair where food trucks line up. The creepy guy tailed us the whole time, trying to get us to roll down the car window. When we pulled up to a valet on Abbot Kinney, he jumped out of his car and ran over yelling, "Don't be scared! I'm just the paparazzi!"

Flash! Click! Flash flash click!

Oh no, I was wearing a tank top with a panda bear on it.

We ran into sushi restaurant Wabi-Sabi to escape.

After dinner, more paps surrounded us as we left the restaurant and strolled down the street. A middle-aged guy sitting in front of a gallery was surveying the scene and as I walked by he remarked dryly, "You're growing on me." I knew right then that if this soccer dad recognized me, probably because his wife forced him to watch the show, I was in trouble.

Three paps stayed with me all weekend and even followed Rachel and me into Bloomingdale's at the Century City mall while we shopped. They were reprimanded by security and told they couldn't take photos inside, so while we went into dressing rooms to try stuff on, they sat on the couches like bored boyfriends. I even felt rushed! At one point I couldn't find Rachel and a pap said, "Oh, she's over there looking at shoes." We managed to ditch them at the mall, but by the time I got home they were parked outside my house. Stefan, a freelancer, was the one who followed me to the airport. Andy worked for *Splash News* and Gaz for *Pacific Coast News*. Gaz eventually gained my trust the most. I actually felt bad that they had to camp out there, so I went outside, introduced myself, and took their phone numbers. I promised I'd call them if I went anywhere exciting. But they didn't budge.

And they continued to not budge. When I landed a Volkswagen GTI print ad they followed me to the set and had to be chased away. I was so embarrassed and worried the client would never book me again. I was getting less work since the show had started airing. The more infamous I became, the less the clients wanted to use me. If they did, it would be more like I was endorsing their products, not just modeling for them. And right then, nobody wanted my endorsement. Thankfully, a Ketel One commercial I shot was renewed and the $20,000 check kept me afloat during the worst slump in my career.

At the end of the weekend, after Rachel left, I called Ben bawling, but he didn't comfort me at all. He was really cold and seemed not to care. We talked briefly before he said he had to go. I was so devastated. I'd done everything I could to make sure Ben knew I loved him. We were both struggling with the press, but he was pushing me away. I asked the producers to put together a reel of all the good stuff I said about him that never aired. I know they gave it to him, but he never told me if he watched it or not. I also put the diamond band he'd given me at Christmas on my left hand on purpose and went out in public to brunch at Urth Caffe so I'd be photographed wearing it. I wanted to send Ben a secret message that we'd make it through this together.

It made no difference. Ben and I were worlds apart already and it would only get worse. I had to fly to New York again for a Stein Mart campaign and while I was there, the tabloids continued their systematic assassination of my already battered character.

In Touch Weekly ran their first cover of me with the screaming headline "Bachelor Ben Tricked! Courtney's Ex Tells All!" Guess who crawled out from under a bar stool to sell dirt on me? Dylan. In the story, he told them that I'd dated an "old rich guy" before the show (Cavan), but the mag erroneously reported that he was fifty. He said that my attraction to Ben was "a complete lie." He had the nerve to say that I used men for money and dumped him because he wasn't rich. (He forgot lazy and bad in bed, too.) "She latches onto guys who can help support her," he said. Which was hysterical coming from the guy I supported for two years and added to my cell phone plan.

I found out later that Dylan was paid about $10,000 for this story and a follow-up in which the bastard gave them the photo of me naked and sick in the bathtub. Adding insult to injury, I also learned that a sexy, voluptuous reporter who worked on Dylan's piece hooked up with him after a long day of barhopping. They started drinking margaritas at El Compadre at noon, got so sloshed at Lexington Social House in the middle of the day they got kicked out, and then moved their party for two to Red Rock, where they made out in the bathroom. I doubt they had sex, since Dylan was often unable to perform after a day of heavy drinking.

Us Weekly wasn't much better. They infamously called me a "Man-eater" on their cover and announced that I was "worse than you think" because I was a lush and had a secret sex tape. How did they know about a sex tape?

The original cover *Us* planned to feature was a family member's mug shot from an arrest a couple years before. When I got wind of this distressing development, we offered up my sister Rachel for an exclusive interview (I wasn't allowed to do press yet) in exchange for never running the mug shot. But that wasn't good enough. They wouldn't drop the mention of a sex tape.

Allegedly, my ex Cavan had been offered $1 million from porn distributor Vivid Entertainment, for a tape, if one existed, but he refused to acknowledge the offer. He called me for the first time since we'd broken up: "I'm a perfect gentleman," he told me. "I would never do that to you. Or my mother." He was a quality guy.

The National Enquirer wasn't about to let that mug shot go and they did end up running it in a despicable story. Needless to say, I was an absolute wreck in New York City. I understood that I was fair game; that's part of signing up for *The Bachelor.* I actually thought the "Man-eater" line was kind of funny and listened to the Nelly Furtado and Hall and Oates songs of the same name to get more insight into what being a "Man-eater" actually entailed. But in no way did my family deserve to be dragged into this mess. I was wracked with guilt that my decision had ended up hurting them so profoundly.

While I was staying at the Off Soho Suites, Ben called me and we had a hasty conversation. He said he was having a hard time and didn't know if our relationship could recover from all of the negative press he'd read.

"Ben, you know me. You know how much I love you." Since Sundance, Ben had been making more of an effort to make me a priority. But when the media shitstorm started, he flipped the switch back to invisible man. He was no J. P. Rosenbaum.

"I need a little space, Courtney. A couple days to think about everything."

I felt sick and heartbroken. But I told him, "Of course, I understand."

Ben was about to dump me, my family was in a shambles, and I was totally alone, literally and figuratively. I decided it was time for me to break the rules and take matters into my own hands. I e-mailed a reporter from Wet Paint and told her to meet me at Freemans, my favorite restaurant on the Lower East Side. I figured if she could just meet me, she'd see that I'm really a nice person. I just needed one person on my side to maintain my sanity. We talked for a few hours over many needed cocktails. I told her when the time was right I would give her an exclusive on the ring. I trusted her and she promised me she wouldn't report that we were engaged. It was a major coup for her to have me as a direct source and she wasn't going to blow that.

I made it through my Stein Mart shoot, barely, then hopped on a plane back to L.A. I wore my sunglasses on the flight, not because I didn't want anyone to recognize me, but because my eyes were as puffed up as pizza rolls from crying so hard. The woman sitting next to me was reading the Man-eater cover story and started peppering me with questions. I pulled my earphones out hesitantly, but realized a complete stranger was the perfect person to unload on. I got us a couple little bottles of wine and purged everything about Ben and the show on this poor, kind stranger.

When I got home, I hadn't heard from Ben in days, so I wrote him a last ditch e-mail:

> My love,
>
> I want you to know I really miss you, and that you're on my mind. What a mess we're in, to say the least! I understand 100 percent where you're at with everything. I know you're scared and I'm right there with you. My heart has already been broken by all of this. Words cannot describe how disappointed I am with the way this has all played out. After going through something so traumatic, I can so clearly see what's important in life, and what's not. I have been in survival mode, and have found a strength within that is pulling me through. I put myself in your shoes every day, and have felt your pain. I care about you so deeply and find peace in knowing you will be okay, with or without me. Lately I picture losing the life I dreamed of having with you, as well as the feeling of not knowing what could have been.
>
> I don't want to live my life with any regrets. And as of right now, I'm choosing to focus only on the positive side of things. I'm alive; this will all go away. I fell in love with the man of my dreams . . . I'm willing to fight for you and our relationship. The thing that's strongest in my heart is my love for you. We have so much to learn about each other, and that will be the fun part ;). I hope you can trust in everything I say to you, and know I've always had your best interest at heart. I just wanted you to know where I'm at, before it's too late. Know I love you more than anything.
>
> All my love, C
> P.S. I wish I could be with you on Valentine's Day. I made you a mix CD. I hope you listen to it ;).

Ben never responded to this e-mail and he never got me a Valentine's Day gift. For anyone else who cares, here's the playlist of love songs I made for him on iTunes:

"Forever" by Ben Harper
"Dreamin' " by Feldberg
"This Year's Love" by David Gray
"When the Night Comes" by Dan Auerbach
"Paradise" by Coldplay
"Conversation 16" by the National
"Wasted" by Angus and Julia Stone
"Where Dirt and Water Collide" by the White Buffalo
"I Would Do Anything for You" by Foster the People
"50 Ways to Leave Your Lover" by Paul Simon

This is a terrible thing to say, but on February 11 Whitney Houston died suddenly and tragically, and I was thankfully forgotten and not followed by the paparazzi for a few weeks.

Around this time, I went out to get a haircut and afterward went to Earthbar on Santa Monica Boulevard for a smoothie. I noticed the paps mingling around but they weren't there for me. They were following Russell Brand, who had recently split with Katy Perry. Funny enough, Russell and I had on matching outfits: black fedoras and denim shirts (hey, it was a hot look at the time). He turned around, we locked eyes, and I smiled. We did kind of look alike. He marched right over to me and put his face close to mine.

"You've got little eyebrows all over your face," he said in his adorable British accent.

"Oh, I just got a haircut!" I said, laughing and brushing the little hairs off my face. "They say I look like you in the media," I added, not knowing if he had any clue who I was.

"Well, my mum tells me I'm very handsome, so you should take that as a compliment," he said. "Why are you in the media?"

I told him I was on *The Bachelor* and had just gotten engaged. "Wait, you mean to tell me you got engaged on a television show! So you're engaged to a total stranger!" Yep. Nail on head.

Actually, I didn't even know what I was. On actual Valentine's Day, I met a *Bachelor* producer at a Coffee Bean & Tea Leaf in the afternoon to discuss me going on the "Women Tell All" episode. It would be a *Bachelor* first: the final two women had never appeared on it before, as it created more mystery surrounding the finale. But the producers wanted to give the women the chance to confront me and also give me a shot to defend myself. I really didn't want to do it and my contract didn't require it. I definitely had to appear on "After the Final Rose" no matter what, but this decision was totally up to me. I was leaning against it.

I still hadn't heard from Ben and was crying throughout the meeting.

As the producer tried to convince me to do the show, I finally received a text from my fiancé, who was in Las Vegas to promote his wine:

"Happy v day. It's a really awkward day for me right now and not sure how to approach it with you. Just wanted to say hi."

I handed the phone to the producer to read the message.

"I'm done," I said flatly. "And I'm doing the 'Women Tell All.' "

I went home and drank a few glasses of wine so I wouldn't send an impulsive, rage-filled response to Ben's emotionless text. An hour later I was ready to be civilized: "All I wanted to hear today was that you still love me, and it's clear you don't feel that way anymore. I think we need to talk about this tomorrow."

"I agree," he wrote back. "I will call you at 5:00 when I get home tomorrow evening."

I finished the bottle of wine, so incredibly pissed off. And then I finally stopped crying. I was over Ben Flajnik and his bullshit.

THE NEXT DAY at 5:00 on the dot, he called. We had another one of our quickie convos, as if we were talking about one of his gourmet grocery lists and not the painful end of our relationship. I turned the tables on him. This time I was the one being short, snappy, and unemotional.

"I'm done. I can't do this," I said, not a tremor in my voice.

Of course, now that I was over and out, he dragged his feet, pausing awkwardly and trying to be nice. But I'd had it.

"And I'm doing the 'Women Tell All' for myself."

"Oh, okay," he said, surprised.

That was pretty much it. Mr. Communication had little else to say so we got off the phone. And we were officially broken up. All that was left to do was watch ourselves fall in love and get engaged on TV.

12

RANTING, RAVING & CHEATING

Less than a week after Ben's and my engagement imploded, I faced the firing squad on the "Women Tell All" special.

When I arrived on the set, in another new Alice and Olivia dress, I was kept far away from Ben, who had to face the wrath of the rejected himself. I had gotten a text from him the day before while I was at lunch with Casey. He asked to meet me after the show at a Happy Couple safe house to talk. I reluctantly agreed.

"I feel like we owe it to ourselves to talk face-to-face," he texted. "Even if it's a straight-up cry fest."

Jeez, Ben, like this day wasn't stressful enough?

I was also given my own trailer, separate from the other women, who were all together. To keep calm, I guzzled white wine. I went over my game plan in my head: apologize, be humble, and show vulnerability. Do *not* be defensive, and most of all, do not cry on-camera.

Chris Harrison stopped by my trailer. He hugged me and said, "Don't worry. It's going to be fine." The only problem was he wasn't fine. He felt really sick and was as pale as a ghost. But he was a pro and, as we all know, the show must go on.

While they got a shot of me pacing in the parking lot, a producer, one who'd always managed to say the wrong thing to me, came up to me and gave me unwanted and idiotic advice: "Just be a girl."

I finally got my cue. I walked into the studio and though there was some clapping, I only heard the loud boos from the audience. It made my soul hurt. It got so quiet you could hear a pin drop. I scanned the room. Fans were shaking their heads in disgust and my old roomies were huddled with each other whispering. This was an absolute nightmare. Unfortunately, I was wide awake. The tears started rolling down my cheek. So much for not crying on-camera.

Jenna Burke, the Over-Analyst blogger who got sent home after she passed out in a bed, broke the ice by saying she wanted to give me a hug. She walked across the stage to embrace me.

Chris abruptly told the crew he needed to stop taping. He was so ill he had to go lie down in his trailer. After he walked off the stage, I was left alone in the middle of the studio like the lamb for the slaughter. Audience and cast members hurled insults at me like I was on *The Jerry Springer Show*.

A producer came to my rescue and sat with me face-to-face so I wouldn't have to look at anyone. My mike was still on and a pool of reporters camped backstage overheard our conversation.

"I don't know if I can show that emotion again," I said.

"You have to," the producer said. "This is for you. This is for you and Ben."

I was crippled with fear and bowed my head again so nobody could see me cry.

As my shoulders were shaking, Monica Spannbauer shouted out, "Look at her! She's laughing!" Elyse, who by now had seen the "sight for sore eyes" episode, shouted, "You love the paparazzi! You love the attention! This is what you want!" Samantha the Chihuahua was shrieking at me, too, but I was so traumatized I blocked out what she said.

I found it fascinating that they claimed that I was in this for the fame. Nothing could have been further from the truth. Plus, during filming, when the cameras weren't there, so many of these same women sat around talking about what it was going to be like when they were "famous" after the show started airing. They were excited about being recognized and hoping for lucrative opportunities.

One audience member made a heart shape with her hand and mouthed, "I love you!" But the verbal abuse became so bad I was taken back to my trailer until Chris was ready to shoot again. When he felt well enough to give it another go, the torture continued. It didn't help when he started off with, "The women are understandably pissed. I mean *pissed* at you," then left me hanging in the breeze. I'm going to forgive him for not coming to my defense that one time, because he was sick. But he didn't seem to have my back at all.

I started off by apologizing: "I have many regrets. I'm disappointed in myself and the way I acted and treated the women. Looking back there's so many things I would have done differently." Eye rolls from the peanut gallery. It was obvious there would be no forgiveness tonight no matter what I said.

Blakeley was one of the first to confront me: "Courtney, what did I ever do to you for you to call me a stripper? What did I ever do for you to say I'm the kind of girl your boyfriend cheats on you with?"

In Utah, after the fly-fishing date, a bunch of the girls were dancing around and I saw Blakeley jokingly give Kacie B a very skilled striptease and lap dance. That's where that came from, but I couldn't say that on-air.

Elyse pounced next, calling me "trashy" for going skinny-dipping right after she was sent home.

Jaclyn, who I thought was my friend, jumped on the attack: "When I hear you drag my friends' names through the mud, that's what really gets me."

Jennifer called me out for not knowing her name for six days. I barely knew her name now.

Kacie B was the most civilized of the bunch, asking me why I made constant jabs. Casey, my best ally, jumped to my defense, pointing out that I wasn't the only one shit-talking the whole time. But then they all jumped down her throat. Emily ripped me to shreds when I said it was intense living with all of the girls. She refused to accept my excuse that the process was hard for me. "It was hard for every last one of us!" she ranted. "Did we all react by making these jabs or being negative and rude to everyone?"

Um, yes, you *hypocrite*? I kept that jab to myself.

"Guess what we did," righteous Emily continued. "We made friendships to support one another and get through it. Courtney did exactly the opposite. We were human beings and tried to make connections to get through it."

I absolutely despised this walking disease expert, but this time I had no choice. I had to swallow my pride, bend over, and take it up the tailpipe. I wanted so badly to talk about how they all alienated me from the very start and talked constantly behind my back and in their ITMs. I wanted to say that Emily threatened me in the hallway in Utah and said I had a personality disorder. It took every fiber of my being to not be defensive as they attacked me, but I let them put me through the ringer. "I want to say I'm sorry," I said, more tears streaming down my face. "I came into this with the same hopes and dreams. I'm sorry if I hurt your feelings. I'm really sorry for that. I hope you can find it in your hearts to forgive me. I'm not a meanspirited person. It brought out the worst in me. I can't apologize enough."

After Chris said there was nothing left for me to apologize for, they mercifully ended the segment, and I walked off the stage defeated. Some of the girls were still rubbing salt in the wound. Nicki leaned over to Kacie B and said, "I'm *not* going to hug her." Samantha barked, "She's a bitch, end of story."

I was already emotionally drained and now I had to wait for Ben to finish the taping so we could have our "talk." I was driven over to a small Happy Couple house off Melrose Avenue in Hollywood, crying the whole time. I cried so much I had vertical streaks down my face where my tears washed away my makeup. In the bathroom I looked in the mirror and saw my busted, tear-stained face. I decided not to clean myself up so that Ben understood the pain of what I'd just been through.

Ben walked into the house carrying groceries and a bouquet of flowers. When he saw me, he stopped in his tracks and smiled sweetly at me. Oh boy, I knew that look. He'd come here to get back together. Well, I was not having it. I thought he was a coward and that I was stronger than he was—a major turnoff.

Ben went into the kitchen to prepare a gourmet swordfish dinner. He was trying to be charming and didn't even criticize my knife cuts. But I still was not letting him off the hook or being affectionate toward him.

When we sat down to eat, it was crickets—until he had the audacity to ask, "What are we doing?" Actually I was glad he said it because now I was entitled to go nuts on him.

"What are *you* doing!" I yelled. "I've completely lost all faith and trust in you! I've never felt this bad in my life. You are supposed to be my fiancé and you haven't been there at all for me!"

He looked into my eyes, reached across the table, and grabbed my hand. Then he apologized. I'm embarrassed to say that's all it took for me to cave. We both got up and embraced. It felt so good to be held by him. Then we went into the bedroom and had sex.

Raise your hand like Kacie B if you're disappointed in me right now. Well, what can I say? We had a natural chemistry that was undeniable. I was in love with Ben and he promised to make it all right again. I believed him. Plus, I really didn't want to go on "After the Final Rose" and explain to 8 million viewers that we failed as a couple, that we didn't make it. I couldn't deal with the "I told you so's." I wanted us to work so badly.

Ben even toyed with the idea of us giving the ring back and bailing on our commitment to finish the show. "We'll do our own thing!" he proclaimed. But we both knew contractually that was next to impossible. Plus, I really wanted that darn ring.

The next morning Ben left and it was like nothing bad had ever happened. We flipped the switch again and we were back to being in love and engaged. He left to do a wine tasting event in Detroit but we would see each other in a week to tape "After the Final Rose." I was so excited. We were just two weeks away from coming out publicly as a couple. We wouldn't have to hide or defend our love anymore to *anyone*.

YEAH, WELL, THE BLISS didn't last long. Two days before the "After the Final Rose" taping, Ben called me. "Hey, just giving you a heads-up that *Us Weekly* has some photos of me," he said nonchalantly. "I'm trying to stop it."

"Well, what are the photos?" I asked.

"The paparazzi were following me and I had some friends over. I kissed someone on the cheek to say hello. But they're making it look like I've been kissing girls."

"Were you?"

"No!"

"Don't worry. I believe you," I assured him. I'd seen enough of the garbage and lies that had been printed about me to know it probably was made up.

The next morning I asked my roommate to go to pick up a copy of *Us*. The paparazzi had returned to my front lawn and I didn't want to be seen picking up a tabloid story about myself. That's so Kardashian.

My roommate brought it back and handed it to me nervously. "It doesn't look good, Court," she warned.

I brought the magazine into my bedroom so I could look at the pictures privately. There, in photographic evidence, were three potential women Ben cheated with after he told me he "needed space." While I was home nursing a broken heart, he was out drinking and groping. One picture, dated February 18, was particularly incriminating. He was definitely kissing this girl and it was not a friendly peck on the cheek. He had his hands on her ass and their pelvises were glued together like puzzle pieces. They were walking Scotch together, which really bothered me. *Us* also had photos of the girl, allegedly a friend from college, leaving his apartment the next morning.

I lay in bed sobbing, ignoring phone calls and rapid-fire texts from Ben.

> Fml.
>
> Sorry you had to deal with all of this for so long, you're much stronger than me.
>
> Sorry for being so naive.
>
> I'm stressing big time.

I went online to read stories about the cheating scandal and, again, the headlines and comments were vicious. Especially about Ben. Everyone seemed thrilled that we would have no choice but to break up now. I even heard from my mom, who e-mailed, "Do you really want to be with a cheater?"

Instead of being sad, I got mad and protective of our relationship. I oddly also felt bad for Ben. Now he finally knew firsthand what I'd been going through the last few months with the press. Now he knew what it felt like to be the villain, the bad guy, and be railroaded in the media. To be stalked and hounded and despised. I felt vindicated and decided to stand by him, even though I wasn't sure at this point what really happened with the ass-grab girl.

I just wanted to send a really big *f-you* to the world and confuse the hell out of everyone who was buying into the tabloid frenzy.

I jumped out of bed and got dressed. I had a new mischievous plan. I let the paparazzi follow me to the Mark Zunino bridal shop in West Hollywood, where I proceeded to try on multiple wedding dresses. I posed brazenly in the window for all to see and snap. For shits and giggles, I even tried on a gown that looked exactly like the universally mocked dress Angelina Jolie had just worn to the Oscars, with the giant slit up the leg.

By the time I left the bridal shop, the sidewalk was teeming with photographers, two of whom got into a shoving match in front of me. I tried to drive home, but it was like the Indy 500, with about twenty paps in cars and on motorcycles in hot pursuit. I'd started this madness, but now I was terrified for my life. Andy from *Splash* called me. "You don't want these scumbags to know where you live. Follow me."

He drove up next to me and pointed at the Twentieth Century Fox studio on Pico Boulevard. I drove up and begged the guard to let me in to escape my tormentors. He lifted the gate and I was safe. I drove through the lot and out another exit. Ha! I lost all of them! Special thanks to Andy.

Within an hour the wedding dress pictures were up online and my plot was a huge success. I'd stumped the media. They couldn't figure out why I was trying on wedding dresses the very day Ben's cheating scandal hit. Was I sticking it to Ben? The show? *Us Weekly?* Were we together? Broken up? I was the only one on the planet who knew the answer.

I finally called Ben: "I did this for you. We can get over this."

"I never kissed her!" he insisted. When I didn't believe him, he sheepishly admitted, "She *did* sleep in my bed, but I promise I didn't have sex with her." He even swore on his father's grave.

Nice. We were engaged, yet he let another woman sleep in his bed. I knew it. I'd closely studied the picture of her leaving his apartment the next morning and the evidence was pretty clear. She had her hair in a bun, a classic post-hookup hairstyle—and she had that walk-of-shame look all over her face.

Ben had the nerve to play the victim, as he barraged me with lame excuses. "I've been having such a hard time and I was going out a lot and acting out and flirting, but I swear I never cheated on you."

Ugh. Enough. Like a stupid idiot, I told him I believed him.

Do I think he cheated? Hell yes, I think he cheated.

But I couldn't take any more pain and lies. There were only three days until we taped the "After the Final Rose" special and we had an interview for the cover of *People* magazine to get through. There was no *way* I was going to give up now. That'd be like Sid in *An Officer and a Gentleman* and we all know how that ended. He went DOR with less than two weeks until graduation, and then killed himself. (Sorry for the spoiler for anyone who hasn't seen the movie. But really, if you haven't seen it, that's not right. Netflix it now.)

When the "After the Final Rose" taping day arrived, I hadn't heard much from Ben and had no idea what we were going to say when the cameras rolled. I called him and asked, "Do we have a game plan?"

"The story is that we're good," he said simply.

Only it wasn't so simple. It had definitely crossed my mind to completely blindside him and dump him right there on the spot. "Once a cheater, always a cheater!" I thought about screaming at him.

But, deep down, I was in love with Ben and not ready to end it. I didn't even see him until just before we walked out on the stage. It'd been almost four months since Ben got on bended knee, so they had us watch the proposal together again to get us back to that fairy-tale bubble, to be in the *Bachelor* frame of mind.

Usually on "After the Final Rose" the runner-up goes first and gets a chance to ask the Bachelor why she was rejected. Poor Lindzi showed up, but got bumped—and never got her day in court. They wanted the entire episode to be about Ben and me. Lindzi got her revenge by doing press in New York City the morning after the finale. While she was gracious and her usual chipper self on *Good Morning America*, she joined forces with that little freckle-faced troublemaker Kelly Ripa, who got her to say Ben needed a new hair stylist and that I kept him on a short leash.

I don't blame Lindzi. We deserved that. And she deserves a guy who will appreciate her quirkiness and unique sense of humor. She's got a good heart. I have nothing but respect for Lindzi and the way she handled herself after the show—just like a lady who'd never chew gum.

The audience at "After the Final Rose" obviously did not respect me; they booed worse than at the "Women Tell All" taping. I felt like I had no support from anyone. Though Ben confirmed during the interview that we were definitely together and on the path to marriage, we both had tears in our eyes almost the entire time. Sure, he slid that $80,000 engagement ring back on my finger, but it was obvious to anyone with a pulse that our future was about as shaky as a dog shitting razor blades. (Full disclosure: I stole that one from UrbanDictionary.com.)

As Ben and I watched the proposal again—for the camera this time—I whispered to him, "I can't stop crying." I wanted him to comfort me, but he kept watching the screen and wouldn't look at me.

I threw him under the bus about abandoning me when things got really tough and for not getting me a gift on Valentine's Day. "He didn't send flowers or a card or anything," I said. "It was awful. There were days where I didn't leave the house, and I just laid there and cried . . . I needed him."

Ben admitted he messed up, swore on his father's grave again that he didn't cheat on me and promised to be true to me from now on. "There was never anything wrong with us," he claimed. "What's wrong was everything that surrounded us."

We were pretty much doomed.

After the taping (and giving the ring back yet again for safe-keeping—it would be returned after the finale aired), we went back to the little Happy Couple house off Melrose. That night, "Women Tell All" aired. I couldn't stomach watching it so I went to take a bath while Ben plopped down in front of the TV.

I submerged myself in the tub, trying to drown out the angry chorus of estrogen-fueled insults. But I still caught snippets of their bitching and moaning.

"These girls are *awful*!" Ben bellowed from the other room.

Ya think, Benny Boo Boo?

13

ENGAGED & DATING

I watched the *Bachelor* finale and "After the Final Rose" on March 12 by myself in my apartment. When it was over, there was no fanfare or celebration or congratulatory e-mails, just an empty wine bottle and a pity call from my dad. The end result of the show was so depressing and unpopular that the interview we'd done for *People* magazine was bumped off the cover for *The Hunger Games*. I didn't even care. The stylist for the magazine put me in a preppy pink sweater, something I'd never wear, to make me look sweeter. The shoot itself was awkward. I was so proud to be in my element and show Ben the modeling ropes, but he was as stiff as a board and ignored my advice to move a little in every frame. The inside story, with the optimistic headline "Can They *Really* Trust Each Other?" just rehashed all of the old drama.

Ben was so burnt-out by the entire experience that other than the *People* interview, he didn't want to do any other press, morning or daytime talk shows, nothing. In fact, after "Women Tell All," reporters witnessed him throwing a temper tantrum about doing more interviews. "One more of these fucking things and I'm done," he complained. "I have so many better things to do with my life."

Now that the full season had aired I wanted everyone to see the real me, but I never got a chance to defend myself or try to change people's opinions or misperceptions of me.

The day after the finale, my three-carat engagement ring was messengered to me at home and I could now wear it publicly and proudly. The day after that, I told the crew of paps on my front lawn that I was going to see Ben tomorrow and booked my flight (which I paid for) up to San Francisco. I hadn't been to his hometown since the very first week of taping. I was so nervous and excited. He picked me up at the airport in his BMW, gave me a bouquet of flowers he bought at the grocery store, and took me back to his place in the Marina, a hipster neighborhood near the Golden Gate Bridge with a lot of bars.

On the drive, I told Ben I had a big surprise I'd been holding off telling him until we were together in person. I had a secret meeting with the producers of *Dancing with the Stars* and they wanted me as an alternate, just in case anyone got hurt. The payday was incredible: $125,000 just to show up and $30,000 for every week I made it through. Cha-ching!

"They offered it to *you*?" he asked incredulously. I noted a tinge of jealousy. I hadn't even thought about this kind of stuff yet and how it would affect our relationship. I was just excited the opportunity was there.

"If you do it," he added coldly, "you won't have a fiancé."

I felt like I'd been punched in the gut.

"I can't believe you'd even bring it up," Ben growled, even more pissed off.

This was not a good start.

I dropped the conversation and ultimately dropped out of the potential *Dancing with the Stars* casting, even though we could have bought our first house together with that money.

Instead we spent the first three months of our public engagement staying in his frat house of an apartment when I'd visit. Ben explained that since he'd been gone for so long on *The Bachelorette* and *The Bachelor,* this was just a temporary living situation. It better be. His two winery business partners lived there, too. Ben and one guy had their own rooms, but the other slept on a queen mattress in the living room. The apartment only had one bathroom, and it looked like a bathroom used by three guys. It felt like we were in college.

I learned very quickly that in Ben's world, the days were jam-packed with activities and his entourage. After cooking dinner together the first night, we didn't have any alone time for the rest of the weekend. The first night we spent in the frat house one roommate had a hookup drop by. This was the "real life" relationship I'd imagined while we were locked up like inmates? The next day, Ben had a wine event scheduled at a restaurant in Sonoma, forty-five minutes away, where his mom lived. He decided not to take me to the tasting. Babs thought I would be hounded by the guests. So he left me with Babs at her condo while he worked the party. "This is better for you," she insisted. "So you don't have to answer so many questions." We both took naps to decrease the amount of time we had to spend together.

That night Ben and I drove back to the city and had our first public dinner with his sister, Julia, and her boyfriend, Garrett, at Park Tavern. We were so lovey-dovey. After, we went back to his apartment and had sex. We were both so tired—him from going, going,

going all day and me from having to be "on" all the time in front of his friends and mom—that it was just . . . *fine*. "It's only going to get better," I told him hopefully.

Early in the morning, Ben and I helped Julia and Garrett move into their cute new apartment. I was a little envious that they were at this step and we weren't even talking about it. The paparazzi had found us in San Fran, which Ben blamed me for, and many of the tabloids mistakenly reported that we were moving in together. Afterward we had lunch then met ten of Ben's closest friends in a park for an afternoon of drinking and kite flying.

The next morning one of Ben's friends had to take me to the airport because Ben had work to do. The guy came to get me before the sun came up and dropped me off on the curb, even though my flight wasn't for hours. It ended up being delayed and I sat in the airport for most of the day.

So, Ben wouldn't "let" me do *Dancing with the Stars,* and didn't want to do any press—but without telling me he arranged for a free trip to Puerto Vallarta, Mexico, in exchange for promoting the resort, a favorite destination of Elizabeth Taylor and Richard Burton. A telling sign, right? I thought we were just going on vacation, but the first day we were there, Ben informed me that we had to take a few pictures and then we could have the rest of the time to ourselves. Did he make money from this setup? To this day I don't know.

Regardless, we had an amazing time together. It really felt like we were on our honeymoon. It was one of the rare times in our relationship—maybe the only time, come to think of it—we were completely alone for five days in a row. Ben, as painful as it was for him, attempted to relax as much as possible. We drank beer and sunbathed all day, and made love all night. We were super affectionate and intimate. We spent the whole trip holding hands and kissing.

There were a couple of hiccups. First, he made the mistake of checking his e-mail after dinner the first night. A friend had forwarded a photo of *In Touch Weekly*'s latest cover; it was the photo of me naked in the bathtub that Dylan had sold to them for a few thousand dollars. The headline was about my "Dirty Secrets" and the rag promised nude photos (yep, there it was on the cover), details of a *Playboy* spread (never happened), and a boob job (unashamedly true).

After the first story had come out, I'd fired off nasty texts to Dylan:

Me: I can't believe you're selling stories about me.

Dylan: I can't believe you'd go on a show like that.

Me: Just remember, there are two sides to every story.

Dylan: Don't you ever threaten me.

Me: I just did.

Dylan: Just leave me alone.

Me: Same to you.

This time I decided to ignore him. Though Ben never offered to beat Dylan up for me, he also didn't freak out about the naked bathtub picture and was surprisingly supportive. "Can you sue that guy?" he asked. It felt like a turning point in our relationship. That no matter what garbage anyone threw at us, we were now a team and strong enough to get through it.

The other issue was that after three days of being by ourselves, we were running out of conversation. That troubled me a little bit. Over drinks one night, we fell back on old reliable, reminiscing about *The Bachelor.* Ben, for some reason, brought up Nicki. "She was really cool," he glowed. "When we were on her Hometown, I looked over at her and it was like I was with one of my buddies."

Seriously? Here we were, on our first vacation alone together and he's fondly talking about an "ex" who treated me like crap. "Do you want to be friends with her?" I said, my voice trembling and on the verge of tears. "She wasn't nice to me, Ben. And you were with her!"

"We said we'd never talk about that," he said quietly. That was a nondenial. I mean I wasn't surprised. Ben made out with like sixteen of the eighteen girls who made it past the first Rose Ceremony.

I pulled out the fiancé card he'd thrown in my face about *Dancing with the Stars*.

"If you want me in your life, you cannot be friends with her."

"In all fairness, you talk about your exes a lot," he said.

"I think the reason I talk about them so much is that I want you to know the truth, that I have had good relationships."

"Okay, I got it," he said and the conversation was dropped like an AT&T call.

In the beginning of our relationship, the offers to make money were rolling in. I turned down a lucrative opportunity to endorse a diet pill company, because I thought it sent a bad message to young girls. Without telling Ben, I turned down $50,000 each for us to appear on VH1's *Couples Therapy* because I knew he'd never agree to it. Ben had several secret meetings about doing a reality show about the wine business called *Young Sonoma* and signed on without telling me. Only after he agreed to do it did he ask me to be on it. I felt blindsided. Already bitter about his *Dancing with the Stars* ban, I told him I didn't want to be on it. I told him that I thought it would create problems in our relationship.

At the end of March, Ben and I had our first paid public appearance together for "Night of a Billion Reality Stars," hosted by Svedka vodka, at SupperClub in L.A. Instead of staying with me at my place, which, unbelievably he'd still never seen, Ben went down to San Diego the night before the event to hang out with friends. When I picked him up at the train station, he looked like shit. I recognized a filmy haze around him and detected a scent of cocoa butter.

"Did you go to a strip club last night?"

"How did you know?"

"It's written all over you."

At the event, we had to walk the red carpet together and a reporter asked Ben about our plans for marriage. It was the first time we'd been asked about setting a date since right after the show ended.

"We're taking it slow," he said. "We're engaged-dating."

I was shocked. What the heck was "engaged-dating"? I'd never heard him say that in my life. Either he made it up on the spot or had been thinking about it and neglected to fill me in on our new status. Silly me, I was under the impression that we were engaged to be married.

I put that on the back burner as we entered the party. I rubbed elbows with Bravo Housewives Teresa Giudice, Kyle Richards, Brandi Glanville, and Gretchen Rossi, and sperminator Jon Gosselin. *Dancing with the Stars* pro Maksim Chmerkovskiy mingled with Mob Wife Angela "Big Ang" Raiola. And it was my first event as an official member of Bachelor Nation. I was introduced to Bachelorettes Ali Fedotowsky and DeAnna Pappas, and the adorable Stagliano brothers, the breakout stars of *Bachelor Pad*. Jesse Kovacs, from Jillian Harris's season, was also there, wandering around looking extremely hot.

Then I met Ashley Hebert, who I knew from a very reliable source had slept with Ben in her Fantasy Suite. My first impression, well, I was really surprised that she was so short. A lot of people look small next to me, but she was just a teeny tiny little thing!

It was the first time Ben had seen her since their "After the Final Rose" taping, and they had a nice chat. "I'm sorry," Ashley told Ben again. "I felt bad about it." She was also very nice to me, but she had a nervous energy.

So what's it like to be in Bachelor Nation? It's a private high school on steroids. There are cliques within cliques, politics and hierarchies to wade through, and at least one secret Facebook group where alums plan exotic vacations together. There are official *Bachelor*-sponsored parties and a lot of charity events organized and attended by alumni. Of course, there is a ton of intermingling, cohabitating, and shocking hookups. For instance, not many people know that Vienna Girardi and country-singing bad boy Wes Hayden had a thing after she broke up with Jake Pavelka.

The *Bachelor Pad* franchise has been a breeding ground for cross-pollination as well. At least two of my cast mates have dated Polish pretty boy Chris Bukowski (Emily Maynard's season). Rachel dated a Stagliano and Jaclyn dated Ed Swiderski. Lindzi dated her *Bachelor Pad 3* costar Kalon McMahon (also from Emily's season), but that went down in flames, too.

As we all know too well, being on *The Bachelor* and/or *Bachelor Pad* doesn't guarantee everlasting love. Several of the women who were on my season are still single: last I heard Jaclyn, Lindzi, and Jenna were still on the prowl. It's a lot different for the guys though. They have women coming out of their ears after being on the show. They get stalkers and marriage proposals, and their mailboxes overflow with X-rated e-mails and tweets. One guy I know even got a request to strip at a bachelorette party.

There is sort of an unspoken rule in Bachelor Nation that we don't bad-mouth each other and keep it in the family. Which is why it was so nasty when Trista Sutter trashed me on Twitter and Ben's best friend Constantine Tzortzis wrote, "Never respect a girl who takes her clothes off" on his blog. And yet, in April, Ben dragged me to Atlanta to visit Constantine, which was really uncomfortable. We slept in his basement next to their other BFF from their season, bartender Mickey McLean. That was one of my biggest concerns about Ben. It seemed like we were never alone.

By the time Easter rolled around, the honeymoon period was long gone and there were more serious problems. Before, my main concern had been the tabloids judging me, but now, I often felt like Ben was the one cutting me down. It was so blatant that I asked him if he'd studied a book called *The Game: Penetrating the Secret Society of Pickup Artists*, in which a guy insults, or "negs," a woman to make her more vulnerable. Ben almost never complimented me and anytime I said I wanted to do something out of the norm, he'd poo-poo it and give me five reasons why I couldn't. I told him I wanted to do a vegan cookbook and he laughed. I told him I wanted to write a memoir and he said, "Don't you think you're a little young to write a memoir? They'll never let *you* write a book."

Ben also didn't respect my modeling career, which was hanging by a thread after the show. He didn't understand that part of my job is to take care of my appearance, which meant going to the gym, getting a facial, or getting my nails done. When we'd be apart, he'd call me and ask, "What are you doing today?" When I told him, he rarely liked the answer. He seemed annoyed and resentful. "Why don't you do something dynamic? Why don't you paint? Why don't you go to a museum?"

He'd also quiz me about my financial situation, which was not great at this point. "I thought I fell in love with a successful model and I'd get to travel with you," he complained once. I needed him to be understanding of my situation and support, not criticize, me. I was still living off the Ketel One residual and building up a little bit of credit card debt. But I wasn't too worried yet. I knew if I booked one good job, I could pay it off completely. "You're too young to have credit card debt," he'd lecture. "We need to talk about your spending."

My spending? How about his spending? While the show had only given me a small amount after the finale to cover some bills, Ben made much more. He'd also made more than $1 million from an online marketing company he sold when he was younger, but he'd blown a lot of the money living large and traveling all over Europe. So, it's not like he was as fiscally prudent as Suze Orman or something. He always bought himself nice things, especially cars. He'd recently won $5,000 gambling in Vegas and used it to buy himself a used Jeep Cherokee, even though he already had a new BMW and would buy another vintage BMW during our relationship.

I was also having money issues because I was constantly paying to fly up to San Francisco. That was the only way I'd get to see Ben. He hadn't once made a special trip to L.A. to stay with me, and he had not yet offered to pay for even one of my plane tickets to see him.

I almost always went to him. For Easter, Ben threw a big party for about twelve of his friends on a ranch/winery near Solvang, California. Because that's what people do on Easter. They party really hard.

As usual, Ben spent more time hanging out with his friends by the grill than by my side. At one point, he blasted a rap song he had made between the *Bachelorette* and the *Bachelor* seasons. Apparently he was so horny because he wasn't allowed to hook up with anyone that he channeled his sexual energy into a vulgar song (and video) called "Cream Dreams." Yes, it's about exactly what you think it is. He obviously was trying to emulate Andy Samberg and Justin Timberlake's "Dick in a Box," but Ben's song wasn't clever, brilliant, or even funny really.

You can Google it, but if you don't want your ears or eyes to bleed, just picture Ben naked in a bed with lotion and a box of Kleenex, singing:

> *Well, if you just let me fuck you right*
> *I can be your cream dream every night*
> *My dick can fulfill your bedtime fantasies.*

It really turned me off, but I just put on a happy face whenever he played it because he was so proud of it.

You may be asking why I was still with Ben. It's hard to explain. On one hand, I did really love him. We had that unexplainable connection and I wanted to get married. On the other hand, I kept learning new things about him that I really didn't like.

KEEPING IT REAL

Confessions of a Villain

By Michelle Money

While filming the show, I was absolutely true to myself. I am a confident woman. I am sarcastic. I am not easily offended. I have no problem making friends with girls. I am not dramatic. I don't take life too seriously. I know who I am, which is the furthest thing from a villain.

I decided to go on *Bachelor Pad 2* to show America the real me. It was a huge risk, but in the end, my dad, who was battling the later stages of colon cancer, convinced me to do it. And it was the best thing I could have done.

Graham Bunn was my partner from the start. He still is to this day. He saved me. He helped America look at me with different eyes. While the show was airing, my sweet father passed away from cancer. It was Graham who came to my side through all the heartache. He and his company helped me raise money and awareness for colon cancer. He taught me how important it is to give back and do good in this world. I've now raised $200,000 for the Chris4Life Colon Cancer Foundation. I look at being a villain as a huge blessing to me now. Do I wish I could have been remembered in a different way? Yes. But I am happy people remember me. It gives me an opportunity to talk about much more important things then reality TV! And people listen. And since I have your attention, please remember to get your colonoscopy by the age of fifty, if not sooner. It can save your life!

In mid-April, we took a trip to the East Coast together to see Ben's friend, who played for the Boston Red Sox, and to see his grandma, who was very sweet and lived in Connecticut. We also went to NYC to attend the launch party for Mark Zunino's wedding gown collection for Kleinfeld Bridal. Ben was rude to the organizer, who was my friend, and barely said thank you when he was given a custom suit. He was so used to getting free stuff by now that he didn't think anything of being handed something so extravagant.

We had dinner alone at Benjamin Steakhouse in Grand Central Terminal but the sparks weren't flying. We had very little to say to each other, other than recapping the trip or talking about the food. Kris Humphries, who had just broken up with wife Kim Kardashian after seventy-two days of marriage, was at a nearby table and I remember feeling a kinship with him for some odd reason. Maybe it was because we were both in made-for-TV relationships and both got the raw end of the deal.

Making matters worse, Ben sprung it on me that he'd arranged a double date with Ashley and her fiancé, J. P. Rosenbaum, who lived in New Jersey, on our last night of vacation. I was so disappointed. The mush in me wanted to explore New York City alone with Ben like in a romantic comedy: a walk through Central Park, maybe he'd spring for a carriage ride, kissing at the top of the Empire State Building. Instead, Ben spent our last morning in the hotel lobby on his laptop and we spent our afternoon at French Connection so he could buy a pair of socks.

So when I heard about J. P. and Ashley taking over our final evening, I snapped. "I think it's weird that you want to hang out with them," I told Ben.

"It's not a big deal. I'm good friends with J. P.!" he snapped back.

"Well, it's weird for me," I said.

Clearly, I had no say in the matter. That night we met the couple for cocktails at Mulberry Project on the Lower East Side. Ashley, like the last time I met her, was still a miniature bubbly Energizer Bunny. She was very handsy and playful with J. P. and kept slapping him in the face with a french fry and pinching his cheeks. His eyes would twinkle and he'd just smile that Cheshire Cat grin that could melt butter.

Not to be outdone, Ben was very handsy with me and I felt like we were in the middle of a cute-couple competition. I really did not want to be there and I was grateful we were only having one drink with them before they left to go to another dinner. But then Ben invited them to our next spot, my favorite restaurant, Freemans. Ugh. *Fine*.

Once we all got to Freemans, Ben had another surprise for me. He'd also invited his manager, a college friend, and his cousin to dinner. Everyone ordered a ton of food and Ben, acting as sommelier, made a production of choosing an expensive bottle of wine. "Babe, this is sexy," Ashley said to J. P. "I wish you knew more about wine." I thought it was a little inappropriate, but J. P. just laughed it off. They left after a glass.

When the check came, after rounds of drinks, appetizers, and entrées, Ben looked at me and mouthed, "Should we split this?" I was so pissed off. These were his friends and he had the gall to make me foot half the bill, which was more than $800! I was already annoyed that he'd let me pick up the tab for the hotel. I didn't want to make a scene in the restaurant in front of his friends, so I tossed my card down.

After dinner, we went dancing at a club with Ben's entourage. Ben ignored me all night and kept disappearing into the crowd. He was wasted and as we walked back to our hotel, he got the munchies. We ordered pizza and meatballs from one of my favorite late-night spots, and sat on a nearby stoop to wait for our food.

"You look so sexy," he slurred. "I love that you know your way around this city." Finally, Ben had complimented me. But he was drunk and it was too little, too late for damage control. I couldn't wait to be away from him.

At the end of the trip I went to the airport alone, which was fine by me because we were recognized more when we were together. Sometimes when *Bachelor* viewers spotted us they'd follow us. Ben hated this side effect from being on the show and often told me, "Pick up the pace," so we could lose curious fans. We couldn't avoid everyone though. Every time we were asked to take a picture with fans, Ben would clam up and leave it to me to chat with them and be friendly. I never minded taking pictures. I appreciated anyone who supported us, and I knew it wouldn't last forever.

I once even took a picture with an emergency room doctor when I went to the hospital for a painful UTI. "We're not allowed to ask patients for pictures," he said. "But . . ." I took the darn photo, even though I looked and felt like shit. You know who the guy turned out to be? Dr. Larry Burchett, *Bachelor* superfan and future cast member on Desiree Hartsock's season. He was cut in the first episode.

KEEPING IT REAL

Tales from Bachelor Nation

by Chris Bukowski

My craziest encounter with a fan happened on a flight from L.A. to Chicago. When the plane landed, the flight attendant announced over the PA that someone on the plane had a big announcement. I was at the back of the plane, anxiously waiting to get off. A girl, who was in tears, got on the PA and asked me to marry her. She said she was in love with me since I walked out of the limo. Everyone was staring at me so I said yes jokingly. The whole cabin was applauding and then it got dead silent. The girl got back on the PA and asked if she could have my babies and if we could start right now.

When I finally met her in the terminal, she literally got down on one knee and proposed to me again. She got up, grasped my arm, and wouldn't let go. Her mom finally got her off me, and then told me it was her sixteenth birthday. Ever since then I will no longer sit in the back of the plane."

The only time I ever had to say no to a photo op was during an event in Las Vegas. Ben and I were hosting two parties: one at Pure in Caesars Palace and one at Wet Republic at the MGM Grand, for $10,000 each. When we arrived at Caesars Palace, Ben sprinted ahead through the lobby when he saw we were being trailed, leaving me behind to deal with the eager fan.

"I'm so sorry. We're in a hurry," I said.

"How rude!" she sniffed.

When I caught up to Ben, I told him I felt really bad about leaving the fan in our dust. "I think we should go back," I pleaded.

"Oh, whatever!" he said dismissively.

Ben invited two of his friends to tag along for the weekend and they had one of those adjoining rooms where they could walk through a door into our room. And they did. Frequently. Casey Shteamer was in town for a bachelorette party and joined in as well. Used to being surrounded by Ben's entourage, I was so happy to have one of my friends around to hang out with. During the day, we took over a private pool at Wet Republic that overlooked the whole club. We had such a blast splashing around, taking pictures and drinking cocktails together.

That night, we all partied at Pure in a VIP booth overlooking the crowd. That was the cool thing about these paid events. All we had to do was show up and stand there like animals in a glass cage, and we got cash, free booze, and even our own bouncer for the night. When I had to pee, my personal security guard escorted me to the bathroom and cut the line so I could go first, which, of course, was greeted with a chorus of angry "aw, c'mons!" It was all enough to give me a big head, until I saw that the billboard advertising the event had spelled my name wrong—Robinson instead of Robertson.

Ben was a big shot that night at the club, too. He kept getting bombarded with screaming girls who would try to run past the velvet rope to hug him, grab his ass, and scream, "I love you!" in his face. Now, *this* attention he didn't seem to mind.

We'd been drinking all day and all night, so it wasn't long before we were hammered.. His drink of choice was Fernet, a bitter aromatic spirit from Italy, which tastes like rocket fuel. In fact, the company found out he was a fan of the liquor and made him an ambassador of the brand. Ben had cases of the stuff at his apartment.

Around 2:00 A.M., I'd had enough and wanted to go back to the hotel room. But Ben wanted to hit the tables. We got into a drunken fight. It was a conversation we shouldn't and wouldn't have started right then, if not for the alcohol.

"We're never alone!" I screamed over the thumping, deafening music. "I want more of just you!"

"We don't have anything in common!" he yelled back at me.

"Stop calling me to tell me to be more dynamic!" I shrieked.

After fighting in front of everyone, Ben apologized and we both calmed down. I told him I was going back to the room. Instead of going with me, he said he was coming in fifteen minutes and let me wander drunkenly through the gigantic hotel on my own in the middle of the night. Sure enough I got lost. I couldn't remember our room number, and I was scared and pissed off.

When I finally made it back to our suite, I crawled into bed and fell asleep. At 6:22 A.M. I woke up and Ben was still not back. The thought crossed my mind that he might be with a random fan girl, a stripper, or a hooker. I mean this is Vegas, right? I texted him:

Where are you?

Fifteen minutes went by.

Walking up. Made some money. So tired.

By the time he walked in the door, it was 7:00 A.M.

I was enraged and stormed out of our room and wandered around the casino sobbing, with Ben frantically calling and texting me.

Babe. Can you please call me back? I'm freaking out a bit.

I feel awful.

I'm sick to my stomach.

I'm such a fuck all. I'm so sorry.

For all of his apologies, Ben never attempted to fix the underlying problem with our relationship. He never made me a priority. On Mother's Day 2012, he flew down to L.A. with Babs and Julia to take them for a special day of pampering on the rooftop of the Thompson Beverly Hills hotel. First, they met me at my house, which I'd cleaned frantically the day before. I wanted to impress Babs with my decorating and housekeeping skills, but they only stayed for ten minutes. After a quick brunch, we all went to the event.

Ben had asked me to bring my mom, but I didn't even pass along the invitation for two reasons: (1) The thought of Babs and my mom in the same room was terrifying, and (2) I didn't feel right about working on Mother's Day. What Babs didn't know is that the event sponsors, Joico and Voli Light Vodkas, paid Ben and me each $1,500 to show up. So he basically made a profit, then shuttled them right back to San Francisco. They didn't even stay overnight to spend time with me.

Once again, I'd found myself in a long-distance relationship that wasn't very satisfying. It's funny how you repeat behavior, even when you know it's bad for you, because it's the only thing you know. It's like a comfortable misery. We'd stopped talking about moving in together completely. There was no way we could. We just had too many issues and problems to deal with first.

Ben had some pet peeves when it came to me—surface-level things like I wasn't very punctual or organized, I believed in luck, I shopped at Whole Foods excessively, I talked about my exes too much, and I was always complaining about being cold. He also was extremely annoyed by my "baby voice," and would constantly point it out, saying, "There it is!" On a deeper level, he didn't respect my career or how I spent my free time. He didn't think I was sophisticated or smart. He even told me I was naïve once for not realizing that he'd done the show to promote his winery. I know there were other issues he didn't voice to my face—but for more of what he didn't like about me, he'll have to write his own book.

I, of course, had a few surface-level annoyances about Ben. Like it bugged me that he never remembered his dreams. He wouldn't go for walks with me and he started to get a little fluffy around the middle. Even though I love going to the movies, we only went to one, *Celeste and Jesse Forever*, during our relationship. He also gave me a lot of grief about my TV habits, especially when I'd make him watch my favorite show, *Keeping Up with the Kardashians*. I loved Khloe but he'd make fun of her, saying, "Blech!" or "Woof woof!" I thought that was totally shallow. Khloe had the best personality of all the sisters. Ben finally changed his tune about the show when he saw the episode where Rob started his own sock collection. "The sock thing is pretty cool," Ben admitted.

On a more serious level, I didn't feel like Ben was as sexually charged as I'm used to and he seemed dispassionate. The chemistry just wasn't there anymore. A few times, I'm sorry to say, I resorted to faking orgasms. We just really never hit our stride in that department. "I need more sex," I'd tell him.

"I'm really sorry," he'd say. "I've just been so busy."

He also wasn't a snuggler. It's not that we weren't comfortable next to each other in bed. "The sleeping is easy between us," Ben would say. And we cracked up every morning, when he'd wake me up with his first toot. But night after night, after sex Ben would just roll over like clockwork. I love falling asleep in a man's arms. For me there is no greater feeling of security and closeness. Ben just wasn't into it. I'd try to spoon him, massaging his calves with the balls of my feet, but he'd give me a gentle nudge to get off. That hurt.

My biggest issue with Ben wasn't about sex though. Hands down, it was that he never made me feel like a priority. It was Ben's world and I was just living in it. During our yearlong engagement, he visited me in L.A. three times and all three of those times were either for paid events or for meetings. He only met my parents twice. Ben needed to be surrounded by *his* people at all times, and he often ignored me. I once spent an entire Giants baseball game getting the silent treatment from him. The only situation when Ben was reliably attentive and lovey-dovey was in front of other *Bachelor* alumni. Like me, I think he secretly didn't want our relationship to fail because he wanted to be perceived as better or above all of the other couples who came before and after us.

Ben's handler from *The Bachelor* got married during our engagement and we had a wonderful time at the wedding. It was held at *Bachelor* creator Mike Fleiss's gorgeous beachfront estate in Malibu. Ben and I got to stay in the guesthouse next to the main house, which was incredible. The guest list was like a *Who's Who* of Bachelor Nation. Chris Harrison (who'd recently separated from his wife); DeAnna Pappas, who is so warm and down-to-earth; Ali Fedotowsky; and J. P. and Ashley were all in attendance. Ashley barely spoke to me all night, but Ben and J. P. threw down so many shots of Fernet that Ben ended up "pulling the trigger" later.

New couple Emily Maynard and Jef Holm, who were only a few weeks into their post-*Bachelor* life, were also there. They'd just come back from doing charity work in South Africa and seemed exhausted.

I'd only met Emily once before and totally randomly. I bumped into her and a *Bachelor* PA in L.A. at the Magic Touch Waxing Salon in Beverly Hills. Emily was about to embark on her overnight dates and apparently needed a little tune-up. This was interesting because on the show she said that she wasn't going to sleep with any of the guys in the Fantasy Suite. She wanted to be a good role model to her daughter. Not that she shouldn't keep her bush trim and tidy at all times, especially since she was off to her destination shoots, which meant bikini central.

"So nice to meet you!" she'd said. "If you ever need to talk, I went through the same thing after I got engaged to Brad [Womack]."

I thought she was really sweet at the salon in L.A. I definitely saw another side to her at the wedding. She and Jef sat right beside us, but were not getting along at all. Emily kept trying to make Jef jealous by flirting with Ben, avoiding eye contact with me the whole time.

Jef opened up to me that they'd been having a rough time already. "There are some differences between us," he complained.

"She likes to be inside and not do a lot. I'm more social."

"Oh, you'll be fine once you get into a normal routine," I lied. I could tell Emily and Jef were doomed.

Fed up with her flirting, Jef, who is Mormon, stormed off and sat in his car to cool down. As soon as he walked out, Emily called him "Jef Boremon." Ruh roh. They were already annoyed with each other and I could tell they had realized how little they had in common. Plus the green-eyed monster was obviously an issue.

This all sounded very familiar, but I didn't tell Jef that. He just seemed a little shady to me. Besides, Ben and I were on fire at this wedding: we tore up the dance floor, then tore each other's clothes off in the guesthouse at the end of the night. Then Ben puked. We were so hung over the next day.

But that was just one great night. Like Jef, I had my suspicions about Ben. I was concerned that he was fooling around behind my back when I wasn't in San Francisco. I'd noticed that he had a very flirty text relationship with the PR rep for Fernet. And once, when we went to Ben's favorite watering hole, a girl who had been caught by *Life & Style* giving Ben a massage in a local park was there. She tried to keep her distance, but I confronted her right in front of Ben, who laughed uncomfortably.

"I recognize you!" I said, with a fake smile. "You're the girl from the massage pictures!"

"I'm really sorry," she said nervously. "Ben said it wasn't a big deal at all."

Oh really, so you've talked about it together? I thought. "Honestly, it wasn't great," I said, still sticky sweet. "My family saw that and it didn't look good. So, no more massages, mkay?"

She laughed it off, but left the bar right after. I'm pretty sure she was in love with Ben.

By Memorial Day, Ben and I were on really shaky ground, and sort of on a mini break. We quietly canceled an appearance in Vegas that would have paid us each $2,500, but I still wasn't ready to announce anything official about a breakup. In early July, I toyed with dumping Ben around my birthday, but we had so much fun with my sister Rachel and her boyfriend, Moe, who flew up for the weekend, that I put it on the back burner again. I forgave him for having to remind him to wish me a happy birthday. I forgave him for making a reservation at a trendy new Japanese restaurant he wanted to try, even though I'd told him on numerous occasions that I always had a special lobster dinner on my birthday.

I forgave him because he picked up the check, bought me lovely flowers, and made an effort with my sister and her boyfriend. He also wrote on my card: "I love you so much it hurts."

But love shouldn't hurt. I don't subscribe to the notion of "no pain, no gain" in relationships, yet I continued down a path that caused me anguish because I thought we could make it work if we just tried harder. I kept giving him chances because I didn't want to give up after we'd overcome so much. And I didn't want to admit to myself that maybe he truly would have been better off engaged to a woman like Nicki.

Ben and I mistook the constant drama for passionate love. We had some great moments, but they were flashes of happiness, and quickly came and went. My favorite times with Ben were always driving in the car together, just the two of us. We'd listen to our favorite music and sing and laugh. When Ben drove through the famous Rainbow Tunnel in San Francisco, he'd honk the horn—an old tradition—and scream at the top of his lungs with such joy. The car was the one place where we really did forget all of our troubles.

After my birthday weekend, I felt so reconnected to Ben that

I stayed in San Francisco for a couple weeks, the longest we'd been together ever, and helped him move into a new apartment. It was a step up from the frat house apartment, but he still had a roommate—and it wasn't me. He also had no furniture. So Ben brokered a deal with *Life & Style,* the same rag that had published the incriminating massage pictures. They offered to give us $5,000 and furnish Ben's new place in exchange for an exclusive article about the status of our relationship and (now nonexistent) marriage plans.

A reporter and the furniture arrived and we did a photo shoot and interview. The reporter asked the usual questions and Ben said that he didn't like my voice again in response to one about his pet peeves. She asked us the last nice thing we did for each other. I was the kind of girl who would call the restaurant and have dessert sent over if Ben was out for dinner with friends. But I seriously couldn't think of anything Ben had done recently, so I made up a story about him renting a hotel room for my sister and her boyfriend when they came to visit for my birthday. In reality, Ben had promised to get them a good deal at the Fairmont and cover half the bill, but when it came time to pay, he wandered off again. As usual, I wanted people to think we were doing great, so I fibbed and exaggerated my way through the interview.

I almost didn't get my $2,500 for the interview though. When a few weeks passed and I still hadn't gotten a check, I asked Ben where it was and when I could expect it. Ben said his business manager had accidentally deposited the check in his business account and it would take some juggling to figure out how to pay me. Ben had this image of me as a rich model, but I was struggling after the show and I needed every penny we earned together. It was very annoying having to beg him for *my* money.

A few weeks later, I told Ben I needed the money and asked if he had figured out how to pay me.

"Why do you need it?" he asked.

"What do you mean, 'Why do I need it?' " I said, puzzled. Ben gave me another lecture about my spending. "I don't understand why you need it," he repeated.

"Ben, it's *my* money. I need to pay my bills, too."

It seemed kind of fishy to me. Turns out *Life & Pile* was fishy, too. After they got the story, they said it was never their intention to let Ben keep the new furniture. Before it was all hauled away, Ben decided to throw a housewarming party for forty of his closest friends. I was terrified the furniture would be destroyed and we'd have to pay for it, but he wasn't worried.

In typical Ben style, the party was a rager and I spent half the time running around picking up beer cans and begging people not to sit on the new white couch. Ben's dog, Scotch, was so freaked out I had to tuck him under the covers in the bedroom. The *Life & Style* reporter and the park massage girl both showed up, but I was okay with it. As time went on, I'd gotten used to Ben's girl-space-friends hanging around.

Bachelor and *Bachelorette* alum Ali Fedotowsky, who was in town, popped by with a twelve-pack of beer, her hair in a bun, wearing a touristy San Francisco sweatshirt she bought at a CVS. I thought she was hilarious, cool, and laid-back, but Ben wasn't a fan. He ironically didn't like that she always traveled with a sycophantic entourage. He used to make fun of her name, drawing it out like a *Downton Abbey* butler: "Ohhhh, I'm Ali Fedotowwwwwwsky."

Ali and I got along great and she opened up to me about the demise of her engagement to Roberto Martinez. She was very upset about rumors that he might be the next Bachelor because their breakup was still fresh. To make her feel better, I told her that Ben and I weren't doing well either. It felt great to be honest about our situation with someone other than my sister.

At one point in the night I spotted Ben on the outside staircase by himself, texting. Um, Ben was never by himself. And he had the posture of a man trying to hide something. Around 1:00 A.M., the party was dying down and he said he was going to grab some food with the boys down the street at Pizza Orgasmica (yeah, Kacie B's parents would have loved Ben) and would be right back.

While he was gone, I cleaned up his apartment. An hour later, he came back and didn't even say thank you. "Where have you been all this time?" I nagged. When he went to the bathroom, I saw the PR girl's name pop up on his phone. I'd met her once when he went to pick up some cases of Fernet at her office. She was cute, but a little standoffish with me. Ben told me she was married, but I never checked if that was true or not.

It read: Are you at Hi-Fi?

He'd responded: Darn, I just missed you.

When he came out of the bathroom, I ripped into him.

"Were you just at a club?"

"No! Why are you going through my phone? We just went out for pizza!"

I told him that was bullshit and asked if he was cheating with this PR rep. He denied it, but then added, "I have to maintain relationships! Sometimes for my job I have to be flirty!"

I was drunk and pissed so I said, "Oh really? Well sometimes Chris still texts me!" It was true. I'd actually told Chris he couldn't text me anymore, but Ben didn't need to know that right now.

"What!"

"We're just *friends,*" I said sarcastically. "I'll show you the texts and pictures. You can go through my phone."

"That's not okay. This is a problem."

"Every time I see your phone her name keeps popping up!"

"Everyone knows I'm in love with you," he said, starting to soften. "I don't want you talking to your exes anymore. It makes me feel like they gave you something I'm not giving you, which makes me want to try harder."

And then we had sex.

14

BUILDING & BREAKING

We kept building up the relationship and then breaking it. Build and break. Build and break. At this moment, we were building toward something, though I wasn't sure what. Ben was starting to be more supportive of my career and when I'd come up to San Francisco he drove me to castings for Gap and Old Navy. I spent time exploring the city and taking the bus all over, meeting Julia for lunch, and trying to get used to the fact that San Fran would be my new home soon.

Ben seemed very happy with me lately, and had no clue that I was unsatisfied in our relationship. I felt like there was no end in sight, in terms of moving in together, and the long distance was getting old. At the end of August, Arie Luyendyk Jr., the sexy race car driver from Arizona who was the runner-up on Emily Maynard's *Bachelorette* season, tweeted Ben and me that he was coming up to San Francisco for a race. It was funny, because at brunch once with Ben's sister, Julia, we'd both admitted that we had crushes on Arie. To get even, Ben said his celebrity crush was Zooey Deschanel and

Garrett admitted he liked Kate Upton. It was one of those harmless hall-pass conversations.

I private messaged Arie that I was going to be out of town, but Ben would love to meet up with him. I'm not going to lie. I was a little flirty. I'd heard through a very reliable source, another former contestant, that Arie was the best sex she'd ever had. "Next time we're in the same place, let's rendezvous," I teased. Eeek.

Ben met up with Arie and Lucas Daniels, from Ashley's season, and had a blast. Arie even took him for a spin around the track. After they hung out, Arie tweeted that he had fun with Ben and that seeing how happy we were together renewed his faith in love. Ben also told me that he gushed to Arie that our relationship had never been better, bragging, "We are in such a great place!" Then he made the mistake of telling Arie that I had a crush on him. "I better keep you two away from each other," Ben joked.

Ben wasn't worried about telling Arie I had the hots for him. In his mind, we were happy and moving toward marriage. He was thinking fall 2013 and now wanted an over-the-top, glamorous affair. "We should have a fancy black-tie wedding!" he said, all excited. "It'll be really cool! Everyone will get dressed up to the nines and it'll be really chic!" I was confused. He knew I'd always wanted a rustic, outdoor wedding at the Farm.

"I guess so," I said, totally deflated.

Then we had the other big conversation.

"I have baby fever!" Ben said out of the blue one day while we were driving to get him new furniture. "Me, too!" I said. We talked about our parenting styles and we agreed that Ben would be the disciplinarian and I'd be the pushover.

This was a thrilling turn of events, but it scared the shit out of me. We'd been up and down so many times—and now he was actually talking about marriage and babies? I didn't know if I should get my hopes up. Ben had recently joined not one, but *two* co-ed softball teams. He did whatever he wanted at all times with no real consideration for me. Was he mature enough to be the father of my children? I mean the guy was constantly showing me dick tricks, like his famous fruit bowl or "the stork." (Sorry for the visual.) I pictured him out having beers with his softball team(s), while I was home with our colicky baby. I'd text him and ask, "Where are you??" and he'd say, "I'll be right there . . ." And we all know how that goes.

Anyway, marriage and babies were both moot because he still had not officially asked me to move in with him. And there was still the issue of his mother, who I was convinced had tried to kill me on an extreme bike ride through Sonoma. As she whizzed through narrow paths and rugged terrain, she yelled at me like *Biggest Loser* trainer Jillian Michaels: "Keep up! Come on!" At a stoplight, she brought up *The Bachelor* again, reminding me how Ben almost gave up on me when the negative press got to be too much. I didn't understand why she'd want to rehash the past, other than to stir the pot.

"You know Ben came to me and said, 'I don't want to have to defend this woman for the rest of my life.' "

"Well, I think when you love someone unconditionally, you do anything for them," I responded. "I think he was very weak."

Babs was flabbergasted.

"And by the way," I continued, "I get asked constantly about him being a cheater. Perfect strangers walk up to me and tell me to get rid of him. I *always* defend him."

When Ben heard about this argument, he called Babs and warned her that she better get on board and be nice because he was in love with me. Ironically, she agreed to make more of an effort and bought me a beige scarf as an olive branch. But the truce didn't last long. And Ben's support of me was short-lived, too.

I'd always had Ben's back throughout our entire stressful experience—both on the show and after. I was always supportive of him. And, ironically, the one time I wasn't became the breaking point in our relationship. In the end, I was the one who totally blew it and caused the thin ice of our relationship to break. I made an incredibly insensitive mistake.

On Ben's thirtieth birthday his beloved family dog, Sophie, had to be put down. Ben, Julia, and Babs went to the vet and I met up with them afterward for lunch. They cried and told stories about Sophie. I gave Ben his gifts, a set of All-Clad pots and pans, a Boos cutting board, and a beautiful framed photograph of him and Scotch on Baker Beach heading toward the Golden Gate Bridge. "Look, he's running away from you," Babs said to me.

That past weekend we'd already had a fun pirate-themed party on Angel Island for Ben, so he spent the evening of his actual birthday sitting on his couch, tooling around on his laptop. I sat next to him, wiping his tears away and rubbing his head. He seemed so sad. I thought he might want to be alone. And to be honest, I was exhausted from spending the day with his mother. I changed my flight and left that night instead of early the next morning. He didn't seem to be bothered by it at the time.

On the way to the airport, Julia texted me.

Why did you leave?

Only then did I realize the gravity of what I'd done. I'd just left my fiancé alone on his birthday, after his dog died. This was very bad.

And that one decision marked the end of my "fairy-tale" romance. Ben's feelings changed for me that day and we never recovered as a couple. I apologized over and over again for leaving, but we spent the next three weeks apart, barely speaking. He canceled a trip down to L.A. to see me, and I didn't go back to see him until early October, to help him with his winery's grape harvest in Sonoma. Of the countless flights I'd taken up there, this was the only time during our relationship that he'd bought my ticket. Normally I would have considered it a lovely gesture, but I had a hunch it was an ominous sign. Unbelievably, my flight was canceled and I ended up buying the replacement ticket.

The weekend was truly abysmal. As soon as he picked me up at the airport, I could tell he was still mad about the dog incident and wasn't happy to see me. He was cold and quiet, and barely looked at me.

"I can't do this back and forth thing much longer," I said.

"I agree," he said. "It's getting old."

We had dinner and the silence was the worst it had ever been. He again brought up his reality show *Young Sonoma*. He really wanted me to be on it, but I told him I wasn't ready for another reality show. He also talked about a falling-out he'd just had with a very close friend. The guy had written him a Dear John e-mail. "You've changed," it said, reaming him out for being selfish and a bad friend.

We had to be up at 5:00 A.M. for the harvesting so we slept on a bed in Ben's office in Sonoma. After picking the grapes, which was actually quite fun, I changed out of my dirty clothes in the backseat of the car and Ben didn't even look in the rearview mirror once. I was waiting for him to look back at me, so I could flash him or do something sexy and playful, but he stared straight ahead at the road.

That night, Ben had an event at the Envolve tasting room and his mom tried to interfere with our relationship again. She told Ben that my friendly good-bye to one of his friends was inappropriate. "Bye!" I'd said innocently to his business partner. Babs gave me a death stare as we all walked to the car and Ben picked up on it. Later, he asked me, "What happened with my mom? That was the meanest stare she's ever given anyone in her life."

"I have no idea!" I said. "What did I do?"

"She told me, 'You didn't hear what I just heard.' "

"I don't even know what she's talking about!" I complained. "Your mom is never going to like me. I feel like she's trying to sabotage me!"

"Your mom is no walk in the park either," he retorted defensively. "I have no respect for your mom. I'll never have a relationship with your mom."

Where in the world did that come from? How did my mom enter this conversation? Once I told her that I was in love with Ben, she'd gotten completely on board with our relationship and had been nothing but nice and complimentary the two measly times they met. She would say to him, "Let me give you a smooch!" or "You have the best smile!"

He knew he'd crossed the line with me and tried to backpedal with a ludicrous plan to estrange himself from his own mother.

"I can't lose you," Ben said. "I just have to cut her out."

"You can't cut her out. She's your mom! I can't be the reason you don't have a relationship."

The next day we spent the day in a park back in San Fran with Julia and Garrett. Ben was in a horrible mood, and would switch between ignoring me and being overtly nasty. When I said that we should be cowboys and Indians for Halloween that year, he got overly pissed off and barked, "That's a dumb idea!"

"Whoa, Ben," Julia said. Even she could see he was being unnecessarily mean.

We went to a bar for his favorite activity, day-drinking, and Ben spent the entire time blatantly with his back to me. He wanted to go to a friend's pizza party, but I'd had enough of his silent treatment and verbal abuse.

"I can't go anywhere with you right now. I'm too upset," I said. "You go."

"That's not fair," he moaned. "It's a trick. I'm not gonna go."

"Go, I'm just sad."

"I get it," he said with a bad attitude.

Instead, we went to get a burrito and we had another fight about my spending habits. I think Ben was looking for any excuse to break up with me. Then a *Bachelor* fan came up and interrupted us, making Ben even tenser. When we got back to his apartment, of course, his friend and his brother were there, so we went into Ben's bedroom to continue the fight in some semblance of privacy.

"Nobody has ever treated me this poorly," I told him, heartbroken, as we lay side by side. "You talk to me the way your mother talks to you and that scares me. I have concerns."

"I know. I have concerns, too. I'm stressed about my mom. And it really bothers me when you talk in your baby voice."

Tears rolled down my cheek.

"I need a break or a breakup," I said.

"I don't want to talk about this now," he said.

When we woke up in the morning, we had sex, but it was quiet and there was no talking. I took a shower and asked Ben if he'd take a walk with me but he said he wanted to sleep longer. Before I left to go to the airport, we stood in the garage. Ben asked me to call him as soon as I got home.

"No, I'm not going to call you later. You've treated me so poorly I need a couple days to figure out what I want and you need to do the same."

I gave him a quick hug. I got in his Jeep to drive myself over to Julia's so she could drive me to the airport. He got in his BMW and drove behind me for a short time on his way to work. I never waved and I never looked for him in the rearview mirror.

He sped off and that was the last time I ever saw Ben Flajnik.

15

REBOUND & RENEW

Two days after I got home, Ben texted me. "Hey babe, just wanted to let you know I'm still doing some soul-searching and straightening out my life. Hope you're well, love you."

I wanted a few days to talk myself back into this. I kept replaying our relationship in my head. There was so much silence and crying. There were so many deal breakers that I'd tried to ignore like the way he was always cutting me down. I really don't think he liked anything about me. The kicker was my voice: I couldn't change that if I tried.

I texted him that I was ready to talk.

He asked if it could wait, because he had two softball games that day.

"Haha," I wrote back, not even slightly amused. "Call me."

Ben and I had a five-minute conversation.

"It's over," I said. "It's not working."

"You're right. It's not."

"I'm sorry. I love you and I wanted this to work."

"I totally understand. This has nothing to do with me wanting to be with other people or single. I just turned thirty and my relationships are changing and I'm having a hard time with it."

"I can't talk to you for a long time."

"You are the best thing that's ever happened to me."

"Stop. I can't hear you say that because you sure as hell haven't been treating me like that."

We talked for a minute more about putting out a joint statement together, agreeing to take the high road. I told him to have a good softball game and then we hung up.

I let out a guttural cry. I knew my mind was made up. I'd seen enough.

Ben did not fight for me.

On October 5 we gave the exclusive to *In Touch Weekly:* "After meeting over a year ago, we have decided to end our romantic relationship. The ups and downs weighed heavily on us both and ultimately we started to grow apart because of the distance, time apart, and our need to focus on our respective careers."

Not wanting to deal with the impending shitstorm, I decided to get the hell out of Dodge. Before I left L.A., I told the waiting paparazzi outside not to bother following me because I was driving home to Arizona. On the way there, I played Mumford and Sons "Holland Road" on repeat like fifty times.

With your heart like stone you spared no time in lashing out
And I knew your pain and the effect of your shame
But you cut me down,
You cut me down

Zoned out, sobbing, and singing, I accidentally drove over a blown tire in the middle of the highway and basically ripped apart the underside of my car. I was stranded in the middle of the desert near Joshua Tree, thirty-five miles from the nearest service station, my cell phone at 5 percent. Now I wished the paps had been following me. I was so isolated that AAA couldn't find me. Big rigs kept slowing down when they passed me, and I was terrified I'd be kidnapped and skinned by a serial killer trucker. Four hours later, I was saved by a police officer, who helped me get my car hauled to a garage. Around 11:00 P.M., $1,300 down the tubes, I arrived in Scottsdale, sweaty and spent.

It was the worst day of my life.

MY PLAN WAS to hide out at my parents' house for as long as necessary and do some serious soul-searching. Not only about what went wrong with Ben, but also about the destruction of my career, my reputation, even my personality, since I went on the show. I was at a very low and dark place; thankfully I got a ton of support from several of my old cast mates, deserved or not. Casey, Rachel, and Jaclyn all checked in. Lindzi Cox, who I hadn't talked to since the end of the show, sent me the sweetest message: "Hey woman, sorry to hear about everything! Sending happy thoughts your way, my dear." I thanked her and joked, "You didn't miss out on much."

Of course, there were always the haters. Trista Sutter had to butt in her big nose, giving an exclusive reaction to RumorFix: "Why did they go slowly if they knew they were in love? A big reason Ryan and I worked out is because we didn't take it slowly, we jumped right into starting our future together." *Right, because you're perfect.*

I had good intentions of having an introspective Zen retreat at my parents' place, but that all got thrown out the window when I checked social media. Note to self and every woman in the world:

turn off all social media after a breakup! It's so essential to your sanity! I made the mistake of checking Ben's pages the first weekend after the split. He and his friends kept posting pictures of him partying his face off on rooftops, having a blast. He obviously didn't care about me. It felt inconsiderate and like he was throwing it in my face.

Feeling devastated and lonely, I was pretty vulnerable when Arie, a fellow Scottsdalian, reached out to me within those first few days. I had this uncontrollable urge to act out and there he was. First Arie tweeted publicly that he was bummed about the breakup and thought we were going to make it: "I guess it just takes the right couple." Then he tweeted me privately, "Heard the news. Hope you're doing ok." I messaged him my number and told him I was in Arizona hiding out at my parents' house. He called me and we made plans to meet up.

When I told my parents about Arie, they were extremely pissed, especially my dad. "Don't do that, Bug," he warned. "It's a really bad idea." He had gotten a nice text from Ben right after the breakup.

> Ben: Sorry it didn't work out. Thanks for letting me be a part of your family.
>
> My dad: I can't believe you let her get away.

Ben didn't respond.

I ignored my parents' warning to stay away from Arie. Three nights after I got home, they left for a vacation in Maine and I immediately, and recklessly, invited him over to their house, like a naughty teenager (and a serial rebounder). He brought over takeout from Postino and two bottles of Brassfield's Eruption wine and we closed the blinds. After we ate, we sat in the backyard talking.

I found out that he'd dated someone connected to the show a few years ago and that's how he ended up auditioning for *The Bachelorette*. During his casting weekend in North Carolina, my finale had aired. He and a bunch of the guys watched it and he said he knew then that I was his "dream babe." He said from that moment on he had a crush on me.

He was rewarded for that touching story with a make out session that lasted for what seemed like an eternity. Though he is an expert at lip locking, known among fans of the show as the Kissing Bandit, I was getting hot and bothered, and needed more. "Arie, I feel like I'm in high school. I can't just keep making out with you."

He was hesitant, for a millisecond, but then we headed into my childhood bedroom, into my canopy bed, for what can only be described as *the best sex I've ever had*. Why was it so good you ask? Arie's incredibly passionate and utilizes his entire body in his lovemaking. And he knows exactly what positions make a woman comfortable and satisfied.

KEEPING IT REAL

Arie's Kissing Tips

"I have to say as a romantic person, the kiss is only as good as the feeling behind it," the Kissing Bandit himself says. "That being said, if you're a terrible kisser we need to work on some things regardless." Here are his tips to make sure a first kiss isn't the only kiss.

1. Fresh breath is a must. Don't think I need to elaborate on this one.

2. Timing is everything. Make the most of a romantic moment, like on long walks, candlelit dinners, being wrapped in a blanket by a fire.

3. Eye contact is key. Tell your partner with just a look you want to be kissed.

4. Never, absolutely never, ask permission. Take "can I kiss you?" out of your vocabulary.

5. Go slow and don't overthink it. Relax your lips.

6. Kissing is not just done with your lips. Pull her close and be assertive.

7. Confidence is sexy. Be bold and in control.

8. Run your hand through her hair; brush her hair from her face.

9. A first kiss should be short and passionate. Leave her wanting more.

10. Last but not least, if you love someone, tell them through your lips.

When it was over, I gave him a massage and I could tell he was smitten. "Will you be my girlfriend?" he joked. He told me he was going to cut all ties with the different women he was seeing. "That's the first lie you've ever told me," I joked back. After he left, he posted to Twitter: "Amazing what can happen if you take a chance."

I quickly learned that Arie liked to post every single detail of his life on Instagram and Twitter. Arie's need for attention was a little off-putting, but I admired his zest for life. Ben was so private, cold, and unemotional.

I was in Scottsdale for twelve days and I spent most of that time with Arie. I felt safe with him and liked that he understood what it was like to be on the show and a member of Bachelor Nation. One night he told me to wear warm, comfortable clothes because he was taking me somewhere special. I was terrified of being spotted with him in public. "Trust me," he said.

He picked me up in his truck and took me to Arizona's only drive-in movie theater to see *The Odd Life of Timothy Green*. We lay on an AeroBed in the back, eating popcorn, snuggling under blankets, and kissing. It was the cutest date ever. Spontaneous and romantic.

In one week, I felt closer to Arie than I had to Ben in a year. Though I knew Arie was another rebound, this was the kind of relationship I'd been craving. He was attentive and kind and complimented me. And he wasn't bored staying in watching movies. He actually enjoyed my company and didn't need his friends around him 24/7. When I'd complained about Ben's entourage, he said to me many times, "This is my lifestyle, Courtney, and it's not going to change."

I got sick of hiding out with Arie and decided to tempt fate. I wanted to take him to my favorite restaurant at the Farm. I called ahead and asked them to reserve the most secluded table and made them promise that my visit would be confidential. But when we got there, they sat two couples right next to us. While we were eating dinner and kissing, one of the couples took our picture. When I went to the bathroom, Arie politely asked them to erase the picture, but they denied they snapped us. We both knew we were screwed.

The next day I left to drive back to L.A. and all hell broke loose. I got a call from my friend at Wet Paint, who told me the picture of us kissing had been sold to TMZ.com. I panicked.

I texted Julia, Ben's sister, to give her a heads-up. "Is he a good kisser?" she asked jokingly. That eased my mind a bit. Until a producer from *The Bachelor* called me and said "I just talked to Ben and he is totally flipping out."

"Should I call him?"

"No, let him cool off."

Ten minutes later I got a text from Ben: "Really? Please don't ever contact me again. Low blow."

I tried to temper the explosive situation by being apologetic.

"Please understand I have been so brokenhearted. I wanted us to work. I'm so sorry I hurt you. It was never my intention. I would have loved you forever and ps I'm still in love with you. I care for you deeply and only want to see you happy."

That just made him spitting mad.

"You just dug your own grave. Good luck gaining respect from anyone. I'm not here to protect you from negativity anymore. You lost all credibility that you built up after the last media disaster. It's really disappointing. Don't expect me to be on your side anymore. Our 'united front' is out the fucking window. Have a nice ride on your own. Tata."

"That united front has been out the window for quite some time. You're the one that gave up, not me. Remember that."

"You kissed the guy!!! How does that make you still miss me? It's been a week since we stopped talking and you're already going on dates in public!? How stupid are you?"

"I do miss you, badly. I wake up in the middle of the night crying. Not that you care. Looks like you've been off living it up. You let me go so easily."

"Last weekend was an escape for me. You going on a date with Arie is the prime example why we didn't work. You never think about your actions."

"Everyone makes mistakes and I've forgiven you many times."

"Whatever. This is your bad not mine. You're in a pickle. Have fun with that."

"It was one date; he called me," I lied, trying to diffuse the situation. "Again I'm sorry. I will always love you and be there for you, whether you like it or not."

"Not so sure anymore. Anyway have fun with this. I do feel bad you put yourself in this situation. Frankly, I'm shocked."

Ben called Arie and left him a message. "Hey man, I'm not mad at you. I just have a few questions." Arie never called him back. I warned Arie that he should be prepared to be blasted in the media but he just said calmly, "Don't worry." Unlike Ben, he didn't let these things bother him or change his opinion of me. He tweeted a picture of himself shouting from a mountaintop with a caption saying he had no problem telling the world what an amazing woman I was. He seemed so much more passionate than Ben.

The Arie incident started a vicious war between Ben and me. Back and forth insults were flung through the media. He said that he owed an apology to the women on the show for not believing them. That he dodged a bullet. His sister posted nasty messages on Arie's Instagram pictures, calling him a C-list fame whore. She texted me, too, demanding to know how I could do this to Ben. Before Halloween, ABC ran a video online called "The Hatchelor" and they used film from our season to make a horror movie starring me as the monster.

I retaliated by setting up a paparazzi photo shoot "catching" me returning the $80,000 engagement ring to Neil Lane.

I also did a story in *Life & Style*, in which I ripped on Ben. I did another exclusive in *Us Weekly*, saying I felt "brainwashed." Ben unleashed more fury, and questioned publicly if I were only interested in being famous. "Did I ever really know her?" he said about me, saying all the things he knew would cut to the bone. "Maybe she was just that good at fooling people."

After a few weeks of this, I couldn't take anymore. I waved the white flag and gave up, totally bummed out. Ben had pushed all of the right buttons and hit me where it hurt most. Like Ben said, "Things don't end, unless they end badly." Boy, did we crash and burn.

I called a producer friend and told him to tell Ben I would break up with Arie if it would stop our hateful war of words. He never responded to my offer, but I knew that my tryst with Arie was toast. In early November, a bunch of Bachelor Nation alumni came to L.A. to attend Ashley and J. P.'s wedding, which would be televised a month later in December. Arie was also in town, though we were not invited to the wedding. I tagged along with him when he visited his buddy Jef Holm, who was staying at the Ritz-Carlton. It was strange that the two were friends, when both had fought so hard to win Emily's heart. But such is the nature of the beast. Ben and J. P. were buddies, too.

Jef and Emily had split up a few weeks ago as well. Emily had not so secretly turned her attention to Arie, bombarding him with jealous texts about his relationship with me. Jef found out about the texts (so did I, there are few secrets in Bachelor Nation). Jef was furious, but he wasn't so innocent either. He may have adhered to his strict Mormon teachings about alcohol, but he certainly didn't abstain from womanizing. The guy was a total player. During the wedding weekend, I know from very reliable sources that he hooked up with *three* women—a one-night backslide with former fiancée Emily, Over-Analyst blogger Jenna Burke from my season, and his new hookup, a twenty-three-year-old named Katianna.

I knew the guy was shadesville the moment I met him. My intuition was confirmed again when he told me, "You got a bad rap. Come build a well with me." He said his People Water charity would do wonders for my reputation. He told me that I could shake a baby and everyone would still love me. Ew, what a cocky bastard.

I couldn't deal with this love triangle or quadrangle or whatever I was involved in with Arie, Emily, and Jef. I wanted out, no part of this incestuous *Bachelor* drama. At the end of the weekend I told Arie we were done. He was disappointed and asked me to think about it overnight, and then attend the iHeartRadio concert with him the next day.

After sleeping on it, I called Arie and told him I'd overreacted and that I'd love to go with him. "I don't think it's a good idea," he said. I was surprised and confused, until I checked Instagram later that night. He'd flown in another girl to take to the show and because he just couldn't help it Arie posted pictures of them together. I clicked on her name and figured out that he was dating this woman, a born-again virgin, the entire time we were together. He'd often seen both of us on the same day. It was all right there on social media, if I'd bothered to check.

Once word got out that I was single again, all sorts of *Bachelorette* guys contacted me. I was asked via Twitter and through mutual friends to "hang out" with a long list of alumni, but I decided to try to stay away from *Bachelor* guys.

A lot of (random) guys also wanted to be my savior. As soon as the news broke about the breakup, my ex Cavan sent me flowers. The comedian David Spade, who got my number from his friend

Mike Fleiss, called me out of the blue and asked me to come see his comedy show. He texted me a lot, and he was so sweet and funny and charming, but I just wasn't ready. After I blew him off a bunch, he wrote:

> Well, I have to admit you are sort of tough to date. First have to figure out if you're single, then I have to get you to answer the phone, then you have to say yes. Lining up all three of these things is sort of difficult.

I declined all invitations and on New Year's Day, after everything had died down, I reached out to Ben in an e-mail. I wanted to come clean and apologize. But he never responded to me. I reached out to Chris, always my source of comfort in times of trouble, but he was living with someone and disappeared on me. I never felt so alone in my entire life.

I sank into a serious depression for months and for the first time in my life, I didn't turn to a man. I turned into a recluse. I was sick of the drama and I was sick of myself. I felt I had lost my voice and sight of who I was. I felt like I had become a bad friend, sister, daughter, and person. I genuinely cared what people thought about me. I was so disappointed in myself for the way I'd handled everything and couldn't face the world.

The show, and everything that happened around it, was the experience of a lifetime. But it also changed me forever—and I wasn't sure I liked the change. Was what I'd gone through worth the pain I felt now? Was it worth destroying my modeling career? Or my reputation? I didn't think I was ever going to feel unconditional love again and wasn't sure I deserved it.

At the end of my rope, my faith in love and in myself completely lost, I decided to see a psychic. I was desperate and I'd had good luck before. In Tempe, Arizona, I'd seen the famous Mrs. Rita, who was immortalized in a Gin Blossoms song, and she told me I would wait until I was older to get married. I'd also seen a guy named Yogi in Miami who handed me a piece of paper and said, "This is who you're going to be with." The name on the paper was "Chris."

I scrolled through Yelp and found a medium named Shirley Lipner, right down the street from me in Santa Monica. She had all five-star reviews and cost $150. When I walked in, she said to me right off the bat, "You're not depressed. You're in a fog."

"Oh, thank God," I said. "I was so worried." I had to pee so I asked to borrow the key to the bathroom. I didn't know if she knew who I was, but while I was gone I became concerned that I'd picked this woman randomly. What if she sold our conversation to a tabloid?

As soon as I got back from the bathroom, she put my mind at ease: "I was channeling your energy when you went to pee and don't you worry, everything is completely private, much like a doctor."

I asked her to channel Ben and she did. She said he was standing there with his arms crossed, pouting like a little boy. She said he had a mental block because of his mother and that we were possibly together in a past life. She said he just didn't know what he wanted, but he really did love me. I would hear from him again when I turned forty.

I had tears in my eyes.

"In the past, you've always been like, 'Pick me!' " the psychic said. "But now you're going to have your pick. Take your time."

She was right. I'd jumped right into most of my relationships impulsively, without even taking the time to ask myself the right questions. What was the type of man I wanted? How did I want him to treat me? How should he treat my family? What type of parent would he be? All simple questions, yet all questions I'd avoided most of my life, just to avoid being alone.

In the months after breaking up with Arie, I was alone for the longest stretch of my life. And you know what? Once the depression started lifting, it was a revelation. I found a new sense of faith and started praying again and giving thanks for my life. Instead of going on dates with guys, I went on dates with myself. I treated myself the way I always wanted a man to treat me. I stopped beating myself up for my past actions and was nice to myself. I realized I wasn't the character "Courtney Robertson" on *The Bachelor.* I wasn't a Man-eater or a cold marble statue or a villain.

I slowly started remembering only the happy moments with Ben and stopped feeling anger toward him. And when that release was true and genuine, in July 2013, he finally reached out to me in an e-mail with the subject "Long time . . .":

> Hey Courtney,
>
> Just wanted to reach out and say a quick hello . . . I just wanted to clear the air a bit in case we ever run into each other at any point . . . I don't harbor any negative feelings about you and wish you nothing but the best in your future relationships, endeavors, and life. With the little bits of info I hear about you through the grapevine it seems you're super happy and that makes me happy. Take care.

I was genuinely heartbroken when Ben and I broke up. The failed relationship was the greatest disappointment of my life. I loved being engaged to Ben and that peaceful feeling knowing the search was over. I thought he was my forever and was scared I would never love or care about someone so deeply ever again.

But I'm not scared anymore. It'll happen when it happens and there's no rush.

Like my mom always says, "You have the rest of your life to let a man screw it up!"

The two biggest questions I always get from *Bachelor* fans is, "Is it real?" (yes) and "If you could to do the show over again, would you?"

The answer to that question is . . . Hell no! Meaning, of course, I wouldn't do it again if I knew then what I know now. But that's not how life works. I think it's okay to live with regrets and learn from failures. Even when things are over, they continue to influence and inspire you. This experience made my life fuller, my beliefs stronger, and gave me the patience to wait for the right person. In that way I'm "winning!" (I couldn't resist.)

So, no, I probably wouldn't do *The Bachelor* again. But you know what? I'd be thrilled to be the Bachelorette, so I can do the picking.

My only requirement for the guys?

Must. Love. Skinny-dipping.

EPILOGUE

April 2014

Ben Flajnik reached out to Courtney via e-mail on July 30, 2013, to clear the air. She wrote back to him and told him about this book. "Am I in trouble?" he asked. Within weeks, he'd auctioned a date with himself for $2,500 on Gilt.com, shot down rumors he was boning fifty-nine-year-old Kardashian momager Kris Jenner, and told a gossip site that he'd begun dating a "great girl" in the wine business who is "super smart." No release date for his reality show *Young Sonoma* has been announced.

Emily O'Brien was briefly linked to Mike Burns (Ashley Hebert's *Bachelorette* season), but they called it quits because Emily was getting her Ph.D. in North Carolina. She is currently engaged to a Duke Orthopaedic chief resident named Donny.

Nicki Sterling went back to her normal life after *The Bachelor*. She isn't on any social media sites (at least publicly) and has a serious boyfriend who reportedly auditioned to be on Emily Maynard's *Bachelorette* season.

Kacie "B" Boguskie appeared on Bachelor Sean Lowe's season, but was eliminated in the third episode. She did not say "fuck" in her second limo exit interview. She was surprisingly friendly to Courtney when they both appeared on Katie Couric's daytime talk show in June 2013. While they were sitting in their makeup chairs, she told Courtney, "They pinned us against each other." Kacie B got engaged to music producer Rusty Gaston in February 2014.

Blakeley Shea Jones was briefly engaged to *Bachelor Pad* star Tony Pieper. She's back in North Carolina waxing away as an esthetician at her new business Couture Artistry. She's a big commenter on *Bachelor* alums' Instagram accounts.

Lindzi Cox lives in Seattle and is really happy. She's single but looking for love and "gypsetting" around, as she calls it.

Casey Shteamer is still Courtney's best friend. Her passion is traveling and she recently spent a month backpacking in Peru. She lives in Chicago and runs her fashion blog ImperfectWonder.com.

Jenna Burke not only hooked up with Jef Holm, but she also hooked up with Sean Lowe after a charity event sponsored by her iced coffee company RealBeanz in September 2012. A week later he was announced as the next Bachelor. Jenna was devastated. She truly thought they had a connection.

Emily Maynard, perhaps after being burned by so many tools from *The Bachelor*, is now engaged to the preacher of her local church in North Carolina.

Ali Fedotowsky is now a host for E! News—and even appeared in the Woody Allen movie *Blue Jasmine*. Ali, who is dating Kevin Manno, still defends Courtney to this day. In a recent interview she explained, "Courtney Robertson was portrayed as a complete bitch on-camera but she's very sweet. I really love Courtney."

Trista Sutter avoided Courtney like the plague at an event at the *Bachelor* mansion. Coward.

Arie Luyendyk Jr. is still racing Indy cars and super trucks. He dated Bachelor Nation's Selma Alameri (from Sean Lowe's season) for a short time. She called Courtney to commiserate, but got over him pretty quickly. Courtney and Arie are good friends and still keep in touch. PS The Kissing Bandit is currently single.

Cavan helped Courtney heal from her breakup with Ben and became her boyfriend briefly again in the spring of 2013. Courtney moved in with him in San Francisco, only to realize within two months that they still weren't right for each other.

Dylan texted Courtney on February 9, 2014. "For whatever it's worth thank you," he wrote. When she replied, "For what?" he never responded.

Chris lives in Palm Beach, Florida, and runs the raw food empire Christopher's Kitchen. He had a baby boy in December 2013.

Jesse Metcalfe's career was resurrected by his starring role on the revamped TV series *Dallas*. He's engaged to *Beverly Hills Chihuahua 3* actress Cara Santana. Courtney is happy he found the right girl to settle down with.

Adrian Grenier still booty-call texts Courtney to this day. The last time he wrote her, he asked, "Are you still on that show?" There's a good chance he has no idea she wrote this book. Or that he's in it.

Courtney Robertson (that's me!) is still single and ready to mingle. Her modeling career is on the upswing again after booking a DirecTV commercial in the summer of 2013 and signing with Wilhelmina Models in 2014. She is still a hopeless romantic and looking for a man who actually wants to get married.

ACKNOWLEDGMENTS

COURTNEY ROBERTSON

I would like to thank my sister Rachel for being my rock; my mom, Sherry, for her strength; and my dad, Rick, for being such a fine example of a man. I'd also like to thank Amy Bean, Elan Gale, Casey Shteamer, Jaclyn Swartz, Arie Luyendyk Jr., Kalon McMahon, Ashlee Frazier, Graham Bunn, Michelle Money, Chris Bukowski, Mike Fleiss, Julia Flajnik, Garret Fitzpatrick, Chris (for his support and not selling me out), Sara Steinmetz, Darienne Arnold (my Mom away from Mom), Carrie Tivador, the entire Robertson family, Linda and Chuck Robertson, Grandma Angie, Liz Dysart, Ally Walsh, Kirsten Neuhaus, Brittany Hamblin, Heidi Metcalfe Lewis, and Michael Barrs. Most special thanks to Dibs, my friend for life, I'm forever grateful. We got this!

DEB BAER

I would like to thank my parents, John and Linda Baer, for making all in life possible, Kirsten Neuhaus at Foundry Literary + Media, Brittany Hamblin and Heidi Metcalfe Lewis at HarperCollins, Rick and Sherry Robertson, Rachel Molina, Marisa Sullivan, Mary Pender-Coplan, Khali MacIntyre, Potsch Boyd, Brett and Cathy Baer, Rachel Biermann, Hotel Valley Ho, Catalina Coffee Company, and, last but not least, Courtney Robertson, who is not only hardworking, smart, and kind, but now a lifelong friend. We, indeed, got this!